DO-IT-YOURSELF HOUSEBUILDING
Step-by-Step

DO-IT-YOURSELF HOUSEBUILDING

Step-by-Step

BY

CHARLES D. NEAL

Macmillan Publishing Co., Inc.
NEW YORK

Collier Macmillan Publishers
LONDON

To my wife, Fairy, whose encouragement was ever a constant stimulation and whose patient understanding made this endeavor a most pleasant writing and photographic experience.

Macmillan Publishing Co., Inc.
866 Third Avenue, New York, N.Y. 10022
Collier-Macmillan Canada Ltd.

Unless otherwise identified, the photographs and drawings in this book are by the author.

Library of Congress Catalog Card Number: 72-91256

THIRD PRINTING 1974

Printed in the United States of America

CONTENTS

KEYS TO BETTER BUILDING

ACKNOWLEDGMENTS

To Frank Steh, Jr., a master teacher of the West Frankfort, Illinois, Community High School Building Trades class, I shall always be grateful for his patient understanding and forbearance during our many conferences about the manuscript and the kinds of techniques and skills necessary for the layman during the construction of a house.

To the following cooperative manufacturers and other organizations, I wish to express my gratitude for their assistance and information, which made possible an up-to-date, technically accurate book: the Selz Organization, Chicago, Illinois; Masonite Corporation, Chicago, Illinois; Thomas Industries, Inc., Louisville, Kentucky; Al Fol, Inc., Charlotte, North Carolina; Stanley Power Tools, New Britain, Connecticut; Markel Electric Heating, Buffalo, New York; Weston Photographic Instruments, Newark, New Jersey; Crane Company, Chicago, Illinois; Christopher Advertising Counsel, Lake Bluff, Illinois; Kwikset Sales and Service Company (Locks), Anaheim, California; Vega Industries, Inc., Syracuse, New York; Whirlpool Corporation, Benton Harbor, Michigan; Iron-A-Way, Inc., Morton, Illinois; Fiat Products Dept., Plainview, Long Island, New York; Marsh Wall Products, Dover, Ohio; Reasor Corporation, Charleston, Illinois; Morgan-Wightman, St. Louis, Missouri; Sears Roebuck and Company, Chicago, Illinois; Montgomery Ward and Company, Chicago, Illinois.

For an illustrated book involving all of the building trades, one must have many subjects to photograph and draw. To the many contractors, their workmen, and the building-trades students of the West Frankfort Community High School, I wish to express my sincere thanks and my regrets that they are so many that I cannot list all their names.

Finally, I wish to pay special tribute to my colleague, Dr. C. William Horrell, Professor of Cinema and Photography, Southern Illinois University, Carbondale, for his helpful evaluations of the photographs during the preparation of the book.

FOREWORD

Since the beginning, man has thought of his home as basic to his life—as his castle. For early man, as for us, there was a time for providing food, a time for making clothing, a time for fighting enemies, and a time to raise and provide for a family. And even though early man was nomadic in nature, he found a base of operations—a home—a necessity. His base might have been a cave, a place under an overhanging rock ledge, or a crude hut made from adobe blocks, broken stones, or chunks of ice. Today, the base of operation of civilized man is a dwelling place inside a house.

So by now man should be pretty good at building houses. But in fact, often the building of a house, one of the most important steps in the life of a man and his family, is taken in the dark, and sometimes with unfortunate results. Many of us take common risks into account—loss of employment by the head of the family, unexpected sickness, a sudden spiraling in the cost of living, fire and theft. But sometimes we fail to recognize risks connected directly with the construction of the house itself, such as undesirable building site, faulty or substandard materials, poor workmanship, rapid depreciation and obsolescence, expensive maintenance costs, taxes out of proportion to property value, and so on—risks that over a period of years can cause enormous losses as well as chronic dissatisfaction.

What I have tried to explain in this book is how to build a house—how to plan it, construct it, and finish it. I wanted to illustrate the structure of a typical one-story house or other single-story building that a reader might want to build. This required more than just making an analysis of the building steps of a single-story house selected at random during its period of construction. The sample house might have a basement, and the reader might want to construct a house on a concrete slab. He might want to build a fireplace, and the sample house might not have one. So I have used three different houses, and I believe that any reader can find in this book just about all the detailed information he needs to build any one-story house, weekend retreat, or garage of his choice from his set of working drawings or blue prints.

Although this book explains a vast number of building procedures accepted by the various building trades, it is not intended to be a treatise on each individual building trade. Rather, it is a guide on *how* to build a house especially written for the person who enjoys working with tools. It contains step-by-step, up-to-date, and down-to-earth basic information along with specific recommendations for building a one-story house, cabin, or weekend retreat. Because complete building plans are available from architects, from various magazines and other periodicals, from house-plan books, and from literature published by the manufacturers of home-building materials, a minimum of such information is treated here.

To meet my objective, I have, in most instances, selected a single procedure for every step of the house-building operation. For instance, when the builder is confronted with the framing of 2×4 corner studs, I have not confused him by explaining two or more ways in which he might construct them, leaving him to wonder which method is the best. On the contrary, I have made a single recommendation that ensures sound and permanent construction for every step of the way.

Wherever possible in the text, I have tried not to tell the reader things he already knows. For those who need no instruction in basic building techniques, Part I of the book, with its step-by-step pictures, is all that is required. On the other hand, for the beginner and for the builder who might feel unsure in certain areas of construction, Part II, the Keys, explains basic techniques and the reasons for them. Beginning with Chapter 5 in Part I, references to the Keys appear in the text, to shed additional light on the how and why of certain specific building operations.

Also, wherever possible in the text, common words are used rather than technical trade terms. Certain trade terms that the builder may have to know are clearly and concisely explained in the Glossary of Housebuilding Terms. To make the book more practical and meaningful, the different phases of construction are arranged logically, in sequential order in the text exactly as they were in the building of the three houses that appear in the photographs.

I hope that this book will enable the home builder to provide himself with a house that is ideally located, of excellent design and construction, satisfactory to his family's needs, and priced within his budget—a home that is truly his castle.

BUILDING

PART I | A

ONE-STORY

HOUSE

LOOKING
AHEAD
BEFORE
BUILDING

Can You Build Your Own House?

If you can measure a board, saw it correctly, position it properly, and nail it in place, you should be able to build most of the house yourself. Furthermore, if you can cut and bend electric wiring into proper length and shape, handle a propane torch, use a screwdriver, and turn nuts tightly with a wrench, you should have very little, if any, need to employ skilled labor in completing the building operation.

Since this book contains a step-by-step approach to the building of a one-story house from basement to roof, including electric lighting, heating and air conditioning, masonry, and plumbing, a great deal depends on how much skill you have with your hands and how careful and exacting you are in applying it. If you can learn techniques by studying illustrations and reading easy-to-understand instructions rather than trying untested short cuts, you have an additional qualification to build your house.

Do You Need Help?

It is best to have the assistance of a nonskilled helper. Although one man *can* build a house by himself, a second man speeds up the operation, and he is almost essential on certain operations, such as large jobs requiring concrete, positioning joists into place, raising wall studding, and placing and nailing rafters.

Sometimes a home builder finds a good helper in his wife or another older member of the family. Sometimes it is a good friend willing to help— often the friend is contemplating building a home himself and is eager to gain experience or exchange labor with another friend. Still other home builders find it profitable to form a small builders' club. It is best to keep the number small; a maximum of five seems about right. Membership qualifications are clear-cut. Each must have a firm desire to build his own home in the not-too-distant future, be willing to exchange labor with other club members, and possess, if possible, some working knowledge in at least one special building field—carpentry, electrical work, plumbing, or masonry. In fact, except for a stonemason and a carpenter to help speed up the framing operation, one of the houses shown in the photographs in this book was built by the club-member plan.

If your community has a code requiring a licensed tradesman for one or more operations, see what your chances are of hiring yourself to the tradesman as his helper. It is surprising how much work you can do in preparation for his arrival on the job, and how much work he will permit you to do under his supervision while he is on the job. In addition, the tradesman's work helps to speed up the building operation, giving you more time for construction in other building areas of the house.

Deciding How Large And Expensive A House To Build

If you are under thirty, you may just be getting a good start in life. So you think about a house that will meet your family needs five, ten, and fifteen years hence, in terms of your proposed annual income. If you must borrow most of the money before building, perhaps you will lean toward a smaller, less expensive house. You may favor an architectural plan that lends itself to the addition of rooms later on without affecting the overall symmetry of the house. This is one way of allowing for a larger house at the time of family expansion. On the other hand, you may want to build a small house, then a second or third or even a fourth house, each one larger than the last, before you are old enough to think about retirement.

If you are between thirty and fifty-five, your children may be at the most expensive stage of their schooling. But this may be a blessing in disguise, for they may not require rooms of their own; during vacation periods children home from college can make use of guest rooms, and the overall size of the house can be reduced.

If you are over fifty-five, you may want to plan for a retirement house. How large and elaborate it should be depends on what purposes it is to serve. A small house is fine if you plan to travel during most of your retirement years. But if you want to spend most of your time at home, and you have a hobby, provide for it. For instance, if you are a woodworker or photographer, provide for a shop or darkroom as part of your house plans. If your objective is to reduce the cost of fire insurance, taxes, and maintenance, perhaps your house should be small but comfortable.

Building Codes

Building codes are rules and regulations found in most well-established communities for governing the construction details of buildings of all kinds, including houses.

Generally, the first rule requires the builder to secure a building permit. Then local building inspectors see that the various codes are being followed while construction is under way.

It may be argued that some codes are out of date, not sensible, or plain impractical. If this is the case, then it is the responsibility of the citizens of the community to demand code revisions. Codes should be realistic, since they should be designed to protect the homeowner. Also, sound codes must be designed to protect the general health and welfare of the entire community.

It is a good idea to know exactly what you may or may not do in building your house by yourself if local codes exist. Some communities require certain jobs, such as electrical work and plumbing, to be done only by licensed tradesmen. Other communities require only that certain building operations be approved by a local building inspector. Still other communities have very strict requirements about how some installations, such as plumbing, are made and are rather lax for other areas of building the house.

4

Tools For Building

Is it necessary to buy all the tools required to build a house? Fortunately, no. Base the number of self-owned tools on their estimated future use, not just their initial use. For instance, if you plan to use a bulldozer about a dozen times over the next ten years, the initial cost of such a tool and the time spent learning how to use it would be extravagant. In such a case, it is more practical to rent the services of a bulldozer and its operator. On the other hand, tools usually considered as basic for the home, such as a hammer, handsaw, set of chisels, etc., are well worth buying if you do not have them already. For you will find hundreds of uses for them long after the house is completed.

When buying tools, it is always best to select quality tools, for they are cheaper in the long run. Most building tradesmen feel this way; few of them would attempt to build quality houses with bargain-priced tools. My personal favorite brand for common tools has for many years been Stanley Tools.

Borrowing tools from people you know is one good way of breaking up friendships in a hurry. However, if you have formed a building club, as described previously, each of you can take some

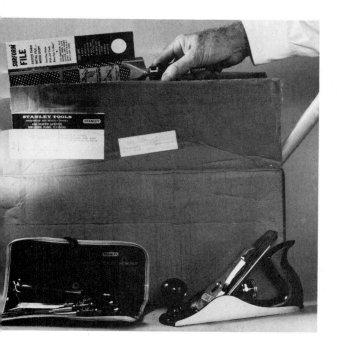

advantage of the others' tools. But for power tools, it is best if the owner operates his own, for trouble-shooting trips to repair shops tend to be expensive both in time lost and in cost of parts and skilled labor. The best of power tools require occasional repairs, but when handled by unskilled workmen they tend to break down more often.

Many do-it-yourselfers find renting tools quite practical in many instances. During the past twenty years, service industries have sprung up all over the nation, with California being the most active area. Whether it is a lawn roller or a power saw, a service agency generally has it, as well as hundreds of other tools for rent. Usually, charges are extremely reasonable. One such agency charges a daily rental fee equal to about 3 percent of the total cost of the tool. For instance, it rents a $60 extension ladder for $2 a day—quite a saving if such a tool is required for only one or two days.

How Long Does It Take?

The time it takes to build a house depends upon the size of the house, the number of helpers involved and their speed of work, and the number of hours daily they and you can spend on the job.

No matter how you approach the building problem, a certain number of man-hours are required. Bear this firmly in mind, for one of the knottiest problems during construction is to become discouraged because of the time required for construction. Actually, this is not as bad as it sounds because it usually points to the eagerness on everyone's part in the family to move in.

One of the most important phases during the preliminary planning stage of building a house is to put your affairs in order as soon as possible so that you can devote practically all your free time to actual construction—not lost motion. Plan to get the house under roof at the earliest possible time. This is particularly important if you live in an area that has cold winters. Working while exposed to the weather can become very frustrating, even to a seasoned construction worker.

If possible, excavate and finish the basement during the fall. Then you can resume building early in the spring without having to wait for the ground to dry out before making the excavation or digging the footing.

Living on the site is another way in which to turn lost motion into working time. By living on the site you save time not only by being on the site of the job, but by eliminating the necessity of getting tools and materials ready at the beginning of a work period and returning them again to storage when day is done. Also, when someone is on the site twenty-four hours a day, it is interesting to note how tools and lumber have a way of remaining on the job and not wandering away during the dark hours of night.

Some families live close at hand by moving a house trailer to the building site. Other families pitch tents and camp. Still other families temporarily cover the subfloor over the basement with roll roofing paper, then move into the basement. Of course, when the walls are tight with windows and doors in place and the roof is completed, you can install necessary utilities temporarily and move into a section of the house, such as the garage. As each room is completed on the inside, your family can spill out into the house proper.

Building Expenses General Costs: Building site $3,500. Construction grade framing materi——

Expenses

As a prospective home builder, gather information on various expenses, if it is lacking, to sharpen your judgment in the preliminary planning stage of building your house. Here are some topics to consider:

GENERAL COSTS. Basic costs of the building site and materials vary within different areas of the nation. Learning early about such costs within the community where you plan to build can save money and eliminate many problems of the future.

INTEREST CHARGES. If you must borrow money, what kind of loans can you secure? Interest on unpaid balances can run excessively high. Always inquire into hidden costs, if any. Sometimes such costs at one lending institution make it worthwhile to borrow from another source even though a slightly higher interest rate is charged.

TAXES. Do not build only to be shocked by your first real-estate tax notice. If you are unfamiliar with the local tax rate, find out now. Check with homeowners within the kind of neighborhood you most likely will build. Find out how

this rate applies to the valuation of actual properties. Check for the current year as well as for the three previous consecutive years to find out if taxes appear to have stabilized or spiraled year after year. Many properties are overtaxed, and your budget may require you to build in a community with a rather stabilized tax rate and property valuation.

INSURANCE RATES. Although this is a continuous cost, some insurance firms must charge very high rates, particularly on properties located beyond community fire districts.

IMPROVEMENT ASSESSMENTS. Are the streets paved, sewers in, and other community projects developed, such as parks, playgrounds, and other types of recreational areas? If so, are they paid for in the price of the building site, or are they to be paid from special property assessments each year for many years in the future? Also, if such improvements are not completed, will there be room for them in your future budget if they are developed later?

DEPRECIATION LOSS. More than likely, when and if you decide to sell, there will be a loss due to depreciation and obsolescence as well as a flat fee or a percentage fee charged by the real-estate broker for selling your house. However, there is not always a loss. Sometimes what was cheap land during the home-development period turns into priceless land when you decide to sell. Or a periodic rise in building materials and labor can mean little or no loss to the seller. And when you build a house yourself, there is a saving of about 6o percent of the total value in labor. This in itself makes it almost an impossibility to lose money on a self-built house. Also, you should remember the rent you have not had to pay during the period you have lived in your own house.

2

FINANCING

Reasonable Total Cost

Many people who are involved in financing homes in one way or another use a person's income on which to base a cost figure. Generally, they recommend a variable amount ranging from 1½ to 2½ times one's annual income as a fair price to pay for a house and a building site. Of course, this assumes that the buyer does not plan to do his own building and that his expenses are "average." You can increase the multiplier considerably, if you wish, because if you do *all* the labor you can make a saving of as much as 60 percent of the total value of the house. Putting it in more practical terms, this means that with $8000 worth of materials and your own labor, it is possible to build a house normally selling for $20,000.

Here is another governing factor. In case you ever wish to sell, consider the fact that generally a three-bedroom house sells quicker than either a one-bedroom house or a $100,000 mansion.

Still another factor to consider is the actual amount of ready cash or borrowed money you wish to invest in a home. After all, when the time arrives to sign on the dotted line, each individual must turn to his own sense of values and decide exactly how much to allocate.

The Cost Of The Building Site

There is no doubt that many building sites are overpriced. Here shopping around really pays dividends. Basically, you should obtain a site for as reasonable a price as possible in terms of the type of house you expect to build. For instance, locating a $40,000 house on a $50 lot adjacent to the city dump is a perfect example of false economy. Building a very cheap house on an expensive lot is just as bad. However, if your plans call for skimping on either house or site, all things being equal, skimp on the site.

More detailed information on site selection is given in the following chapter. For the moment, consider the price in terms of whether the site is improved or unimproved.

An improved site has streets, curbings, sewage installations, electricity, and gas. There should be no unsightly utility poles and wires. Sometimes they are planned and installed so well as hardly to be noticed. Such improvements *can* be made without becoming eyesores if forethought and care are given by the land developer.

Generally, 20 to 25 percent of the cost of labor and materials required to build the house is a fair price to pay for an improved lot. Of course, this formula applies to an ordinary building lot, and not, for example, to a 60-acre tract of land.

An unimproved site has none of the improvements mentioned above. Generally, it is not a wise investment to pay more than 5 to 10 percent of the combined cost of labor and materials involved in building the house. Then, too, unimproved sites are the kind to scrutinize carefully before buying. Improvements that must be made in the future can cost plenty, particularly if materials and labor continue to cost more and more.

steer clear of fast-talking operators who promise quick loans at below the going rate for home mortgages in your particular community.

Here is the way reputable lending agencies operate. They furnish money to build your house, and they require a note whereby you promise to pay the borrowed amount back in easy but definite installments, with interest. Generally, the house and the building site are put up as security for the money. If the sum you wish to borrow is not too large, other collateral may be substituted. For instance, you may be able to borrow enough money on your life-insurance policy to make a down payment or to purchase necessary materials to make a start on your house before making the loan proper.

Private loans from a relative, friend, or an individual in the community are perfectly acceptable if carried out in a businesslike manner. Be sure nothing is taken for granted. Have all terms stated clearly in writing. Then have them approved by an attorney of your choice before signing your name.

Financing Plans

If you can pay cash for your house and site, you can skip the remainder of this chapter, except for the last topic, "Final Pointers."

The first requisite for sound financing is to seek out a reputable lending agency. This may be a bank, mortgage loan company, savings and loan association, building and loan association, or a private lender of sound reputation. By all means,

The Maximum Loan

Scarce is the moneylender who has full control over the amount of money he can advance on a loan. Generally, legal restrictions set the maximum amount of a loan in relation to the appraisal value of the house. Although some lending agencies are not restricted by law on this matter, institutional policy prevents the borrower from making a full loan.

If you are hard pressed to borrow as much money as you need, shop around. An 80 percent loan is possible from some lending agencies if the house, the neighborhood, and you are considered good risks. Other loan companies can advance only 60 percent under the same conditions, while others will be able to approve a loan somewhere between these two percentages. Remember, too, that the lender's personal feeling may enter the picture. He might approve a loan no higher than 50 percent of appraisal because of certain risk factors affecting the security of the transaction.

What To Do Before Talking To A Mortgage Specialist

The mortgage specialist will consider your visit strictly as a daily business transaction. As a business transaction, he is certain to pass judgment on you as an individual. For instance, if you are forty now and talk about a twenty-five-year loan, he may wonder if your earnings will be adequate in your later years to meet payments. If this is your case, you should be able to show cause why a twenty-five-year mortgage is for you, instead of a fifteen-year one.

Before the conference it is best to do plenty of homework to avoid delay and possibly disappointment. For instance, think about and prepare complete statements regarding the size and source of your income, your current indebtedness, and your credit references.

To assist the lending agency in evaluating your ability to pay monthly housing expenses from your income, prepare some advance computations on your own.

First list your monthly income or take-home pay. Then prepare a tentative prospectus indicating monthly charges that you can afford, such as payment on principal, interest on the loan, property tax, and house insurance. Then lump them together, for generally they are covered by single, monthly payments.

Now list general, monthly expenses that you anticipate, such as utility charges, insurance premiums (medical, life, automobile, and mortgage), automobile payments, automobile-repair payments, food and clothing expenses, and any other expenses that occur monthly in your household.

Be sure to show why you think your income is adequate for repaying what you wish to borrow. Of course, you cannot expect to receive a loan from a reputable institution if your proposed monthly bills exceed your income. Frankly, your credits should be arranged so as to allow a few dollars monthly for unexpected emergencies. Then when your financial situation is evaluated, most likely you will be considered a good risk.

Finally, be prepared to leave a copy of your building plans with the lending agency. Also, prepare a cost sheet, showing cost of materials, cost of labor you plan to do yourself along with any other labor costs that you anticipate, and the price of the building site, which must be surveyed by a qualified engineer if this has not already been done. The above information is not prying into your affairs. It is necessary before any lending agency can make a fair appraisal of your personal responsibility regarding the possibility of a loan.

Should You Give Up Because You Have No Ready Cash?

No. It is true that no lending-institution executive in his right mind would finance an entire house without the owner putting in a certain amount of cash. But you are a special case, since you are willing to put up your labor, or at least most of it. Yet, everyone knows the world is full of dreamers, and the lending-institution personnel are no exception. They are practical people, and they are interested in working with doers only. So it is well to prove you mean business by getting the house under way at your earliest opportunity. Otherwise, there may remain some doubt about your ability to go beyond the planning stage.

Of course, if you own the building site plus the willingness to furnish the labor, you are steps ahead of the average person seeking a loan. Perhaps all you need to do to establish yourself as a good credit risk is to dig the footing or complete the excavation to show you are ready to go.

If you do not own the site and have little cash and approach the lending agent with your homework completed but indicate only a willingness to work, he may suggest returning later when you have shown good faith by having something tangible completed on the house, such as having the wall studding in place. If this happens you find yourself with six of one and half dozen of the other. For without money the lumberyard is hesitant to send you materials to work with, and without materials you cannot show the lending agent you mean to build.

What do you do next if this is your case? If people respect you and you have a good reputation, you are still in the home-building league. Set up an appointment with the manager of a lumberyard. Then lay the cards on the table. Speak openly and frankly about your situation. Most likely the manager will advance materials to get started on a thirty-, sixty-, or ninety-day consignment. If the first manager you approach throws cold water on your proposition, arrange to see other lumber dealers. In almost every community there is at least one dealer who will go more than half of the building way with an honest, courageous customer of good reputation.

With some materials, you can begin building. Then when you return to the lending agency, you have concrete evidence of a house under construction. If you are doing sound work with quality materials, more than likely you will be considered a good risk for a loan. Thus, you can pay for your materials as they are required.

Sometimes the company for which you work may be helpful. If you work for a large company, your employer may be interested in talking to you about a loan. Good employer-employee relations are considered more and more by forward-looking companies, and they do more and more to help their responsible employees through financial difficulties. Your employer may have funds available for investing in mortgages when the employee is a satisfactory risk.

Types Of Mortgages

There are two elements common to all mortgages, namely, principal and interest.

The principal is the amount of money loaned. It is the estimated amount of money required to complete the house. In short, if you borrow $10,000, this is the principal. The interest is the money you pay for the use of the principal. Interest is expressed in percentage. It varies from location to location and from time to time. For instance, if you pay $600 annually for the use of $10,000, you are paying an interest rate of 6 percent. The interest is paid annually or at some

other interval agreed upon between you and the lending agency at the time of negotiating the loan.

Actually, there are two kinds of mortgages. One is called an amortized, first mortgage, the other a straight mortgage. Most likely you will not need a magnifying glass to read the word "mortgage" on either one, but do not pass up the fine print. Not only is it necessary to read every word, but you should understand the meaning of every word you read.

An amortized, first mortgage is recommended if cash to build your house is hard to come by. This is the method favored by most home builders who require financing. Here payments are made monthly or every three months as agreed upon by both parties for as long as is required to pay off the principal. Each payment is apportioned among the principal, interest, fire insurance, and taxes. With this payment plan, the interest is always computed on the unpaid balance of the principal. As payments are made, the loan is gradually reduced. The interest portion becomes less and less, which means more and more is applied on the principal because the total payment is always the same. Of course, this is based on the assumption that fire insurance and taxes do not fluctuate greatly.

A straight mortgage is designed for a short term running for five to twenty years. Here 75 percent is the borrowable maximum of the appraised property value, and full repayment is made at the termination date of the loan. Installments are paid semiannually, quarterly, or monthly as agreed by the lender and borrower, and the installments include interest, fire insurance, and taxes.

If the repayment of the principal cannot be met at the termination of the mortgage date, the lender *may* renew the mortgage for another term, but he is not under legal obligation to do so. Even if he does, he will more than likely expect some specified amount to be paid on the principal. On the other hand, the lender may foreclose the mortgage. Legally, there is no reason to give cause for not renewing the mortgage. However, an economic condition is sometimes cited as a reason for foreclosure, such as a national recession. At other times, the lender simply allows the borrower to make a choice—either repay the principal or accept foreclosure.

Generally, here is what happens when a mortgage is foreclosed. Property ownership passes from the borrower to the lender. Then the property is offered for sale. Following the sale, the lender is paid the principal. The balance, if any, is paid to the borrower.

If by now you still believe a straight mortgage is for you, are you considering a second mortgage? Sometimes a second mortgage appears to be necessary to obtain additional funds if the borrower needs more than 75 percent of the property value, the maximum allowable with the straight mortgage.

Also you should know that a second mortgage is subordinate to the claims of a first mortgage. For instance, foreclosure on a second mortgage does not jeopardize the position of the holder of the first mortgage. But if the first mortgagee forecloses, the claim of the second mortgage holder is eliminated. Only by satisfying the claim of the first mortgage holder does the second mortgagee protect his interest. Before seeking a second mortgage, know that because of the nature of the lien and because of lack of established or recognized market there is no check on the lender's charges. Therefore, the interest rate is generally much higher than that of first mortgages. Generally speaking, it is best to avoid second mortgages if at all possible.

Here is another thing to consider, and more reason why you should sign nothing in the nature of a legal paper without the approval of your attorney. Do not accept a mortgage where the principal is required "on demand." This means you must pay the full amount of the principal at any time the lending agency demands it or have your property foreclosed. If your finances were as flexible as this, there would be little point in your securing a loan in the first place.

FHA Loans

In 1934, the Federal Housing Act (FHA) was passed by Congress. It provides for government insurance to guarantee lending agencies the amount of loans made to approved borrowers. Thus, the FHA does not make actual loans. If the house meets FHA standards, is priced within the lender's means, and appears to be a good long-term risk, any person with a steady job or business with a good credit reputation can secure FHA approval on a loan for building a house.

The FHA is much like any other insurance company. After the appraisal of the property, it insures itself against loss on the loan if it seems to be a good risk. It does this by requiring the borrower to pay an insurance premium of 0.5 percent per year on the average balance outstanding in each year during the life of the loan. Thus, the annual amount of interest becomes a little smaller each year until the loan is completely repaid.

There are several benefits derived from having FHA insurance. First, an FHA valuation of your property provides an objective measure of its long-term value. This provides the home builder with a guideline for determining how much he should request for a loan to pay for building materials.

Next an impersonal evaluation of your liabilities and your assets helps prevent you from entering into an unrealistic transaction.

Another advantage is that you may obtain a larger loan at a slightly lower rate of interest (even considering the 0.5 percent premium mentioned above) than you might secure by making a conventional loan.

Finally, if and when you decide to sell your property, FHA approval means that your property has met minimum standards and inspections—a good point for your prospective buyer to know about.

Veterans' Loans

In 1966, the Veterans' Readjustment Benefit Act became effective. Eligibility for a home loan applies to most people who served in the armed forces since 1950.

If you are a veteran and feel that you are eligible for a loan and desire one, secure application forms and additional information from any Veterans' Administration Office or active duty station.

Construction Loans

A construction loan is especially designed for the person who builds his own home. Generally, it is a loan covering the costs of material and labor. Since you plan to do all or most of the labor, your construction loan can be tailor-made to meet your particular needs.

If you decide upon securing an FHA-insured loan, know that the Federal Housing Agency does not insure construction loans as such on individual homes. It is possible, however, to secure a conditional FHA commitment on a permanent loan before you begin construction. In turn, this makes it easier to obtain a construction loan from a local lending agency, for both you and the lending agency know that a permanent loan will be insured by FHA when the house is finished. Be sure to obtain an FHA commitment before the construction begins. Otherwise, you may find yourself out in the cold, wondering how you are going to build your house.

Some Final Pointers

Be sure to carry a homeowner's insurance policy. (If you build in Alaska, Hawaii, Oregon, or Mississippi, purchase a Comprehensive Dwelling policy.) During construction, you will need coverage only on fire, windstorm, and hail in certain sections of the nation, and liability (a must if you have other people working for you, or if you allow people to trespass on your property).

Next activate a complete policy when the house is finished. Add to the original policy protection from fire on personal property and household furniture, as well as other common hazards. There are five different kinds of homeowners' policies. Any reliable insurance agent, perhaps the one associated with your lending agency, will be glad to explain the best policy suited for you.

Title insurance is required by many lending agencies before making the loan. Here you are protected against such matters as disagreement over property lines and any flaws that might appear in the property title. If the lending agency does not require title insurance, secure the advice of your attorney as to whether you should buy it, after he has had an opportunity to examine the abstract and title of your parcel of ground.

More than likely you will be asked sooner or later exactly how you want your title to the property to read. Both the phrases "tenants in common" and "joint tenants" may have a pleasant ring as your lending agent talks to you about them, but there is a very important difference between them. If the deed names you and your wife as "joint tenants," you are co-owners of the property. If one dies, his or her title, as the case may be, automatically passes to the survivor without probate of the estate to make transfer to the living heir. Because states differ on exact wording required to create joint tenancy in a deed, check with your lending agent or your attorney to be certain your title will reflect your desires.

3

SELECTING
A
HOMESITE

Generally, it takes considerable time and investigation to find the plot of ground best suited for your particular needs. Your future happiness and contentment rests on going beyond finding out whether the ground is "improved" or "unimproved" as discussed in the previous chapter.

The setting of a house is most important, and naturally the setting has its beginning with the purchase of the building site. Will the design you have in mind look right on it? How will the style as well as the price range appear with relationship to others nearby? Is the size of the plot adequate for the house you have in mind, with the landscaping you want to do, and with the yard you desire for games and cookouts or other outdoor activities?

The elevation of the site can have a great bearing on whether the site is for you. A location at the bottom of a gully can not only spoil a view, but the basement, if you have one, might double as a swimming pool during rainy seasons. This might have several advantages, but furnaces, washers, dryers, and other equipment usually found in basements do not make ideal pool furniture.

When evaluating a site, you are primarily on your own. No one else is either concerned or has the ability to make the decision to buy for you. Then, too, neither the owner nor the realtor is likely to point out the bad features of the site for sale.

Even the best house you can build can be unsatisfactory if located in a shabby or declining neighborhood. So plan to spend time walking through the neighborhood in the search. While there, pay close attention to the homes and the yards. Notice how they are maintained. Observe the proximity of public services and public buildings. Talk with and observe the people. Find out what they do for a livelihood. As you talk, think about how their interests and expectations of life compare with yours. Then while you are in the neighborhood, make a check on the zoning regulations and building codes, if they exist.

Lot Size

First check the boundary lines of the lot. This gives you the size as well as the shape. For instance, suppose you find a lot in a newly developed housing area with a 150-foot front, but because

If zoning exists, does it cover only residential buildings? Probably you will not buy if playgrounds and shopping centers can locate around you. Therefore, it is well to avoid buying a site where zoning or lack of zoning allows all types of commercial buildings within residential areas.

Sometimes zoning regulations are so tight that you cannot build any additional buildings on your lot, no matter how well they are designed or how much they cost. Although a little tool house may be well constructed and serve a useful purpose, it would violate zoning regulations in some communities. At other times, you may not add certain attachments to your house. A greenhouse attached to a house may look pleasing enough, but sometimes it cannot be built because it violates zoning regulations. At other times, the minimum cost and the style of the house is clearly defined. Thus, if you desired to build a $50,000 ranch-type house in an area zoned for $15,000 Cape Cod cottages, you are out of order. You would not be issued a building permit.

the lot faces a curved roadbed, a rear width of only 75 feet. An irregularly shaped lot such as this may be of little practical value to the average home builder. You may want to seek a lot more rectangular in shape.

Most lending agencies making FHA-insured loans require a minimum space of 8 feet between the house and boundary of lot on each side. This is a minimum space that you should allow. Generally, a lot less than 60 feet wide tends to reduce privacy. The minimum length of lot should be no less than 100 feet, and 150 feet is much better.

Zoning Regulations

Zoning regulations are local laws found in many well-established communities. The purpose of such regulations is to govern the type of buildings (residential, business, industrial, etc.) that are erected in specified areas of the community, protecting you and yet meeting your needs and desires.

Although most restrictions are positive protections and should not be considered undesirable, read them carefully now. Do not find yourself later starting to build a swimming pool in your back yard only to discover that it violates zoning regulations.

Deed Restrictions And Zoning Regulations

Deed restrictions do not take precedence over zoning codes. Often the seller of a plot of ground

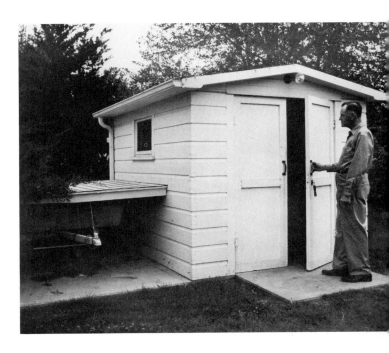

writes certain restrictions in the deed, regarding the type of construction, style of building, and cost. Such conditions may have originated several generations ago, or they may have more recent origin. In either case, the restrictions are binding, although they cannot replace zoning regulations. And if both zoning regulations and deed restrictions exist, be sure that both meet your approval before buying.

Choosing A Convenient And Safe Place To Live

If everything checks out well thus far, find out now if it is a convenient and safe place to reside. If you have children of school age, visit the neighborhood schools. Find out if the facilities are satisfactory and the classrooms not overcrowded. If the schools operate on split shifts, how will this fit into your schedule? Find out if the teachers are highly qualified and if they are using up-to-date methods, especially in teaching the core subjects, such as English, mathematics, science, and the social studies. If your children require transportation to school, must you provide it, or will they be transported by school bus? If you have a child interested in art, or music, or one that requires special education, is the kind of program you have in mind found in the schools?

Inquire if there is a church of your denomination located in the neighborhood or nearby. If so, talk to the pastor, rabbi, or priest. Get his point of view on your moving into the community.

No one wants a fire, but a well-trained fire department is a delight to have around if the house catches on fire. Is the site within the fire district, or must you pay a special fee if the fire truck is required? If so, what is the fee?

How about public playgrounds, street lights, convenient fire hydrants, and police protection? Are they adequate according to your standards? For example, how does the crime rate compare with that in the neighborhood where you currently reside?

Public Utilities And Services

If you are satisfied with commercial and public services now, do not take the new ones for granted. Study the street conditions.

STREETS. Study the street conditions, preferably during rush hours. Find out if anything is done to discourage high-speed driving. Are speed limits enforced? Other things being equal, choose a location that has curved or deadend streets designed to reduce automobile speeds. Generally, the less traffic in a neighborhood the better.

Find out if the streets adjacent to the site are privately owned or public. If privately owned, be sure of the maintenance policy, for the future as well as for the present. For instance, in cold climates what provision is made for snow removal from streets and sidewalks, if any? If the streets show need of improvements, inquire if assessments are planned for the owners, at what cost. Are there foreseeable condemnation possibilities? Since highway departments, public schools, and institutions of higher learning plan well ahead of construction, this is an easy matter to check now with the local planning commission.

ELECTRICITY AND TELEPHONE. Generally, a franchise requires utility companies to furnish service to any resident living within the corporation limits, even if it requires the setting of additional poles. On the other hand, it may be another matter if the site is located on a private road or a public road outside of corporation limits. You may find it necessary to pay the costs of setting poles and stringing wires from the nearest utility pole to your house.

Rates for service can vary considerably from community to community. Find out exactly the electricity rate and telephone charges for the specific services you require. For instance, there still remain building sites in the nation that offer telephone service, but only on a ten-party line.

WATER. A water supply might mean anything from water gushing from a spring at the bottom of a hillside to water flowing from a first-class city main where the supply is adequate even during dry summer months, and is tested and treated if required. Also, the water from a city main might contain a high content of minerals, making it too hard for cooking and laundry uses without the addition of a water softener as a part of the home water system. This would be an added cost that you would want to consider.

While you are checking the water supply, inquire about the water rate. Does a flat rate cover both the water supply and sewage disposal, or are the two services charged separately? If so, how much for each, and on what basis are they assessed?

SEWERS. If flash floods are common, take a good look at the lay of the land, for it will tell you much about the drainage in general. Grading, filling, or building a retaining wall can come high for correcting nature's drainage design. Of course, if the site is located in an area that floods, look elsewhere. Such a plot of ground is too expensive even if it is for free.

If the site has passed inspection thus far, inquire about the nature of the sewers. For best results the sewer main(s) should be located at a lower level than the basement floor, if it is a part of your house plans.

If there is a storm sewer as well as a sanitary sewer, are they large enough to handle the drainage of excess rainwater and the sewage from the plumbing fixtures? Sometimes regulations are such that both sewage and excess rainwater from the roof gutters are piped into one large sewage system. If this is the case, be sure the system is adequate to do the job. Think about a growing community. Will the drainage system, or an improvement on it, take care of the sewage problems of the future?

If sewer mains are lacking, you may want to resort to installing a private means of sewage disposal, such as a septic tank. If so, see your county health officer, who can explain local requirements and will probably have sets of plans.

COUNTRY SITES. Country sites may have some merit, but many a man wanted to become a country squire as he fell in love with an attractive site located in a rural area, only to live in bitter disappointment after the house was finished. If the rural site is without zoning regulations or deed restriction, it is true that you may build anything from a hog house to a castle without it being anyone else's business.

What works well for you works well for other people who build. Sometimes what they build fails to coincide with what you and your family like. After all, each to his own liking in an unrestricted area. Remember that junk yards, filling stations, race tracks, hog pens, commercial airplane landing fields, factories, and poorly managed dog kennels can spring up overnight in an unrestricted area.

You can obtain some protection in unzoned areas by purchasing large tracts of land on both sides of the main road adjacent to the site, but this is expensive unless you plan to make use of the ground for farming or other business purpose.

Forming a land corporation is another way to assure you of protection from obnoxious situations, but here you are right back into zoning regulations if you are wise. Of course, if you are the leadership type, you may develop regulations of your own liking.

Sometimes lending agencies hesitate to make loans on properties located in isolated regions. This is particularly true if utilities, such as electricity, gas, and telephone lines, are some distance away. The nearest FHA office will be glad to advise you on loan insurance for any specific piece of rural land that you have in mind. But if you have the cash, this is no problem. And you can be free of anyone's advice, if you wish.

BORINGS AND SOIL TESTS. If everything else seems satisfactory about the site up to this point, by all means make deep borings and soil tests, especially if your plans call for a basement. Be sure you have the owner's permission before tampering with the soil, however.

Using a post-hole digger, make several test holes on the lot. If convenient, do this during a

rainy season, for the borings at this time will show the depth of the groundwater below the surface, indicating any difficulty you may encounter with a basement. Of course, if a storm sewer is available and is in good working order, this step can be eliminated.

There are several other questions that can be answered by digging test holes.

Is the ground virgin soil, or is it "filled" land? Landfills of tin cans, broken concrete, tree limbs, and other debris with some dirt added is something else again. Are there rock formations between the surface and the proposed basement floor? Rock formations of any consequence can soon price a basement right out of the house plans.

It the topsoil thin, or is it thick? The thickness of topsoil is a determining factor in whether you can or cannot grow shrubs and plants successfully without first hauling in expensive soil.

Is the subsoil sandy or clay? Sandy soil drains well, while clay soil has a tendency to hold water.

Site Evaluation Checklist

The list below is a checklist prepared especially for your convenience in bringing together a summary of your findings. Before looking at sites, it is well to prepare several copies of the list, leaving plenty of space for your observations. Record your observations of each site on a separate checksheet. Then purchase the building site most nearly meeting your requirements.

BUILDING SITE EVALUATION

Site
  Dimensions
  Shape
  Virgin or filled ground
  Topography
  Mine entries underground
  Oil or other mineral rights
  Type of lot (corner or other)
  Street (type and width)
  Alley
  Drainage
  Nature of soil
  Floodwater
  Basement possibilities

Conditions
  Type of neighborhood
  Deed restrictions
  Zoning
  Easements
  Percent developed
  Traffic conditions
  View
  Assessments
  Taxes
  Insurance rates
  Future trends
  Chemicals, dust, smoke, smog
  Foul odors
  Noise
  Condemnation possibilities
Services
  Church
  School
  Transportation
  Time to reach work
  Shopping centers
  Recreation
  Hospital
  Doctor
  Dentist
Utilities
  Sewer
  Water
  Electricity
  Gas
  Telephone
  Garbage and debris
  Truck delivery
  Mail
  Street lighting
  Public transportation
  Improved roads
  Police protection
  Fire protection

Making The Purchase

Before moving into the final buying period, you must find answers to the following questions:

1. Is the title to the property in the clear? Check to see if there are any mortgages or other outstanding indebtedness against it.

2. Does the seller's price include all assessments?
3. Are the taxes paid up to date? Also, find out exactly who pays the taxes for the current year. If you and the seller are to share them, how much are you expected to pay?
4. Have the boundaries of the site been established by a competent surveyor? Sometimes, rural boundaries are quite vague on such matters.
5. Does the title indicate any easements that have been granted to individuals for private roads or utility companies to run poles on the ground or pipes under the ground?

Secure answers to these questions from an attorney of your choice. He will search the court records relative to the site. Then he will prepare a document known as an Abstract of Title, bringing the record up to and including a specified date.

For your protection, have your attorney approve an option to buy between you and the seller. To protect your interest during the interval between your decision to buy the site and the actual acquisition of the deed, sign an option form with the seller. Generally, you can purchase an option for only a few dollars.

An option gives you the privilege of buying the site for a specified amount during a certain period of time, but also it frees you of an obligation to buy, should you decide to change your mind. Be sure the option contains a complete description of the property and defines the method of payment. There is one final point to consider before placing your signature on the option paper. If a down payment is made on the site, the purchase is legally binding on both you and the seller.

There are deeds, and there are deeds. A *tax-title deed* is not advisable to consider if this is all the seller can offer. Such a deed varies; but in the main, it merely shows that the seller paid taxes on the site for a specified number of years. If you buy such a site and make improvements, you can almost be assured of heirs appearing to claim rights to your property.

A *quitclaim deed* passes from the seller to you, the buyer, a site for better or for worse. Sometimes it is for worse. Frequently, claims come up against the property, such as longstanding indebtedness on pavements, sidewalks, and/or sewers. All things being equal it is best not to purchase where the seller can produce only a quitclaim deed, unless your attorney feels that you are really making a sound purchase.

A *warranty deed* includes the description of the site and the price to be paid. Also, it warrants enjoyment of the site. Essentially, this means that the seller and his heirs will defend the title against any legal claims to it. Of course, if and when such suits come to the attention of the courts, the seller and his heirs may not be living, or they may be living and be financially irresponsible. For this reason it is always good advice to seek advice from your attorney about the possibility of purchasing title insurance as described in a previous chapter. Finally, it is best to buy where the seller can produce a warranty deed for the site. After all, you expect to invest a sizable sum of money for building materials and to furnish your labor in building the house.

4

PLANNING
A
HOME

You should not try to design a house from scratch by yourself, unless you are an architect with training in home design. One eager beaver with more nerve than architectural ability completely designed his own house. After it was completed, visitors were always escorted graciously from room to room. At some point during the tour his wife always remarked, "Henry designed the house all by himself." This was a nice gesture on her part, but anyone with half an eye for home design would already know that Henry must have designed it. Hardly anyone else could have come up with a design so poor.

Henry's house had an inconvenient arrangement of rooms, with traffic patterns through the living room, two rooms located between the garage and kitchen, and so on. It lacked sufficient storage places, such as cabinets and closets. It lacked privacy; the living-room picture window faced the neighbor's house located only a few steps away. The living quarters were not located properly with respect to the sun, shade, and wind, which should serve as advantages at different times of the day as well as different seasons of the year.

Planning a house calls for more than putting a few rooms together, each with a few windows and doors. Actually, designing a house is a professional art done by a professional architect, unless you are satisfied with the possibility of having a hodgepodge of rooms between basement and roof.

Sources Of House Plans

Generally, homemade plans, whether the home builder himself or some other inexperienced person draws them, are not good architectural design. Neither are amateur alterations of good plans.

Working drawings, in the form of blueprints, specifications, and material lists may be purchased for homes featured in popular magazines, in home books found on magazine racks, and in stock plan books given by lumber yards in the form of advertising materials.

Securing the services of a local architect who specializes in designing small homes is a sure way of getting a house designed to meet your every requirement. And the additional cost involved may be an economy in the long run. This is particularly true if you build a large house and expect a low rate of obsolescence.

There is a compromise method between hiring an architect outright to draw a set of plans and buying a set of stock plans. If you locate a house plan that almost meets your needs, generally you can obtain professional help from a competent architect to make necessary minor alterations. Here a going hourly fee is charged, and the architect actually serves as a consultant. If you follow this approach, have the architect make an estimate of his charges before hiring him, for you should know in advance approximately what the added service will cost. You may find it more economical to hire the architect to do the complete job for you, or you may find it less expensive to look for another set of stock plans.

Planning Pointers

Whether you look for stock working drawings or seek out an architect to design your house, here are some questions to answer before starting:

1. What is the maximum amount of money you want to spend for a house?
2. What are your expectations in general about the house? Give consideration to such general matters as beauty, convenience, quietness, privacy, roominess, facilities for recreation, facilities for entertainment, facilities for study, and facilities for hobbies, such as a workshop or photographic darkroom.
3. Since you are going to furnish most of the required labor, what kind of construction can you afford and do you feel competent to do? For instance, you should decide on a material for the exterior—wood, masonry, hardboard, etc. Generally, it is not good practice to use more than two combinations of building materials here, such as a combination of wood and stone.
4. What style of architecture do you want? In addition to climate, geographic location, and personal taste, neighborhood houses are a determining factor in what looks best. For instance, it would show poor taste on your part to build a ranch-style house among a group of two-story houses of traditional design. It is a good idea to stay away from freakish or faddish designs. Rather, seek good design, simple and economical to construct.

Also, consider the fact that dormers, hips, and valleys add to material costs and labor. Sometimes, the added cost and time are well spent, particularly if you get exactly what you want.

Specifications Of A Good Plan

TYPE OF ARCHITECTURE. Shy away from outmoded, obsolete, geographically unsuited, or shoddy designs. Otherwise, you may build only to find you own a white elephant if you ever wish to sell. Select a design that is compatible with other houses in the neighborhood, both in price and in architecture.

ORIENTATION. Pay particular attention to the sun, shade, and wind in relationship to the house location. Give forethought to how the house will look and what purpose it is to serve. If it is landscaped correctly, has windows in the right locations, and has properly dimensioned overhangs, then it can be delightful in the summer and comfortable in the winter.

ROOMS. Determine how many and what kind of rooms you require. Then find out if they are of appropriate size and arranged in proper relation to each other, with plenty of wall space to accommodate furniture. Generally, plenty of wall space is needed in the living and dining rooms. The kitchen should adjoin the garage, and if you have a family room, consider having it adjoin another kitchen wall. If you want a fireplace, decide whether it is to be located in the living room, family room, or some other room in the house. If you plan to do much socializing in the basement, consider a second fireplace for it.

SPECIAL ROOMS. If you have hobbies requiring special rooms, now is the time to see that they are properly located in the house plans.

Sometimes the builder has a way of accumulating materials and equipment long before they are needed on the job. If this is your case, plans for their storage and care are most important during the interim. As a case in point, some photographic equipment I had ordered arrived long before my house was completed. I included them in a temporary darkroom, thus solving the storage problem and at the same time putting them to good use.

FURNITURE AND BUILT-IN CABINETS. Naturally, these require space. A good way to determine if they will fit into the rooms without crowding and still allow suitable walking space is to prepare

cutouts representing the objects in question. First make simple drawings of the furniture and cabinets (or anything else that takes up floor space and is not found on the floor plans) on light cardboard, such as 3×5-inch index cards. Use the same scale as shown on the floor plan. Then make cutouts and label them. These serve as paper models when placed directly on the plan. By shifting them about, you can tell exactly whether the space meets your furniture requirements, whether you need the plans altered, or whether to seek another set of plans altogether.

BATHROOMS. Consider two bathrooms, one for the master bedroom, the other one for general use. Adjoining bathrooms, back to back, save both time and materials in construction.

HALLWAYS. Look for a center-hall plan that permits entry to any part of the house without having to walk through other rooms. Hallways should have a 3-foot minimum width. Require a direct garage-to-kitchen route for ease in bringing in groceries and other items stored in the kitchen. The floor plan of the Kingwood house supplied by IBC Homes, Charleston, Illinois, shows how central hallways give direct access to all rooms without going through other rooms.

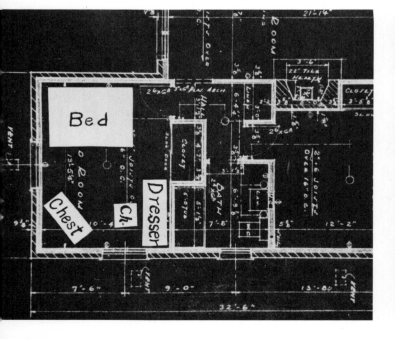

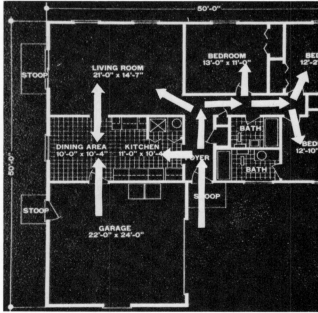

KITCHEN. Using cardboard models, check out the location and arrangement of the refrigerator, range, sink, dishwasher, and cabinets, if not indicated on the floor plan. Find out if the lights are adequate and located in convenient places. Make this judgment after the cardboard models are in place as you want them.

DOORS. Require exterior doors to have a width of 3 feet. Interior door widths of 2 feet, 8 inches are acceptable, but 3 feet is more practical for moving large pieces of furniture in and out of the rooms. You might want to consider sliding doors throughout the house. They are convenient and waste no wall space.

STAIRWAY. The stairs to the basement should not be located in a conspicuous place. Consider the practicality of having both an inside and an outside stairway.

GARAGE. Insist on a floor drain under each car in a multi-automobile garage if it is connected to the house. Otherwise, traffic has a way of tracking mud and slush into the house proper during inclement weather.

BUILT-IN ITEMS. Require built-in items of your choice wherever feasible. There is no reason why kitchen cabinets and sinks, ironing board, telephone cabinet, breakfast unit, dishwasher, electric stove, bookcases, guncases, medicine cabinets, and so on cannot be built in.

PORCHES AND PATIOS. These are items of personal taste. Insist on one or both if this is your choice. Adding them later can be expensive and time-consuming.

HEATING AND COOLING. Insist on plans that show both heating and air conditioning if you live in a weather zone requiring such installations for complete comfort. If you decide on an electric heating system, you will need a separate air-conditioning unit. I installed Markel electric baseboard heating in one of the houses featured in this book because I find it's one of the cleanest, safest, and most trouble-free of systems.

BASEMENT. Insist on a basement if your building site is suitable and you have a desire for it.

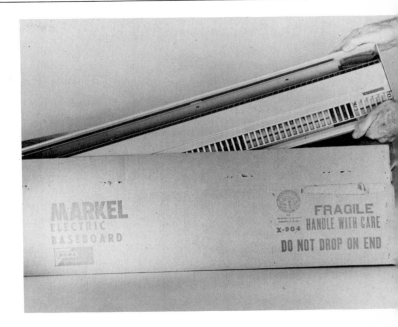

A basement serves the direct needs of the occupants, and it also makes for practically complete control over termites if they exist in your area. Then, too, water pipes are less likely to freeze in cold climates if the house is built over a basement. If wiring and piping are installed underneath the house, a basement makes repairing them much easier.

Working Drawings And Blueprints

You can't learn everything there is to know about working drawings and blueprints in one easy lesson. However, you can learn enough to interpret the blueprints of your own house.

Working drawings for building a house are the way an architect has for showing you exactly how the house should be put together. The terms "blueprint," "working drawings," and "plans" are used synonomously. Sometimes, only the word "plans" is used, but "working drawings" is the correct term. A set of working drawings shows you overall dimensions, room and hallway sizes, location and sizes of doors and windows, location of interior partitions, location of electrical appliances and plumbing fixtures, and other bits of information needed to finish the house.

A blueprint is simply a copy of a drawing, usually a tracing, showing the working plans as they were drawn in ink or pencil. The chemical treatment of the paper produces white lines and lettering on a blue background; hence the name "blueprint." If required, hundreds of blueprints can be made from a single set of working drawings.

As a builder, it is essential that you know how to "take off" dimensions from a blueprint and convert them accurately into the various parts of the house—framing members, windows, doors, and the like. You must recognize water-pipe and plumbing-fixture locations so you can place studding and joists in proper position to allow for the fixtures and their accessories. Finally, from time to time you should check the progress of the house against the blueprints.

Although a set of working drawings may appear somewhat confusing, because of the great amount of detail involved, do not pass up the opportunity of examining blueprints of any house. For, by making a systematic study of different blueprints you will soon gain a basic knowledge of blueprint reading, particularly if you make use of a few general principles explained below.

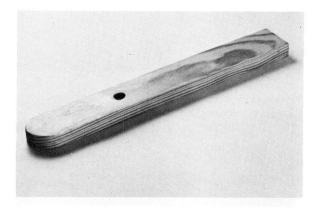

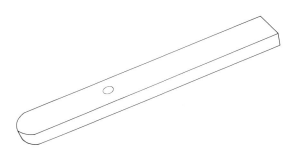

VIEWS. Other than the perspective view (explained later), most views shown on blueprints represent a solid object on paper in such a manner as to describe its exact shape. This is accomplished by drawing true views of the object as observed from different positions and by arranging these views in a systematic order.

Start with the picture showing a shaped piece of lumber. Almost everyone knows what it is and could probably make a good facsimile of it, because it represents a portion of a standard piece of lumber as it appears to the eye. The sketch below the picture shows the same object in what is called a pictorial view (sometimes called a perspective view). A *perspective view* is a view as it appears to the eye. This is the one generally shown by an architect when he wants to show the builder how a finished house will look from a fixed position. In short, it looks much like the view you would get if you took a picture of the finished house. Such views as this, along with floor plans, are shown in the newspapers and house-plan books when the architect desires to give the reader an "eye" view of the house.

Most working drawings are not drawn in perspective, and for a very good reason. A perspective view shows the general and somewhat distorted appearance of an object, but it does not show the *exact* forms and relations of the various parts of the object. In brief, it shows an object (in your case, a house or part of a house) as it appears, not as it really is.

Because you, the builder, need a description of an object to tell its exact shape, working drawings show measurements of a *single* plane only. Sometimes a *top* view is shown as in a floor plan; at other times a *front* or *side* view is shown as in an elevation plan. Such views are called *orthographic projections*. The drawing here shows how an orthographic projection can show three views, using as an example the shaped 2×4 shown previously. Notice that each view shows a single plane of the object as it actually is.

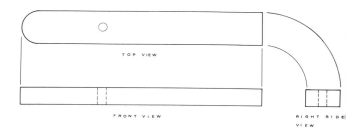

TOP VIEW

FRONT VIEW

RIGHT SIDE VIEW

DOTTED LINES. Because the architect describes every part of an object, all surfaces are represented on the drawings, whether they can be seen or not. Short dashes represent hidden surfaces, as indicated in the case of the hole shown in the front view and right side view of the accompanying drawing.

CURVES. Notice the top view shows the curve. This is exactly what you would see if you looked directly down on the piece of lumber. The front view shows a straight line on the left, because this is exactly what you would see if you looked at it directly from the front.

CENTER LINES. These are lines used to locate centers of circles and arcs. If the top view of the 2×4 were shown in an architectural drawing, it would look like the drawing here.

DIMENSIONS AND LETTERING. These are symbols used to complete the description of the object in question: a radius of 2 inches, a hole 1 inch in diameter, a length of 2 feet 4 inches, a width of 4 inches, and the exact location of the holes.

BREAK LINES. Ruled lines connected by freehand zigzag lines are used to show the cross-section of long, uniformly shaped pieces and for "breaking out" parts. The break lines in the top-view drawing show the breaking out of a part of the same 2×4.

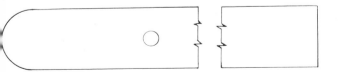

SCALE. Because an object is large or lacks detail, it may be drawn in reduced proportion, called drawing to scale. Generally, architects use a scale of ¼″ = 1′. Where parts cannot be shown in sufficient detail, larger scales are used, and they are indicated on each respective drawing. Thus, using a scale of ½″ = 1′, the architect represents a board 10 feet long with a line 5 inches long.

Reading Blueprints Initially

Examine your set of blueprints. Generally, a set of working drawings made up into blueprints include a plot plan, basement plan, floor plan, section plans, plans of specific details, etc.

Begin by taking a preliminary look at the plans. On your first reading, pay little attention to actual details. Rather, try to gain an idea of how the house is laid out and what it will look like on the building site.

Courtesy Reasor Corporation

If a pictorial view is shown, study it for gaining a conception of the exterior views in relationship to the site.

The architect shows only the top view in the plot plan, foundation plan, and floor plan. When examining any of these, imagine yourself looking straight down from an elevated position where you can see only the top plane of the object represented.

Now examine your plot plan. Note the location and position of the house proper. If there are

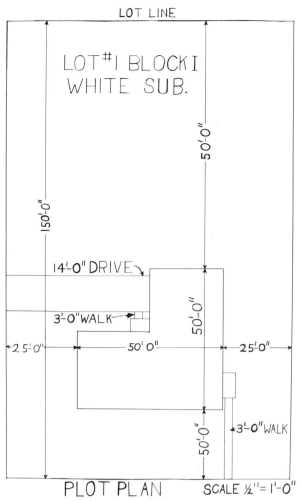

PLOT PLAN   SCALE ½″ = 1′-0″

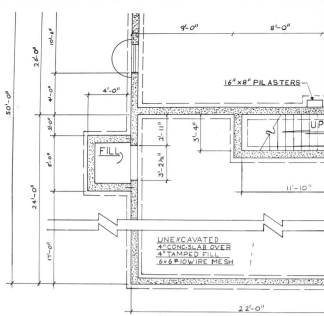

Courtesy Reasor Corporation

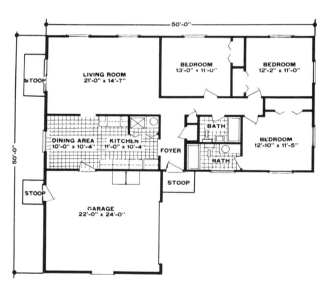

Courtesy Reasor Corporation

other separate buildings, they should be indicated. Many plot plans show accurate dimensions and locations of walks, driveways, and utility services, such as electricity and telephone lines and gas, water, and sewer pipes, along with anything else that is to be located on the building site.

One builder made his own plot plan, using a scale of ½″ = 1′ as shown in the picture. He made the plan large so that evergreens and trees could be shown more clearly when he reached the point of landscape planning.

Next examine your basement foundation plan, shown as a top view. This plan should contain a complete layout as shown in the partial plan here. Any unexcavated ground should be clearly indicated. Foundations for porches, patios, and chimneys along with basement windows should be accurately located and dimensioned.

Now acquaint yourself with the actual floor plan. Although you try to imagine yourself looking directly down on the top view of the floor, further imagine yourself walking through the front door and then going through each room of the house, completing your trip by coming out the back door. As your imaginary trip takes you through the house, note the room and hallway arrangements designated by interior partitions. Also note the locations of doors, windows, closets, built-in cabinets, fireplace, and other details.

Study the different elevation drawings. These show the exterior appearance of your proposed house, such as the floor and ceiling heights, openings for windows and doors, roof pitch, and so forth. Most house plans include four elevations.

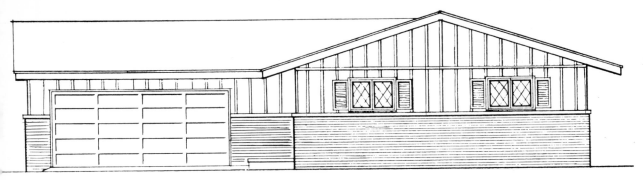

In fact, Federal Housing Administration (FHA) loans require four elevations (front, back, and both sides) as part of the set of house plans. The picture here gives an example of a right-side elevation found on one set of house plans.

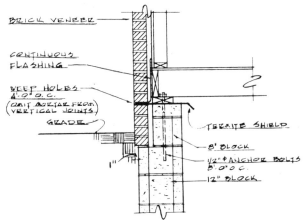

Take a look at your different section drawings. Generally, these are vertical parts of the house, showing the type and size of construction used in a particular portion of the house. Normally these

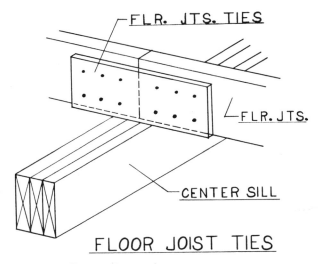

FLOOR JOIST TIES

drawings show side or end views. Furthermore, imagine looking at the part represented as if it were located directly in front of you. In the section plan here, notice the construction details for the foundation wall, studs, floor joist, etc.

Finally, examine the detail drawings if they are included in your set of plans. These show work to be done that may not be clear in a floor, elevation, or section plan. Notice the detail drawing showing floor-joist ties. A detail plan is an enlarged drawing of the object or objects it represents. It is a way that all necessary points of construction can be shown clearly and precisely.

Now read your set of blueprints in more detail, trying for a better understanding of them. If you take measurements from the blueprints, be sure they are accurate. A slight error here can result in an error of several inches or even feet in the house itself. Also, take note of the exact scale used for each print, as well as becoming acquainted with the actual dimensions. For instance, an opening expressed 4′ — 0″ means exactly four feet, nothing less and nothing more, between the two points indicated on the plan.

Because of the small scale used on working drawings, symbols are used where it is not possible to show actual details. For example, an electric floor outlet is shown as a circle with a dot in it, and a circle without a dot indicates an electric ceiling outlet.

Specifications

Specifications are prepared by the architect to explain many of the details about your house not possible to include on the working drawings. Specifications include general information with regard to legal responsibility, who obtains and pays for certain permits, guarantees of performance, supervision of work, who makes inspections and when, etc. Also, a description is given for each trade as to who does the work, how it is done, and what grades and kinds of materials are used.

Since you are doing the building, pay close attention to the detailed instructions as to how the materials are to be applied. If you farm out some of the jobs to tradesmen, doublecheck to see that they follow their part of the specifications to the letter. In fact, it is always a good policy to include those parts of the specifications that apply to a particular trade in the contract or work agreement.

A list of building materials includes, as the name implies, all of the materials required to build a particular house.

In part, Chapter II deals with reaching a decision on the amount of money to spend in building a house. Now that a plan, specifications, and a list of building materials are at hand, you are in a position to find out exactly how much house you can get for the money. Using the materials list, make separate copies of materials required in the different building trades. For example, there would be copies for the kinds and amounts of concrete, kinds and amount of lumber, plumbing supplies and kinds of fixtures, elec-

trical supplies and kinds of fixtures, kinds and amounts of exterior and interior finishing materials, and types of built-in equipment. Then submit copies to the respective building suppliers in your area for bids. Adding up the low bids gives you the cost of the building materials. If the total cost is much greater than the amount you planned to spend, you may want to select a new set of plans and start the bidding all over. On the other hand, if the difference is not too great, you may want to have the plans altered accordingly by an architect. I know of people who have put building material lists of several different house plans out for bids before they arrived at a total building materials cost commensurate with their building budget.

Everything pertaining to building a house cannot be placed on the blueprints specifications, or on the list of building materials. For instance, dimensions of windows and doors are shown, but you must know how to frame the openings. The techniques of the various building trades represented on the plans and in the specifications are definitely not indicated. Here is where this book becomes useful in supplying the knowhow.

5

THE EXCAVATION

empty bags, etc. All such remaining objects are sure to cause difficulties, come landscaping time. Wood of any kind allowed to remain underground is an invitation to termites in many parts of the United States.

 5-2. If your topsoil is not of good quality, skip this step. If it is of good quality, locate the approximate building site by placing a temporary stake at each corner. Now strip the topsoil (approximately 12 inches) in an area somewhat larger than the dimensions shown on the house plans. Then pile this dirt well out of the way, since it is to be redistributed as topsoil when the house is finished.

 5-1. Study area code along with any other restrictions, if they exist, before determining the exact location of your house.

Clean the building site of any roots, stumps, and tree limbs. Also, remove such debris as old bricks, rocks, blocks of wood,

5-3. Using a transit, a farm level, or a hand sighting level fastened to a stand, establish a benchmark, which is a reference mark usually placed on a permanent object, which should represent the elevation of the first floor. However, a stake may be substituted for a permanent object. Be sure the mark is located high enough so that rainwater from the finished house will drain in all directions. Also, keep in mind the importance of keeping the house and the yard at an attractive elevation.

In the photograph here, no permanent object on the lot was as high as the foundation specifications, so I established a benchmark on the street curb, which is 18 inches below the foundation elevation.

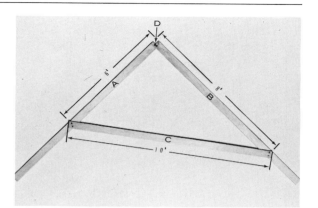

 5-4. Locate the front lot line by stretching a nylon cord between the two front surveyor's stakes.

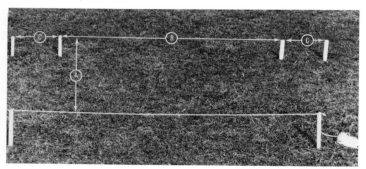

5-5. Using the front lot line as a guide, locate the front building line by driving two corner stakes the required distance A from the lot line and the required distance B apart as indicated on the house plans. Also check the spaces between side lot lines and corner stakes for required distances C. Then drive a 6-penny (2½-inch) nail firmly into the exact center of each stake, leaving at least 1 inch of the nail exposed.

  **5-6.** Use a large layout square to locate the third corner, if your leveling instrument cannot be used for this purpose.

Construct the square from three perfectly straight 1×4-inch boards 10 feet long. Accurately square one end of boards A and B. (Each of these boards may be slightly less than 10 feet in length.) Then make a lap joint at the squared ends of these boards. Now carefully mark 6 feet on A, 8 feet on B, and 10 feet on C. (This board must be at least 10 feet in length.) Next lap boards A and B and place board C on top of both and nail in place. Then notch the square at D so the stake will not prevent placing the outside edges of the square directly under the building lines.

5-7. Stretch a cord from nail in stake A to nail in stake B. Then place layout square on the ground, with one edge exactly under line AB. Now stretch cord from nail in stake B along the other outside edge of the square and several feet beyond point C. Hold in place with temporary stake D. Then, using a steel tape, measure the exact width of the house from nail in corner stake B to point C. Drive a stake at this point, followed by driving a 6-penny nail as before. Next remove cord from temporary stake. Then stretch and fasten the cord to stake C. Before proceeding to the next step, recheck corner with layout square.

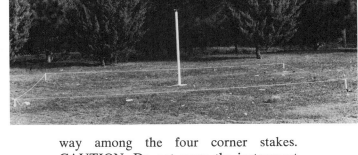

way among the four corner stakes. CAUTION: Do not move the instrument from its original position until the four sets of batter boards are erected.

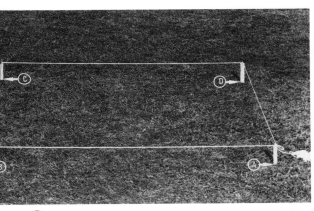

5-8. With a steel tape, measure sides CD and DA as indicated on the house plans. Now drive a stake exactly over the point of intersection. Then drive a 6-penny nail in the center of the stake in the same manner as the other stakes. Finish this part of the layout by stretching the cord from nails C to D, then to nail A.

5-9. Make preparations for erecting batter boards, made from 1×4-inch boards 6 feet long and stakes of scrap lumber, long enough to be firm when driven into the ground. Use two boards and three stakes at each corner. Plan to erect the batter boards 4 feet from and parallel to the building-line layout so they will not be disturbed during the excavation process.

Begin by placing the transit, farm level, or hand sighting level fastened to a stand on a level spot approximately mid-

5-10. Using a hammer, begin driving the first batter-board stake firmly into the ground directly in line with diagonal corner stakes and 4 feet from extended building line.

With the aid of your rod and sighting instrument, locate the top of stake to the required elevation. This is the same elevation as determined previously from your benchmark.

5-11. Using a hammer and a carpenter's level, locate two additional stakes 5 feet from the original stake and 4 feet from the building lines. Be sure these two stakes are exactly level with the original stake as well as located parallel to the building lines.

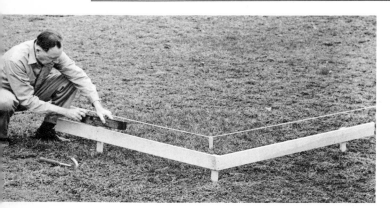

5-12. Nail the batter boards in place with 6-penny box nails. The top of the boards should be flush with the stakes. Now erect the remaining three sets of batter boards in the same manner as the first set.

5-14. Just before starting the actual excavation, if you plan to build a basement, make preparation for preventing rainwater or seep water from filling the excavation by laying most of the sanitary sewer line.

Begin by placing 4-inch 4-foot lengths of bell tile with a built-in sealer, such as Canelock, on the ground close to the proposed ditch line between the sanitary sewer line connection and within 5 feet of where the sewer line is to enter the basement.

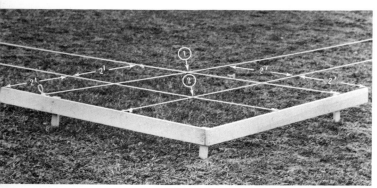

5-13. This is the way a single set of batter boards should appear.

With the aid of a plumb bob, locate and stretch building lines 1 on batter boards located at each corner. Hold lines in place with 6-penny box nails driven firmly into top edge of batter boards at proper locations. Stretch lines taut, being certain not to disturb batter-board elevations.

Next locate excavation lines 2 on batter boards, 2 feet outside the building lines. Fasten and hold them in place in the same manner as the building lines.

Before proceeding, be certain diagonal distances between building lines located on batter boards are of equal length.

Now remove cord from the four corner stakes.

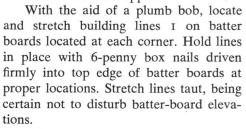

5-15. Dig ditch from the sanitary sewer to a point where the house sewer line is to enter basement. Generally, slope ditch from point of basement entrance to

sanitary sewer tap no less than ⅛ inch and no more than ¼ inch per foot. If greater depth is required to reach the sewer connection, make one or more sharp drops of either a 45° or a 90° angle. CAUTION: Check code. Most likely a licensed plumber will be required to make the connection to the sanitary sewer and to lay line to your lot line.

5-16. Begin laying the bell tile, bell toward foundation, from the sanitary-sewer connection to within 5 feet of the foundation entrance. This is the point where the plumbing drain enters the house sewer line.

Using a paintbrush, apply primer designed for spreading on the end of the tile as you slip each piece into the bell of the preceding tile, making a watertight joint. Since the tile should lie solidly on the bottom of the trench, always scoop out enough dirt under the joints to allow for the bell.

5-17. With the aid of a plumb bob, locate and drive a stake into the ground directly underneath each corner of the excavation lines. Then remove the leveling instrument from the place to be ex-

cavated. Also, temporarily remove the excavation lines and building lines from the batter boards. Now instruct your tractor operator to begin excavating.

5-18. Locate the leveling instrument on a level spot, outside and clear of the tractor operation. Do not move the instrument from its position until the excavation job is complete. Later, use the excavated dirt in backfilling and in forming preliminary grade before depositing topsoil.

If your house calls for a basement, check the elevation of the earth on which the basement floor is to be poured against the elevation as shown on your plans. The above also applies to the construction of footings, whether for houses with basements or with crawl spaces.

6

THE FOUNDATION AND THE BASEMENT FLOOR

A. Concrete wall
B. Concrete footing
C. Keyway
D. Concrete floor
E. Polyethylene sheets
F. Topsoil
G. Subsoil
H. Rock
I. Field tile

If your house plans call for a basementless house, construct the footings no deeper than the depth to which the worst winter frosts penetrate, if you experience frosty weather in your part of the country. Also, lay 4-mil polyethylene sheets on the ground inside the foundation walls instead of pouring a concrete floor as in basement construction. The polyethylene serves as a vapor barrier, holding moisture in the ground rather than allowing it to penetrate the wood in the house.

6-2. Begin by replacing the building lines on the four sets of batter boards previously constructed. Then drop a combination chalk line and plumb bob or an ordinary plumb bob from the suspended corners to locate the proposed foundation corner points on the ground. Be sure the distances between the suspended corners and their counterparts on the ground are equal.

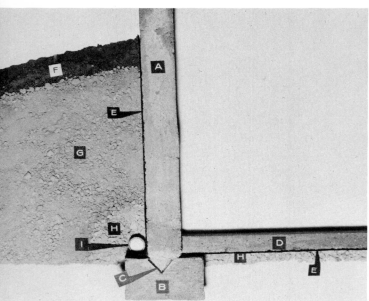

6-1. The cross-section picture shows your objective in the construction of a waterproof basement foundation, including the basement floor. The materials are as follows:

6-3. Next build the 2×4 footing forms, allowing for the projection on each side of the wall. Also allow for the thickness of the wood form material.

Drive a stake at two opposite outside corner points of the footing location. Now stretch a nylon cord between them at the elevation of the forms. Next drive stakes firmly into the ground at the same elevation as the cord and about 1/16 inch away from it. Similarly, drive stakes for the remaining three sides, as well as between the inside corner points.

6-4. Using 6-penny box nails, fasten the stakes to 2×4 form material. Be sure the distance between the forms and the wall corners as located in illustration 6-2 correspond. This completes the carpenter work on the footing forms.

6-5. This is the time to check your house plans for the exact location of footing pads, which are used as partial supports for the girders and fireplace if you have one.

Complete the footing-pad forms in the same manner and to the same elevation as the footing forms.

6-6. Using a long-handled shovel, remove 4 inches of dirt from inside the footing forms and footing pads. Do not disturb wood forms while digging. Make the bottom of the forms square, not round. If your plans call for a footing thicker than 8 inches, remove additional dirt before pouring concrete.

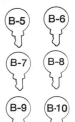

6-7. Do three things before having ready-mix concrete delivered for the footing and footing pads:

Have enough 2×4s to equal the perimeter of the footings and footing pads.

Have necessary tools available. Include a deep-tray wheelbarrow if the truck will not be able to reach all pouring areas.

Figure the amount of concrete required. Then place the order, giving time and day to begin delivery.

6-8. Distribute the concrete evenly by pouring it into the footing excavation at several points. Level the concrete by sliding a short piece of 2×4

back and forth across the top of the wood forms. Do not use a trowel, since a rough finish is desired.

Fill the footing pads with concrete in the same manner as the footing.

6-9. For footings over 30 feet in length, locate 16-inch lengths of ½-inch reinforcement rods 8 inches deep, near the center of the footing at intervals of 8 feet.

6-10. Later, it will be necessary for the wall to tie itself into the footing. So at this point, make a keyway as near to the center of the footing as possible by pressing 2×4s diagonally into the wet concrete. A keyway is not required in the footing pads.

6-11. After the concrete has set (twenty-four hours is generally long enough), remove the 2×4s

from the keyways and footing and footing-pad forms. Then clean and stack them for use later in the building program.

The picture shows a cross-section view of a footing with its keyway. Do not worry about the jagged edges that may appear near the edges of the keyway.

6-12. Now is the time to spread 4 inches of crushed rock, no smaller than ¾ inch in diameter, on the ground floor. Rock should be flush with top of footing.

6-13. Using a plumb bob, mark points directly below each corner of the building lines located on the batter boards. Since these points represent the

outside of the wall, use them as guidepoints to locate the inside corners on the footing. In all three houses in the photographs in this book, the wall lines were 8 inches apart, and 7 inches of footing extended on both sides of the walls.

6-14. Using two opposite corner points at a time as guide marks, snap chalk lines on the footing enough times so the outlines of the inside and outside of the foundation walls are clearly indicated around the perimeter of the footing.

6-15. Inspect wall forms before constructing the basement wall. Remove any hardened concrete from the forms. Then use a clean paint roller to oil the sides of the forms that will be exposed to concrete.

6-16. Begin wall construction by using a 1½-inch concrete nail to fasten a 4-foot corner section to one of the inside footing corners. Be sure inside of section is flush with inside chalk line on footing.

6-17. Set up a regular-sized section on each side of corner-post section. Lock sections together with slotted triangular

keys and wedges made for this purpose. Also, fasten lower sections to concrete footing with concrete nails spaced at 6- to 8-foot intervals.

6-18. Now set up a corner section on top of the inside lower corner section, followed by a regular-sized section as in the previous step. Use keys and wedges to hold sections firmly in place.

6-19. Next set up a similar number of outside forms, being certain inside faces are flush with outside wall chalk lines.

It is not necessary to nail outside wall chalk lines.

It is not necessary to nail outside form to footing.

Forms must be assembled plumb. Use a carpenter's level periodically for checking.

6-22. Instead of wood, use steel window frames, which are prefabricated and designed to be nailed to the inside of the wall forms at proper locations.

6-20. As outside form sections follow inside form installation, locate tierods through holes provided. Tighten by driving triangular wedges in place through slotted keys.

6-21. If you require openings in the walls, provide for them now as inside and outside form sections are assembled. Also provide for items to be mounted flush with the finished wall. At this time consider such items as windows, doors, electric conduits, electric outlet and switch boxes, water pipes, gas pipes, bearing seats for girders, and whatever else requires openings.

6-23. If your plans call for a door opening, prepare frame A from 2-inch lumber the width and height of the finished doorjambs. Add 1 inch to width and height of frame so that finished jamb can be installed plumb. To this frame, nail a 2×4 tapered key B on each side and temporary brace C between.

Next position frame between form. Then drive 8-penny box nails through both sides of forms into frame at 2-foot intervals.

Note that keys are tapered so that later when the frame is removed, they remain in the wall as nailers.

6-26. Prepare wood forms for beam (supporting floor joists) openings in top of wall if required on your house plans. Here three pieces of 2×4s fastened together with 16-penny nails and covered with polyethylene serve as the box. The carpenter in the picture will nail it in the proper location in the top of the wall form.

6-24. Check your house plans for flush-mounted electric switch and outlet boxes to be mounted in the basement. Then using ¾-inch nails placed through the metal box brackets, fasten the required number (connected to conduit of proper size and length) to the smooth side of the sections before they are put in place.

6-25. The picture shows a vent-pipe opening being formed. First a piece of 2×2 the thickness of the wall is fastened in place with an 8-penny box nail driven through the outside wall form. Next a piece of plastic drain pipe whose length is the same as the thickness of the wall is slipped over the 2×2. Then the inside wall section is positioned and nailed to the 2×2.

6-27. Begin pouring concrete at the ends of a wall section. Then move toward the center, being sure to pour concrete against concrete, not ahead of that already poured. In the picture, concrete is just below eye level, so concrete is actually being poured against concrete.

6-28. Using a short piece of 2×4, level concrete with top of form.

6-29. Cast ½ × 12-inch sill bolts (machine bolts with nuts and washers) into the concrete approximately 7 feet apart in the middle of the wall. Leave 2 inches of each bolt protruding above the 1×2 guide board nailed across top of form.

6-30. Remove keys and wedges from form sections only after concrete has thoroughly set. Gen-

erally, between 24 and 48 hours following the pouring job is about right.

A wrecking bar is handy when removing forms from the finished wall.

6-31. Now break off tie extensions from inside walls. If polyethylene or a similar material is to be used on the outside walls, break off tie extensions here. Otherwise, extended ties below the grade line may be left intact.

6-32. Using a white-wash brush, coat the outside of the basement wall (within 1 inch of the finished grade line) and the top of the outside footing with a waterproof material.

If you are building in an area noted for wet basements, follow the outside wall coating with a waterproofing membrane of 4-mil plastic sheeting placed directly on the fresh mastic. Be sure to extend the material down and over the top of the footing.

6-33. Lay 4-inch field tile around the top of the footing next to the outside wall, spacing each tile ½ inch apart. Install a Y joint in the line nearest the sanitary sewer. Then connect bell tile between the Y joint and the sanitary sewer.

Next place 4-inch strips of building paper over the field-tile joints, followed by ¾- to 1-inch rock to a depth of about 1 foot above the tile. As an added precaution against dirt working through the rock into the tile, place long strips of building paper 12 inches wide over the rock. Hold in place with chunks of dirt before backfilling.

6-34. CAUTION: Do not do this step now. Make a note to return to this step after framing

the sill and floor; instructions are given for completing the subfloor installation in the chapter on this step.

Backfill the space next to the outside wall with subsoil in layers approximately 12 inches thick to a point about 10 inches from the finish grade line. Then use topsoil to complete the backfill job.

Use a hose to wet the layers of dirt thoroughly as you backfill. This causes the dirt to pack much better than dry dirt alone. CAUTION: Do not create water pockets, and be certain surplus water drains away from the house.

6-35. Place the girder that supports the floor joists in the bearing seats located in the top of the basement wall. Support the girder with the proper number of steel posts located on center of the footing pads.

A steel I-beam serves the purpose of a girder well. Also, a built-up wood girder of three 2×8s fastened together with 16-penny nails is entirely satisfactory. If your plans call for a wood girder, be certain the joints fall directly over the center of the steel supporting posts.

6-36. If your sewage drain system is to be located underneath the basement floor as in the picture here, refer to the chapter on plumbing.

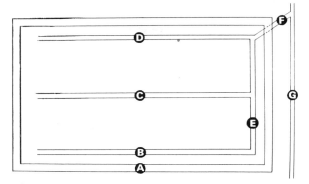

Spread polyethylene sheets, lapped 6 inches at joints, over floor area. Then lay 6×6 #10 gauge mesh reinforcement wire over polyethylene. Do not place polyethylene over concrete footing, as the concrete floor must bond to the footing areas. Also cut polyethylene neatly around floor drains and plumbing stubs if they are sticking up above floor level.

6-37. Next prepare and connect to the storm sewer a drainage system for underneath the basement floor if you are building in an area noted for wet basements or if you just want to be certain excessive water pressure does not form under the finished floor.

Prepare trenches B, C, D, and E by removing temporary rock from these areas. The trenches may all be dug to the same elevation with a minimum width of 4 inches, and they should be located approximately 12 feet apart and within about 1 foot of the footing.

Now install lines made up of 3-inch perforated plastic pipe in 10-foot lengths, joined together with prepared plastic couplings, at locations B, C, D, E, and F. Use a plastic elbow to connect lines B to E, a plastic T to connect C to E, and a plastic Y to connect D, E, and F.

Finally connect line F to a Y in field-tile line G outside basement leading to storm sewer.

Check with a carpenter's level, being certain seep water will flow toward sanitary sewer.

6-38. Next replace the rock over and around the plastic drain pipes, being certain the entire floor elevation is the same as that of the footing.

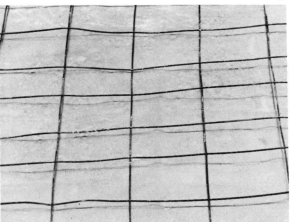

6-39. Prepare the required number of screeds parallel with each other as guides for leveling poured concrete.

Make a screed by driving into the ground in a straight line 1×3 stakes A at approximately 5-foot intervals, allowing 2½ inches to remain above rock floor.

Next lay 1½-inch o.d. (outside diameter) iron pipe B on top of stakes A. Then hold pipe in place by driving 6-penny box nails into top of stakes on either side and flush with top of pipe.

6-40. Order the concrete to be delivered as early in the morning as possible.

When the truck arrives, have the driver begin chuting concrete between screeds at one end of the floor.

6-41. Wearing rubber boots, use a flat shovel or garden rake to place and tamp concrete in place between the screeds. Be sure to keep the leveling job and the concrete coming from the truck on an even keel.

6-42. When 6 to 8 feet of concrete is fairly level between the screeds, level it further with a 2×4 slightly longer than

the distance between them. Either you or you and a helper can do this by slowly sawing it edgewise, back and forth across the screeds until a level, rough finish is obtained.

6-43. Use a wood or an aluminum float on the surface to help push down coarse rock and to bring fine material, including mortar, to the surface. The concrete finisher in the picture prefers a long-handled float. Here the float is more than twice the size of the hand float shown in key B-1.

CAUTION: Do just enough floating to do the job. For best results do not overwork the concrete.

6-44. When all surface water has disappeared and the concrete has lost its sheen, indicating that it is beginning to

stiffen, begin the troweling operation for securing a finished surface. In the picture a troweling machine is used for the finishing operation.

If the concrete is not ready for using the finish trowel, pour, level, and float another 8- or 10-foot section of concrete.

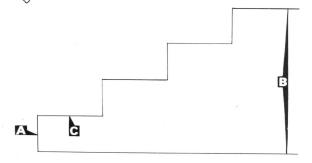

6-45. If you included an outside entrance as part of the basement walls, make preparation for pouring concrete steps.

To find riser height A, divide height of proposed steps B by number of risers desired. Be certain both risers and runs C are of convenient dimensions.

Next use a pencil, carpenter's level, and ruler to locate an outline of the risers A and runs C on each of the two basement entrance walls. Then check bottom and top step for proper head clearance.

6-46. Using 2-inch material of proper riser height, saw one edge to a 45° angle. This makes the bottom outside edge of the risers.

6-47. Now cut riser lengths to fit snugly in place between entrance walls. Take measurements from corresponding riser marks located on basement entrance walls.

Begin by placing top riser. Be sure angle cut, forming bottom edge, faces forward. As each riser is located, hold firmly in place with one or two 16-penny nails between each end and entrance wall.

6-48. When risers are completed they should resemble the picture here. Make a last-minute check for a tight fit of each riser before ordering concrete.

6-49. When the concrete is delivered, instruct the operator to pour it slowly out of the chute down the rear basement entrance wall. Also use a shovel to help prevent the concrete from hitting directly against the risers. Be sure to instruct operator to hold concrete as you work poured concrete in place to form lower step. Continue previous operations until entire series of steps are poured.

6-50. Use a finishing trowel (as described previously for finishing the concrete floor) to finish each step to your satisfaction. Tapping risers of filled steps gently with a rubber hammer brings fine materials toward riser, making for a smooth, professional appearance.

6-51. After four or five days, remove 16-penny nails from edge of risers. Then remove wood forms with the aid of a wrecking bar, being careful not to damage any part of the concrete steps.

If risers are not perfectly smooth, you can make them so by rubbing them with a concrete finisher's rubbing brick periodically dipped in water.

6-52. If you prepared foundation walls for concrete porches, now is the time to pour the floors.

Begin by placing and packing fill dirt to the top of the foundation walls.

6-53. Make forms from 2-inch lumber the required width spiked together with 16-penny nails and braced as shown in the picture. Form a lip over the foundation by spiking 2-inch lumber of the required width to the inside face of the outside form board. The arrow points to a 2×6 used because a 4-inch ledge below the form is to accommodate a 4-inch wall of stone. This allows for proper floor overhang for the stone wall.

6-55. The techniques for finishing the floor and removing the forms are essentially the same as those previously described for the concrete basement floor and steps.

6-54. Before pouring the concrete, be sure 6×6 #10 mesh reinforcement wire and polyethylene are applied inside the form, just as when preparing the basement floor for concrete as described previously.

7

installation has been described in the previous chapter.) Floor joists D are positioned and nailed into place. Next, bridging E is located between the floor joists and fastened in place. The sill and floor framing is complete with the application of subfloor F.

FRAMING: SILLS AND FLOORS

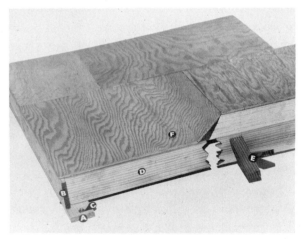

7-1. Begin the job of framing the house by becoming familiar with the construction details as well as the names of the parts of the built-up-type sill, or box sill, as shown in the photograph.

The box sill is made up of 2-inch lumber, sill A nailed to header B. Bolts C fasten the sill to the foundation. (Bolt

7-2. Place the sill plates along the top of the walls and against the anchor bolts. Square the butt joints with a framing square and a saw if not already square.

Now mark lines from anchor bolts across the sill plate. Mark location on each line for anchor bolt hole. CAUTION: Be certain that no joints occur over an opening in the foundation wall.

7-3. Next, bore the anchor-bolt holes through the sill. Make the holes oversize to permit exact sill alignment later on.

7-4. Try sills for size. Locate them on top of the foundation with anchor bolts running through sill anchor-bolt holes. Outer edge of sill should be flush with outer foundation wall.

7-6. Place the joist headers, fastened to the sills (cut square and butted together), flush with the outside of the foundation.

Next, fasten headers together at the corners of the foundation by driving three 20-penny nails through the corner of one joist into the end grain of a corresponding adjacent header.

Place washers over sill bolts. Then screw nuts to sill bolts, tightening with fingers only at this point.

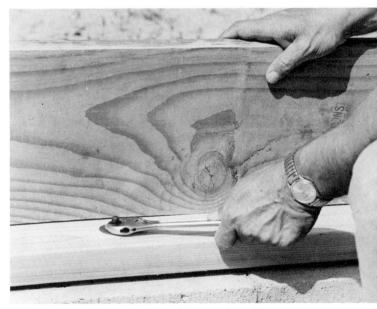

7-5. Remove sills from foundation walls. Then, using 16-penny nails spaced 16 inches apart, fasten sills to corresponding headers. Before nailing, be certain both header and sill materials have squared ends.

7-7. Next, level and straighten the sills over the bearing walls by using a level and a straightedge. Then with the sills level, straight, and square at the corners, tighten the nuts on the anchor bolts, but not to the extent of pulling the sills out of alignment.

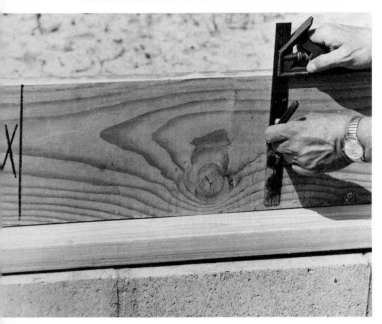

7-8. Using the 16-inch division marks on the steel tape, lay out 16-inch intervals along the tops of opposite headers to which the floor joists are to be fastened. Then, using a combination square and pencil, locate the joist spacing on inside of header. Also, locate the joist spacing on top of girder(s).

The X in the picture here shows the floor-joist location against the header relative to the 16-inch-interval spacing lines.

7-9. Those headers in the previous step not laid out for attaching floor joists require blocks of 2-inch lumber, 1 to 2 feet long, spaced 5 to 6 feet apart, nailed with 16-penny nails to the headers. Top edge of block and top edge of header must be flush.

7-10. Now cut the full-length floor joists to proper size, allowing space for stair, chimney, and other wells if required. Then locate and butt joists onto proper header, driving three 16-penny nails through the headers into the end grain of the joists. CAUTION: Cut joists crossing the girder(s) so they lap a minimum of 8 inches.

7-11. If your plans call for a fireplace, now is the time to locate the opening through the floor so that the laying of masonry later will not present a problem. Also this is the time to mark off partition positions and the stairwell if your plans call for stairs leading from the basement to the first floor.

Do not allow partition, chimney-well, and stairwell markings to interfere with the spacing marks previously made for the regular floor joists.

7-12. Next double-frame stair and chimney wells if called for. The cutaway view shows how.

For fireplace framing, plan a 2-inch space between double frame and masonry. Later, place fire-stopping material within these spaces. Stairwells do not require additional space, since it is not necessary to use fire-stopping material here.

Cut tail beams B and position in place. Next cut and position similar tail beams on the opposite side of the well location.

Cut header joists A and C to size. Also cut two similar joists for the opposite side of the well. Using 16-penny nails, position and nail header joist A to tail beams B. Then nail a similar header to the tail beams on the opposite side of the well.

Position, and nail double header joist C to joist A. Then nail trimmer joist D into end grain of double headers A and C. Nail opposite double header joist and trimmer joist in the same way.

Complete the well framing by cutting, positioning, and nailing trimmer joist E to trimmer joist D. Do the same on the opposite side of the well.

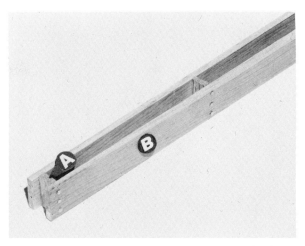

7-13. Next, prepare double joists required under partitions running parallel to floor joists. Cut 2×4s A as long as width of joists B. Using six 16-penny nails, three on each side, fasten double joists to the 2×4s spaced 4 feet apart.

Now fasten each double joist onto the header as previously recommended for nailing regular joists in place.

7-14. Using two 16-penny nails, fasten each set of overlapping joists A together. Then cut short pieces of 2-inch lumber as solid bridging B to fit between the joists. Position the bridging pieces directly over the center of girder C. Now drive two 20-penny nails through two adjoining joists into the end grain of the short bridging pieces. (Arrows point to top and bottom nails.) Then, using three 16-penny nails, toenail the opposite ends onto their adjoining joists.

Use the cutaway picture to check your results.

7-15. Now check the alignment of the floor joists. If you are not sure you can position joists A accurately over large spans, you can use 6-penny nails to fasten temporary strips of wood B, spaced 8 feet apart, across the joists.

7-16. Next snap a chalk line midway between bearing points across the tops of the joists to indicate cross bridging locations.

7-17. Measure the actual distance between the floor joists as well as their actual height. In the three houses shown in illustrations in this book, the 2×10 joists were located on 16-inch centers, making the distance between them 14½ inches.

7-18. Place the 9½-inch mark of the tongue A of the framing square on the lower edge of a piece of 1×4 cross bridging stock and the 14½-inch mark of the body B of the square on the upper edge of the stock as shown by the arrows above. Then mark a line across the stock along the tongue of the square. This line gives your angle of cut for each end, since both bridging angles are parallel. This is the angle for making all bridging cuts.

7-19. Cut the piece of cross bridging stock on the mark indicated by the tongue of the square. Then place the cut end ⅜ inch from the bottom of a floor joist, making a pencil mark on the stock ⅜ inch below the top of the adjacent joist. Then mark and cut this angle in the same way as explained in the previous step.

7-21. Using the pattern, cut enough cross bridging pieces for connecting the joists into a strong, square structure.

Then begin by nailing two pieces of bridging side by side, centered directly under the chalk marks previously located on the tops of the joists. Use two 8-penny nails in each end, fasten the top sides of the bridging only at this point. Nail the bottom sides to the joists only after the subfloor is completed.

7-22. Using 6-penny resin-coated nails, spaced 6 inches apart at joints and around outside edges of floor and 8 inches apart on 16-inch centers between ends, fasten the 4×8-foot sheets of ⅝-inch plywood to the floor joists. Be sure to stagger joints.

7-20. Check cross bridging piece between joists. It should fit with a ⅜-inch clearance. If so, this serves as your pattern. Mark it with a P.

7-23. Fasten short pieces of 2×4s flat between joists at subfloor joints by driving two 16-penny nails through the face of the joist into the end grain of the 2×4. This makes for a more solid floor, even though your floor plans may not call for this type of construction.

7-24. Now that the subfloor is down, level and straighten the entire platform by using a straight-edge and level. If shims are needed, use wood wedges placed approximately every 4 feet between the bottom of the sill plates and the top of the foundation wall and the girder(s).

Now is the time to backfill the foundation. See Chapter 6, step 6-34.

C-13

7-25. You may wish to build the stairs after the house is under roof. If so, skip the remainder of this chapter.

The same principles of stair building (headroom and sizes of runs and risers) apply here as are described in step 6-45 and key B-36.

Once the riser and tread sizes are located as explained in key B-36, on a piece of 2×12, saw out the triangular pieces, including sawing the bottom to fit on top of the floor and the top to fit against the stairwell header. This forms a saw-tooth pattern called a stringer. When the stringer is set in place, it should have the appearance of one of the stringers in the picture here.

Using the first stringer as a pattern, prepare two more exactly the same. Then, using 16-penny nails, fasten the three stringers, parallel to each other, to one end of the stairwell.

Until wall studs are fastened to outside stringers, give additional support by temporarily fastening two 2×4s in place as illustrated.

The arrow points to a piece of shingle used as a wedge to ensure tight fit between stringer and floor. Also, place a piece of roofing paper between the bottom of the stringers and the concrete floor. This prevents moisture from entering the wood from the floor.

7-26. Rather than installing finished risers and treads at this time, you may wish to use scrap 1-inch lumber for temporary treads, because protecting finished risers and treads from traffic at this stage of the building is not easy. The man in the picture is taking this precaution.

7-27. When you wish to finish the stairs, cut risers and tread material flush to the sides of the outside stringers. Then, using 8-penny finishing nails, fasten them in place. Countersink the nails.

This step should be completed before wall studs are located against the stringers, as explained in the next chapter.

D. Header
E. Full-length stud
F. Trimmer stud
G. Cripple stud
H. Rough sill
I. Corner post
J. Partition junction stud
K. Sheathing (plywood here)

Arrows point to width of 2×4 gaps in cap plate. Such gaps allow cap plate from adjoining wall to tie both walls together in a solid unit.

8

FRAMING: STUDDING AND SHEATHING

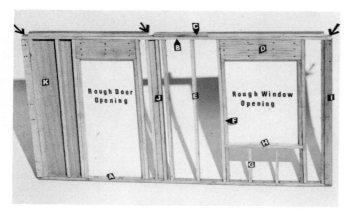

Rough Door Opening

Rough Window Opening

8-1. The second series of steps in the framing operation is the construction of the studding and the fastening of the sheathing to the outside of the studs.

Before beginning actual construction, learn the names of the framing parts:

A. Sole plate
B. Top plate
C. Cap plate

8-2. Begin by placing pairs of straight 2×4s side by side around the perimeter of the subfloor. Eventually you will use the one nearest the subfloor edge as the sole plate, and the adjoining one for the top plate.

Because the joints of the plates should be arranged to come over the center of a stud, delay squaring and cutting them to exact size until all studs are laid out as described in the following steps.

8-3. With ends of both plates square (shown by white arrow), lay off entire length on 16-inch centers. Use an X to show regular stud locations. Use XX to show corner-post locations. Be sure total width of corner post is 5 inches.

Be certain end joints in either plate come in

56

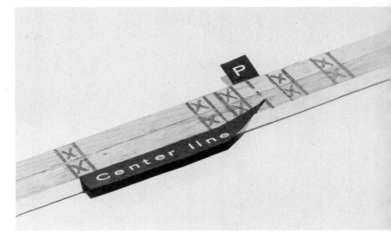

the center of a stud position (shown by black arrow). Also, joints in top plate and sole plate must be staggered.

Before proceeding further, be sure both plates are square at each end as well as cut to proper length.

Remember the total length of plates is equal to the length of subfloor minus twice the thickness of the sheathing.

8-5. Check your plans for locations of partition (P) centers if called for on this side of the house. Measure 1¾ inches on each side of this line. Then mark the position of a regular stud outside these points.

CAUTION: The specifications above are for 2×4 wall studs. If your wall calls for 2×6 studs, measure 2¾ inches on each side of the center line.

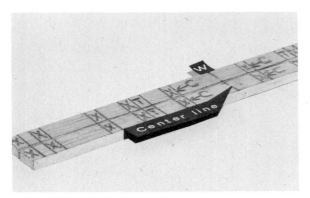

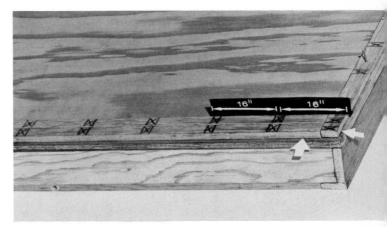

8-4. Check your plans for locations of the centers of door and window openings if they are called for on this side of house. Mark these on both plates by a center line as shown in the window (W) framing example illustrated.

Measure on each side of center line one-half the opening width. Then, indicate trimmer studs by a T outside these points.

Using an X, indicate regular stud outside each trimmer.

When laying out window openings, use a C to indicate all original layout positions between the trimmers for cripple studs.

Ignore original layout positions on sole plate between trimmers for all door openings.

8-6. Next lay out sole and top plates on remaining sides of the subfloor.

End walls will sit between side walls as shown in the picture. Therefore, allowances must be made. White arrows show also where allowances must be made for thickness of the sheathing your plans call for.

Next measure 16 inches from outside edge of side walls. This marks the center of your first stud. Thereafter, mark regular studs with an X as described in previous step describing plate layout.

above the subfloor minus 1½ inches (thickness of sole plate).

Using 16-penny nails staggered 16 inches apart, spike the face of the trimmer studs to the face of regular studs S. The picture shows the trimmer stud and the regular requirements for each door opening.

 8-7. Now you should be ready to cut and assemble the exterior wall frame.

Begin by cutting regular studs to proper size. Do not overlook regular studs required for corner posts, partition junctions, openings, etc.

Next prepare the headers for doors and windows. The length of the two 2-inch pieces is the width of the rough opening plus 3 inches (thickness of two trimmers). Check width of headers from your plans. Cut enough strips ½ inch thick as spacers to be placed 16 inches apart between the two 2-inch pieces (plywood makes good spacers). Using three 16-penny nails, top, bottom, and middle, spaced 16 inches apart, fasten the two 2-inch pieces and the spacers together like a sandwich.

8-9. Now position header between regular studs and on top of trimmer studs.

Using 12 16-penny nails, drive three pairs of nails through the face of each regular stud into end grain of header.

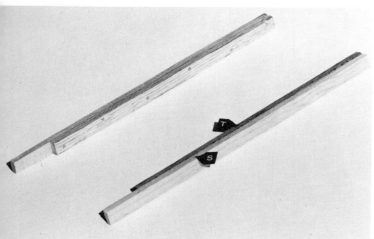

 8-8. Next, cut the trimmer studs T for rough door openings. Their length is the height of the top of the rough opening

8-10. Next prepare frames for rough window openings. The picture shows the similarity between rough window frames

and rough door openings. The header H and the regular studs S are dimensioned and assembled in the same way for both rough door openings and rough window openings. Note the trimmer studs for rough window openings are in two pieces, allowing for the insertion of rough sill S. The rough sill is a 2×4 and is the same length as the header. Of course, if the wall studs are 2×6s, the rough sill is also a 2×6.

Cut lower trimmer studs to specifications. Then spike in place with 16-penny nails. Now position rough sill S and fasten in place by driving two 16-penny nails through the face of each regular stud into end grain of rough sill. Next, cut upper trimmer studs to size and fasten in place with 16-penny nails. Complete by spiking header in place as you did for the door opening in the previous step.

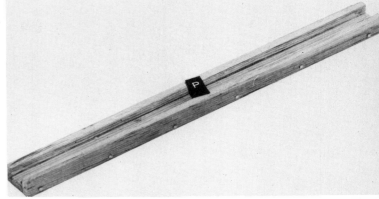

16 inches apart, three regular studs as shown in the picture above.

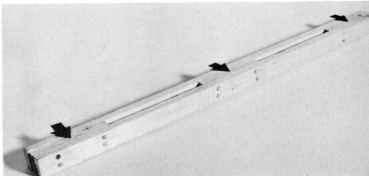

8-13. Next construct corner posts.

Begin making each post by locating the face sides of three short 2×4 blocks (16 inches minimum length) between face sides of two regular studs, shown by arrows in the picture. Be sure the ends of the two outside blocks are flush with top and bottom ends of studs.

Using four 16-penny nails to each block, fasten regular studs and blocks together.

8-14. Complete corner posts by nailing face side of a third regular stud with 16-penny nails, spaced at 16-inch intervals, to both edges of regular studs as assembled in previous step.

8-11. Next cut cripples C for windows. Their length is the height of the bottom of the rough window opening above the subfloor minus 3 inches (thickness of sole plate and rough sill). In the picture, cripples C are located but are not fastened in place. This is done when the window frames are attached to the sole and top plates.

8-12. Now assemble partition studs P by positioning and fastening with 16-penny nails, spaced

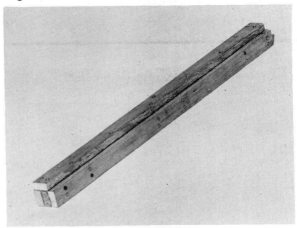

edge, spaced stud length apart. Be sure sole plate is near the edge of subfloor upon which it will rest.

Position regular studs, corner posts, partition studs, rough window frames, and rough door frames where so marked between plates.

Begin assembling regular studs, corner post, and partition stud (if it is called for) as a section of the frame. Drive two 16-penny nails through the face of each plate into the end grain of the studs as shown in the picture.

Fasten tops of rough door frames in place by driving 16-penny nails through the face of the top plate into the top of the header, spacing nails 16 inches apart. Fasten lower parts of rough door frames in place by driving two 16-penny nails through the face of the sole plate into the end grain of each trimmer stud and regular stud.

Fasten rough window frames as assembled thus far in the same manner as described for door frames above. In addition, assemble cripple studs. First, position cripples in accordance with markings on sole plate. Then fasten sole plate to cripples in the same way as described above for regular studs. Second, with cripples square with sole plate and rough sill, drive two 16-penny nails through face of rough sill into end grain of each cripple.

8-15. Beginning now, consider special wall-framing operations, such as cabinet framing, if they exist either on your plans or as extras that you would like to add.

In two of the houses pictured in this book, a self-contained all-electric pressing unit called a Handi-Press was installed. This is a compact space-saving cabinet designed to do a full job of ironing. Preparation for such cabinet installation calls for special wall framing as shown in the picture.

Instructions for complete installation are given in step 14-35 in the chapter on interior wall finishing. Several different models are manufactured by Iron-A-Way Company, Inc., 220 West Jackson, Morton, Illinois 61550.

8-17. With the exception of the cap plate you should have completed the framing of one outside wall. Now raise the assembled wall in place.

8-16. With the laid-out faces toward each other, locate sole and top plates on

8-18. With wall in vertical position, locate bottom flush with subfloor edge minus thickness of sheathing. Do not overlook ends of wall.

Next nail sole to subfloor and joist header with 20-penny nails spaced 16 inches apart as shown by arrow in picture.

CAUTION: Do not nail sole to subfloor between rough door openings.

8-19. Using a level or a straightedge and a level, plumb the wall at its center. Then brace it as shown above by nailing a piece of 1-inch lumber to the face of a stud near the top plate. Fasten the lower end of the brace by nailing it to a block which is nailed to the subfloor.

8-20. Next raise and locate the opposite wall in place.

Now raise and position the end walls.

CAUTION: The two outside regular studs are already in place for the end walls as part of the corner post of the side walls.

With the sole plate located under the regular stud of the corner post and the top plate located on top of it, nail the sole plate to the subfloor.

Using two 16-penny nails, toenail the end stud to the sole plate. Nail the top plate to the end stud as previously described for fastening top plate to regular stud.

With corner post plumb in either direction, brace with 1-inch lumber as shown in the picture.

8-21. Next, lay out partition locations. Snap a chalk line on the subfloor between partition studs to locate sole-plate position. Then assemble and locate partition framing as described for exterior wall framing above.

Erect long partitions, followed by cross partitions. Using 16-penny nails spaced 16 inches apart, fasten partition end plate to partition stud as shown.

8-22. Using 1-inch lumber, brace partitions as shown in the picture.

Now is the time to cut out sole plate between trimmer studs in rough door openings.

8-23. If a fireplace is to be included as part of a partition or wall, position and locate fireplace and chimney studding so as to allow space for in-

combustible material between all masonry and wood framing.

In the picture here, the builder positioned and located a minimum of wall framing around the fireplace-to-be. After the mason finished his work, studding was framed around the masonry.

 8-24. Complete partition framing (with exception of cap plate) by assembling and locating clothes closets, hallways, and stairwells if required.

8-25. In the house shown, the stairway leading to the basement was framed and the interior finished all in one operation.

First the two partitions were framed in the usual manner. Then 4-foot sheets of Masonite

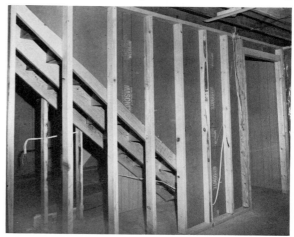

were fastened to each of the two partitions. With the finished side of the Masonite positioned against the stairs, partitions were fastened in place as previously described.

opening, to interfere with a continued line of bracing. If an opening is so located, bypass it, keeping the brace line at a 45° angle, even though it does not reach from sole plate to top plate.

D·13

8-26. Complete tying exterior and interior walls together by nailing cap plate to top plate with 16-penny nails driven through cap plate into top plate. Stagger the nails and drive them at 16-inch intervals.

Always overlap cap plate with adjoining top plate at plate joints. Refer to step 8-1 for further information. Notice cap plate set back 3½ inches or the width of a 2×4 from end of top plate. Also notice the 3½-inch gap in cap plate where partition joins wall.

8-27. If your plans call for plywood sheathing, no additional frame bracing is required.

If you plan to sheath with a softer material, such as insulation board, add corner braces to outside corners of exterior walls as shown.

Use short pieces of 2×4s cut at an angle of 45° and fasten between studs with two 16-penny nails driven through each end of the short pieces into face of stud.

For better stability, run a line of braces at the opposite end of wall in the opposite direction.

Do not allow an opening, such as a window

8-28. Before proceeding, make a final check for straightness of top plates.

Run a nylon line tightly along the top plate, holding it in place around the ends with an 8-penny nail.

Block the line out at each end of the wall with a scrap piece of 1-inch lumber (black arrow). Use another scrap piece as a test block (white arrow). (Remember that 1-inch lumber is really only ¾ inch thick.) Make a number of tests along the line. If the test block shows the top of the wall to be perfectly straight, congratulations. If not, loosen the bracing. Then push the wall in or out until the top of the wall is straight. Now refasten the bracing. Check all outside walls. Also recheck corner posts to be sure they are plumb.

8-29. A sheet of 4×8-foot sheathing is easily carried by two people. Here two high-school boys furnish the manpower necessary to transport sheathing to where it is needed.

8-30. For plywood sheathing, use 6-penny nails spaced 6 inches apart along panel edges and 12 inches apart on intermediate studs to fasten the 4×8-foot panels in place on exterior walls. Cut it flush with studding at all door and window openings. Then staple or tack 15-pound building paper over the sheathing, providing a moisture-shedding layer over the sheathing.

FRAMING: CEILING JOISTS, RAFTERS, ROOF DECKING, AND ROOF FELTING

A hip roof with an intersecting gable roof is shown in the picture here. For clarity, only top and cap plates of wall framing are shown, and repeated roof areas are not shown. The parts have the following names:

A. Top and cap wall plates
B. Main ceiling joists
C. Stud ceiling joists
D. Ceiling nailer
E. Main ridge board
F. Common rafters
G. Main ridge brace
H. Hip rafters
I. Hip jack rafters
J. Supporting valley rafter
K. Short valley rafter
L. Valley jack rafters
M. Cripple jack rafter
N. Minor ridge of intersecting roof
O. Gable rafters
P. Rough facia board
Q. Gable studs

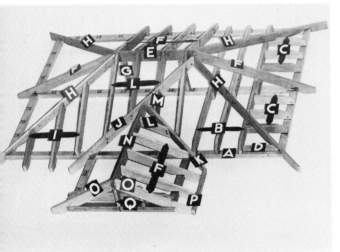

  9-1. Although framing the roof has only a limited number of details, it can become one of the most complicated problems of construction if you fail to become familiar with the names of the various parts of the roof and how to frame each part exactly for the purpose it is intended to serve.

9-2. Steps 9-2 to 9-51 tell how to frame ceiling joists for a hip roof. If your plans call for a gable roof instead, skip to step 9-52.

For clarity only top and cap plates are shown. First, locate major ridge on each of the side plates.

The major ridge equals the length of the house minus the width. Using the measurements of one of the houses pictured in this book as an example, the major ridge equals 10 feet (length, 34 feet, minus width, 24 feet).

Using a steel tape, locate ridge dimensions on each of two opposite top plates. Then locate common rafter locations with an X spaced on 16-inch centers between these dimensions. Also lay out the two common rafters on the end plates. One is located in the exact center of each end plate (shown by arrows). Next locate ceiling joist locations J adjacent to each of the common rafter locations on each of the two opposite side plates.

9-3. Beginning from ceiling joists already laid out adjacent to the common rafter locations, lay out remaining parallel ceiling joists on 16-inch centers toward each end of the house. Usually, the last ceiling joist may be located about 4 feet from the end plate (See step 9-5). Then use angle or pitch of roof as a guide for checking exactly how close to locate to avoid interference of rafters later.

Because hip rafters would interfere with the location of a regular joist at each end of the ceiling, make a substitution in these areas. Lay out stub ceiling joist locations on end plates, beginning on each side of their corresponding common rafter locations, shown by arrow in the picture.

CAUTION: Because the hip rafter would also interfere with stub rafters near the end of the plate,

make a second substitution here. Plan for nailing a short piece of 2×4 on top of the plate, with about 2 inches extending on the inside to serve as a ceiling nailer later, between last stub-ceiling joist and hip rafter.

9-4. Next decide on how the ceiling joists are to be cut to size. Your plans may show either of two ways they are joined over bearing walls: butt-joined, A; or lap-joined, B.

If your joists are butt-joined, plan to use 16-penny nails to fasten a 3-foot piece of joist material over each joint as shown in the picture.

On the other hand, if your joists are lap-joined, be certain joists will lap a minimum of 8 inches. Then plan to fasten them together with 16-penny nails as shown.

 9-5. Because the outer end of the ceiling joists must be cut to fit the roof framing, do two things:

Decide on the pitch of your roof and

the height of the back of the rafter above the plate. Your plans or specifications should show this information.

On a piece of straight ceiling-joist stock, measure up and mark from the bottom edge of one squared end a distance equal to the height of rafter A.

Now locate the framing square on the stock so that the unit rise of the roof (in the case of the example above, 5) on the tongue and 12 on the body touches the mark previously made showing the rafter height.

Now mark along the body. Then cut the joist end on this slope. Mark this piece with a P to serve as a pattern for similar joists.

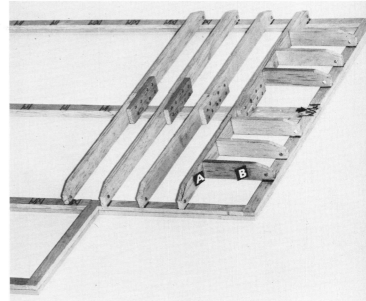

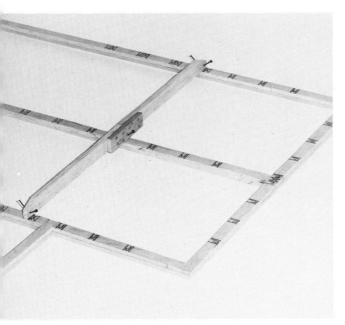

9-6. Position ceiling joists to 16 inches on center. Then using two 16-penny nails, toenail each end to plate as shown in picture.

Now fasten joists over bearing walls as shown in step 9-4.

9-7. Next cut stud ceiling joists B to size. Be sure end angle is the same as ceiling-joist angle. Drive three 16-penny nails through face of ceiling joist A into end grain of stub ceiling joists. Fasten ends of stub ceiling joists to top plate the same way as previously described for fastening main ceiling joists to plate.

The arrow in the picture points to common rafter locations to be located later.

9-8. While installing ceiling joists, provide for holes called for in ceiling plans. Generally, fire regulations require an access hole not less than 24 inches square to the attic, which can be single-framed.

The picture shows two men in the process of building a fireplace chimney access hole in the ceiling. Because of the size of the hole, double framing is recommended here.

Hip Main Roof

9-9. Select a straight piece of rafter stock A long enough for making a common rafter. Be sure material is long enough to allow for the overhang if called for.

Next mark depth B of the bird's-mouth on the face. (A bird's-mouth is an interior angle or notch cut in a piece of lumber.)

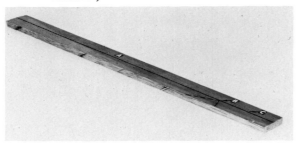

Then through that point, mark line BC from one end to the other parallel to the edges. This is called a measuring line.

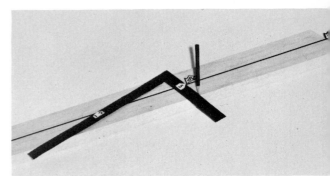

9-11. Beginning from point A where tail cut intersects the measuring line, measure along this line the distance the rafter is to extend away from the plate. This locates point B, the peak of the bird's-mouth.

Now position square on stock, locating 5 (rise of roof) on the tongue and 12 on the body as shown. Be sure the 5 on the tongue touches point B. Locate the plumb cut of the bird's-mouth by drawing a line from the measuring line at point B to bottom edge.

9-10. Now locate the tail plumb cut. Position the square near one end of the stock with 5 (rise of roof) on the tongue and 12 on the body, both touching measuring line A as shown above. Next mark along tongue. Then saw along line to form tail plumb cut.

9-12. Next locate the seat cut of the bird's-mouth. Slide the square toward the tail until 12 on the body touches the measuring line at point B, the peak location of the bird's-mouth. Be sure 5 on the tongue also touches the measuring line.

Now draw a line from the measuring line at point B to bottom edge.

Form the bird's-mouth by cutting out the plumb cut and seat cut lines.

9-13. Again refer to the rafter tail. If your plans call for only a rafter tail plumb cut as indicated in step 9-9, skip this step. However, if your plans call for cornice, a level cut is also required on the bottom of the rafter tail.

Locate required distance A from top of tail cut. Then locate level line B parallel to bird's-mouth seat cut C. Next saw along line B to form rafter level cut.

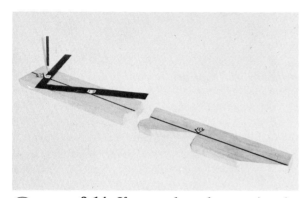

E-12

E-13

9-14. If your plans do not give the length for common rafter, use the rafter table on the face side of your framing square to compute it.

Locate the number along the top of the tongue that corresponds to the unit rise of your roof. Since 5 is the unit rise in the houses in this book, it is used here as an example.

The figure noted on the square under the unit rise number is the line length for 1 foot of common rafter run. In this example, 13. Since the example house is 24 feet wide, the run is 12.

12 (run) times 13 (line length for one foot of common rafter run) equals 156 inches or 13 feet).

Locate length of rafter B by beginning at the peak of the bird's-mouth A

and measuring 13 feet along measuring line.

Now position square with 5 on the tongue touching point B and 12 on the body intersecting the measuring line. Next draw a line along the tongue of the square. This forms the top plumb cut. The distance between the peak of the bird's-mouth and this line is called line length.

Complete step 9-15 before sawing.

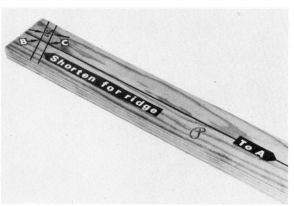

E-12

9-15. Because of the 1½-inch ridgeboard, your rafter is too long at B by half the ridgeboard thickness or ¾ inch. To make proper correction, measure back ¾ inch (half the ridgeboard thickness). Then draw new plumb line C through this point. Complete common rafter by sawing along this line. Then mark it with a P to represent a pattern for all common rafters.

A refers to the peak of the bird's-mouth in the previous illustration.

E-14

9-16. Cut ridgeboard A to length (¾ inch longer on each end than outside rafter markings on top plates if 2-inch lumber is required.) Then place it along side top plate, taking rafter locations from those previously located on top plate.

Drive two 16-penny nails through one of the end ridge spacing marks into the end grain of common rafter B. The top of the rafter must be on the spacing marks and be flush with the top of the ridgeboard.

Nail a second rafter to proper location on the opposite end of the ridgeboard.

position, drive two 16-penny nails through the side of each rafter into the adjoining ceiling joist. Also, toenail one 16-penny nail through each rafter into top plate.

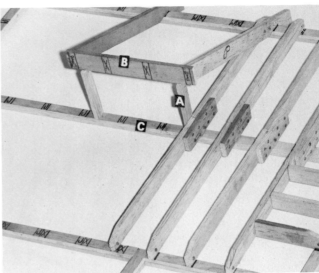

 9-17. The plans of the houses in this book did not call for common rafters on the opposite side of the ridgeboard. If your roof is of the same design, skip this step. However, if your plans require them, now is the time to toenail tops of common rafters in position through the opposite side of the ridgeboard opposite the two previously nailed in place. Use two 16-penny nails to do the job as shown in the picture.

9-19. Plumb and brace common rafters installed thus far. Do this by toenailing one end of 2×4 brace A underneath ridgeboard B and the opposite end to top plate C of inside partition or to a 2×4 block nailed across two ceiling joists. (To show framing details more clearly, joists are not completely installed in the picture.)

9-18. Raise the rafters erected thus far, fastened to the ridgeboard, until the bird's-mouth fits the top plate. Then while your helper holds them in plumb

9-20. Fasten remaining common rafters in place onto the side of the ridgeboard by erecting first one and then the opposite one (if called for on your plans). Here nailing the bottom end of each rafter to the plate first provides a straighter ridge.

CAUTION: Be sure end rafters are plumb before proceeding.

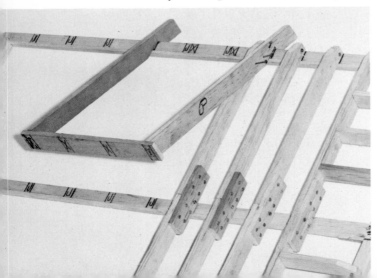

9-21. Next erect the two common rafters at the ends of the house, one each midway between the sides. Toenail the tops as described in step 9-18. Using two 16-penny nails, toenail bottom of rafters near bird's-mouth to top plate.

Be sure top edge of each end common rafter is in line with ridgeboard edge.

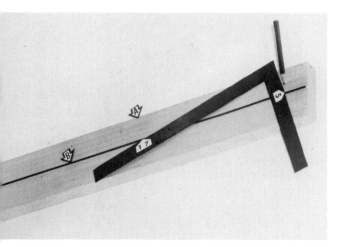

9-22. Next select a straight piece of rafter stock A long enough for making a hip rafter, including the tail if required.

Check your framing square for the per-foot run for a hip rafter. In the house illustrated the pitch is 5/24 or 17.69 inches. Therefore, the line length of the hip rafter is $12 \times 17.69 = 212.28$ inches $= 17$ feet $7\frac{1}{4}$ inches. Add to this length the rafter tail length called for in your plans.

Now mark measuring line B on rafter stock, being sure the distance from the top edge is equal to that for the common rafter.

Locate the tail plumb cut. Position the square near one end of the stock with 5 (unit rise) on the tongue and 17 on the body, both touching the measuring line.

Mark along the tongue. Next saw along line to form tail plumb cut.

If your plans call for a cornice, see step 9-13. Then lay out and cut level cut on bottom of the hip rafter tail.

9-23. Beginning where tail cut intersects the measuring line, measure along this line the distance the rafter is to extend away from the plate. (Note: hip rafter tails must be longer than common rafter tails.) This point locates the peak of the bird's-mouth.

See steps 9-11 and 9-12 for laying out common rafter bird's-mouth. Then using 5 and 17 on the square, lay out and cut bird's-mouth.

9-24. Beginning at the peak of the hip rafter bird's-mouth, measure line length (as found in step 9-22) along the measuring line.

Using 5 on the tongue (rise of roof) and 12 on the body as you did for the common rafter, lay out top plumb cut A.

As with the common rafter, your hip rafter plumb cut requires shortening. From line A measuse back at right angles $1\frac{1}{16}$ inches (half the diagonal thickness of $1\frac{1}{2}$-inch ridgeboard). Then draw a new plumb cut through this point.

line along body of square from the center point to top edge of rafter nearest the corner of the square.

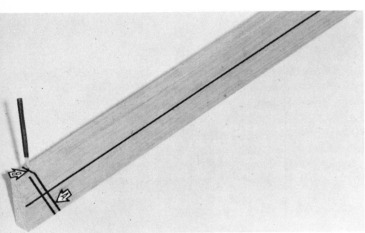

9-25. Now square top edge from top point of shortened plumb cut line A. Then locate center point B. This point must be located accurately, since both check cuts are to drawn through it.

9-26. Again consult the rafter table of your framing square, observing the sixth line under 5. Here the number $11\frac{1}{2}$ is given.

Position square on the stock with 12 on the body and $11\frac{1}{2}$ on the tongue, both touching the same edge. When the body edge coincides with the center point as found in the previous figure, draw a

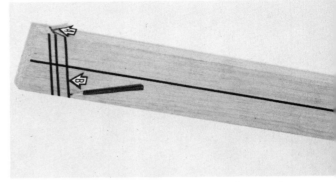

9-27. Using the same figures as in the previous step, draw opposite cheek cut A. Then beginning at the end of each cheek cut, draw a new plumb cut B on each side of the rafter.

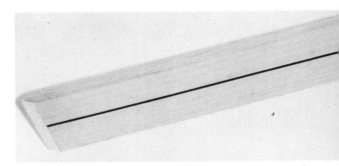

9-28. Saw the two cheek cuts. Now the top of the rafter should look like the picture here.

9-29. Also the bottom of the hip rafter tail requires two cheek cuts, making use of the same angles as shown for top end in step 28. Notice, however, the angle formed on the top end is in the opposite direction.

If a cornice cut is required, it should have been constructed as directed in step 9-13.

9-30. Next, locate the backing angle on top of hip rafter.

Begin by squaring line A across the top edge at any desired place. Then locate exact center of line.

mark line C through the center and parallel to both top edges.

Set electric saw to proper angle. Then cut top edges to the lines. Some builders plane backing angles rather than saw them.

Place hip rafter in place on the roof frame. If it fits, mark it with a P to serve as a pattern for other similar hip rafters.

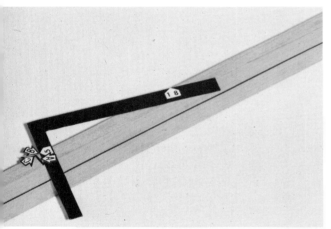

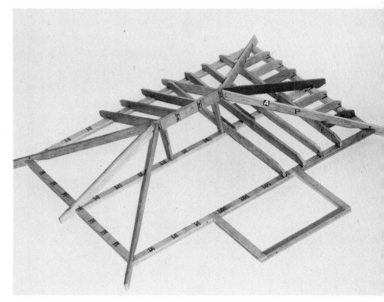

9-31. Position the square on rafter edge with unit rise 5 on the tongue and the length of the hip rafter per foot run 18 on the body both touching the same edge, when edge of tongue coincides with the center point as found in the previous step. Then draw line AB along the tongue. Distance CB is the backing distance.

9-32. Using distance CB in the previous figure, measure it off from the top edges of the rafter on both faces.

Next mark lines A and B through these points from end to end parallel to the top edges. Also

9-33. Next erect pattern hip rafter A as well as other similar ones. Fasten tops of rafters by driving two 16-penny nails through face into face of ridgeboard.

Toenail bottom of rafters in the same way as you previously fastened the bottom of common rafters.

Be sure top edge of hip rafters are flush with top edges of ridgeboard and adjoining common rafters.

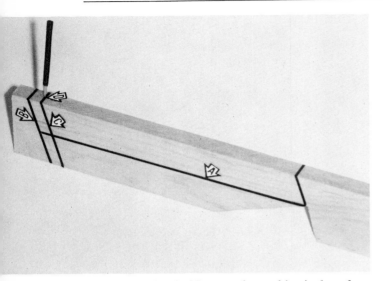

square on the edge of the stock with 11 1/16 on the tongue and 12 on the body, both touching the same edge of the stock when the edge of the body is located through the center point as found in the previous step. Mark along the body completely across the edge.

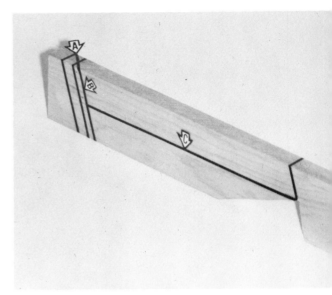

9-34. Next make a hip jack rafter. Begin by drawing measuring line A as you did for the common rafter. Then mark and cut the bird's-mouth and tail the same as for the common rafter previously cut.

Check under 5 (rise of roof) of the third line of the framing square. The difference of hip jack rafters 16 inches on center is 17 5/16 inches, which is also the line length of the first jack 6 inches from the corner.

Beginning at the peak of the bird's-mouth, measure along the measuring line A 17 5/16 inches. Then mark plumb cut B in the same way as you did for the common rafter.

Now shorten by dropping back from plumb cut B half the thickness of the hip (1 1/16 inches for a 2-inch-stock ridgeboard). Then mark new plumb cut C.

Next square across the top edge and mark center D.

9-35. On the framing square 11 1/16 is found under 5 (unit rise). Position the

9-36. From the far end of cheek cut A mark and saw new plumb cut B. Measuring line C now shows the true length of the first hip jack rafter. Each of the following jacks fitting against the same face of the hip rafter will have its length increased by 17 5/16 inches.

Note: Jacks fitting against the opposite face of the hip must have their cheeks marked and cut in the opposite direction.

Use the set of jacks prepared for one hip as patterns for other similar hips of the roof.

9-37. Position hip jack rafter A in place. Then using two 16-penny nails, fasten bottom of rafter

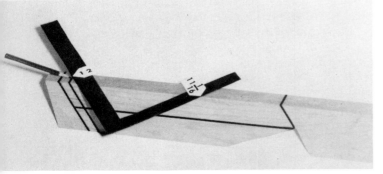

to ceiling joists in the same way as previously described for nailing bottom ends of common rafters in place. (For clarity, ceiling joists are not shown in this section of the roof frame.)

Next drive two 16-penny nails through the face of the hip jack into the face of the corresponding hip rafter.

the hip, or ¾ inches. Also, the valley rafter is without cheek cut at top end C. Next saw line CB.

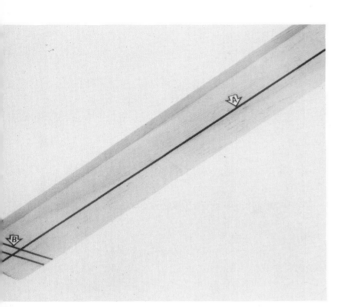

9-38. If your roof plans call for an intersecting roof, one or two valleys are required, depending upon the roof design. If your roof plan does not require a valley, skip this part of the chapter. The houses in this book called for a span of the addition less than the span of the main roof, so one of the two valley rafters (supporting rafters) was framed against the hip rafter of the main roof. Line length A is 17 times its common run 10, which equals 170 inches or 14 feet 2 inches. To this add the line length of the rafter tail, which is the same as previously done for the hip rafter.

5 (unit rise) and 17 are used on the square because the layout for the tail plumb cut, bird's-mouth, and top plumb cut is the same as for the hip rafter previously constructed. Since this valley rafter meets the hip rafter at right angles, in the example above shortening B for securing the true length (right angle to the plumb cut) is half the thickness of

9-39. Notice in step 9-1 that the bird's-mouth plum cut is so constructed as to fit into the corner.

With rafter upside down, locate center point of bird's-mouth plumb cut. Using the figures 12 and 11½ on the square (same figures as previously used in constructing the hip rafter), mark two cheek cut lines.

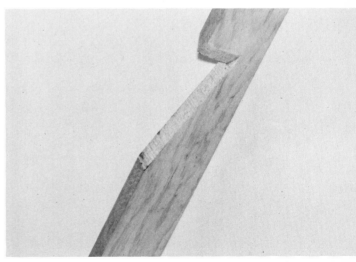

9-40. Next draw plumb cuts on both sides of stock from lower end of cheek cut lines. Sawing along these lines should produce bird's-mouth's plumb cut similar to the picture here, and it should corner on top of plates.

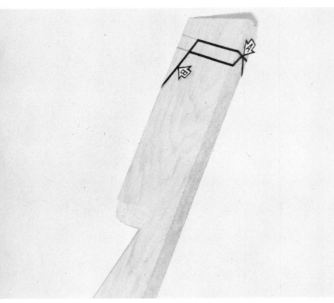

9-41. The same angle as required in the previous step for cutting the bird's-mouth is also required for the tail cut. However, the forked tail here is cut in the opposite direction.

Locate center point A across the top edge of a plumb cut line. Draw two cheek cuts through this point, using same figures as previously used for hip rafters. Also, draw new plumb cut lines from their lower ends.

Lay out cornice cut B, if required, in the same way as previously described for common rafter cornice tail cut.

Next saw along proper lines to form tail.

9-42. Position supporting valley rafter A in place. Then using four 16-penny nails, two at the bottom and two at the top, fasten in place as shown above.

9-43. Lay out and cut short valley rafter (shown by arrow) in the same way as the supporting valley rafter previously constructed. Here the common run is 6 feet. Its line length, therefore, is 6 times 17 inches, which equals 102 inches or 8 feet 6 inches.

Position and nail bottom of rafter to plate the same as for the supporting valley rafter. Then drive two 16-penny nails through face of supporting valley rafter into end grain of short valley rafters.

9-44. Lay out and cut valley jack rafter A next. Since the valley jack extends from the valley rafter to the ridge, it does not have a bird's-mouth or tail. Here the run is the same as that of the common rafters. The line length is 12 times 13 inches, which equals 13 feet 0 inches.

Bottom end of rafter requires a cheek cut to meet the valley rafter. Make these cuts exactly as you did for the top end of hip jack rafters, steps 9-34 to 9-36. The shortening distance is half the diagonal thickness of the valley rafter.

Top end of rafter fits against the ridge piece. Shorten and draw plumb cut lines at top the same as for common rafters.

Now position and nail rafters in place with 16-penny nails.

ceiling joists and mark rafter locations on top wall plates as previously done for main section of roof. For clarity, only first installed ceiling joist A is shown in the picture here. Notice this joist extends over the end plate, thereby serving later as a ceiling nailer. Location is made by leaving the thickness of a piece of 2-inch stock between joist and gable rafter location.

If your plans call for an intersecting hip roof, frame it as previously described in this chapter for hip roof framing.

9-45. The last rafters to construct for a hip roof are valley-cripple jacks A. The run is 4 feet. Therefore its length is 4 times 13 inches, which equals 52 inches or 4 feet 4 inches.

The length of valley-cripple jacks is from the center of the hip to the center of the valley rafter. (The example shown is from center of supporting valley to the center of short valley rafter.) Therefore shortening at top and bottom is half the diagonal thickness of the valleys. To save time twice this thickness can be taken off one end of the rafter.

The valley-cripple jack has a cheek cut at top and bottom and is laid out and cut as you did for the hip jack rafter cheek cuts.

Position in place. Then use 16-penny nails to fasten in place.

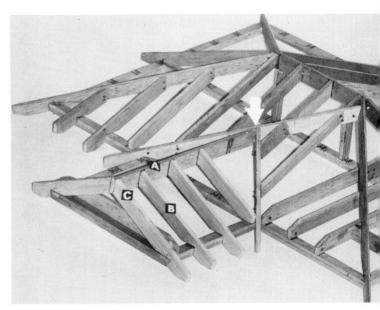

Intersecting Roof

9-46. If your plans call for an intersecting roof, lay out, cut, and fasten intersecting roof

E-3D

9-47. If your plans call for a gable intersecting roof, the picture here shows such a roof style with a span of main roof.

Select a straight 2×8 for minor ridge-board A. Then locate rafters with an X. Now lay out and cut valley end (shown by arrow) with a double cheek. Cheeks are cut at a 45° angle.

Lay out, cut, and fasten common rafters B in place the same as previously described for the hip roof.

CAUTION: Select two straight common rafters for the gable rafters C. After gable rafters are located, be sure ridge is level and outside of gable rafters plumb and flush with outside edge of top plate.

For clarity, except for gable rafters, common rafters are shown on only one side of intersecting roof.

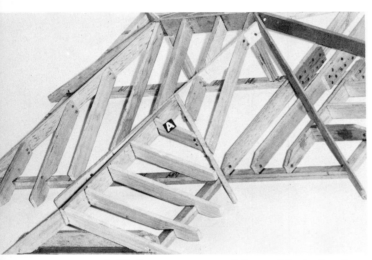

9-48. Lay out, cut, and fasten hip jack rafters A similarly to those previously described in hip roof framing.

9-49. A gable intersecting roof requires gable studs extending from plate to gable rafters.

Using a combination square, square line A directly below the center of the gable ridgeboard. Also locate a center line B on top plate below ridge.

If your plans call for an opening in the gable, such as a window or a ventilation louver, measure one half of the opening on each side of plate center mark. Square a line across the plate on both

marks. These lines represent the outside edge of the first full-length stud on each side of the opening. Later complete opening frame with two 2×4s fastened between these studs, one across the bottom opening. If no openings are required, the first center line represents the center of the first stud as shown in the picture.

Beginning at the center line(s), lay out the stud spacing 16 inches on center to both outside plates of the house. Use an X to show stud spacing.

9-50. Next lay out and cut gable studs to fit vertically between plate markings and gable rafter. The picture shows how gable stud is notched to fit flush, inside of rafter. Cuts A and B are made on the same slope or pitch as the roof.

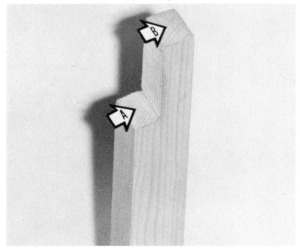

plate and the ridgeboard. Next place the ridgeboard alongside the plate on the opposite side of the house and locate rafter locations here. Be sure outside of end plate rafters are located flush with the outside of wall frame as shown in the picture.

Next locate ceiling joists exactly as directed in step 9-2 with respect to adjacent common rafters. Then cut and fasten ceiling joists as directed in steps 9-5 and 9-6. Be sure end ceiling joists also serve as ceiling nailers later, as described for intersecting roof ceiling joists in step 9-46.

9-51. Locate gable studs A. Then, using two 8-penny box nails, fasten top of each gable stud of rafter, toenailing bottoms in place with 16-penny nails. For clarity only half of the required gable studs are shown in the picture.

Gable Main Roof

9-52. Lay enough boards A (2×8s unless your plans call for different dimensions) along plate B of one side of the house. Saw ridgeboard when necessary so that joints come halfway between rafters.

Beginning at the outside edge of plate at one end of house, lay out rafter locations on 16-inch centers on both the side

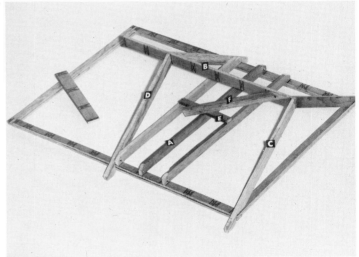

9-53. Measure and cut common rafters as previously described for hip-roof framing. (For clarity only three ceiling joists A are shown in the picture.) Choose four straight rafters for the two gables.

Nail the first length of ridgeboard B to an end rafter C. Then nail a second rafter D on the same side of the ridgeboard but about six rafter spacings away. Be certain that top of rafters are flush with top of ridgeboard and that they are located exactly over the rafter markings. See step 9-16 for nailing instructions.

As your helper raises these rafters fastened to ridgeboard, adjust the bird's-mouth to fit over the proper rafter markings on the plate. Then nail in place. See step 9-18 for nailing instructions.

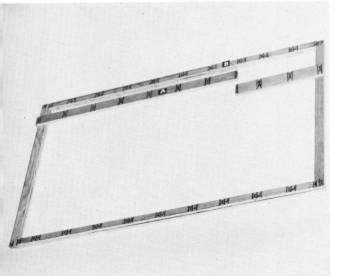

Now position and nail the bottom ends of two rafters to the opposite plate so they will line up with the two rafters already installed. Raise or lower the ridgeboard as the case might be until the top is flush with the top of the rafters being installed. Then nail rafters to ridgeboard. See step 9-17 for nailing instructions.

Be sure end or gable 2×6 is flush with the side of the wall framework. Plumb and brace this section of roof framing by temporarily nailing 2×4 E over at least three ceiling joists. Then nail one end of 1×6 F to it with the opposite end nailed to the top of the ridgeboard as shown in the illustration for step 9-29.

Fasten remaining rafters of this section of roof in place, first by erecting one and then the opposite one. Nailing the bottom end of each rafter first results in a straighter ridge.

Next locate and install a section of rafters, including gable rafters, at the opposite end of house. Nail and brace exactly as described in step 9-29.

Now locate and install remaining rafters between gables to the ridgeboard and plates.

CAUTION: As a final check, be certain ridgeboard is straight and level from the top of one gable to the other and that they are plumb before proceeding.

Complete roof framing by marking location of gable studs on top plates located at each end of house. Then lay out, cut, and fasten gable studs in place. See steps 9-49 to 9-51.

Shed Roof

9-54. If your plans call for a porch where a single-slope roof is required (referred to as a shed roof), only common rafters are required. The layout is the same as previously described for the common rafter in hip-type roof framing.

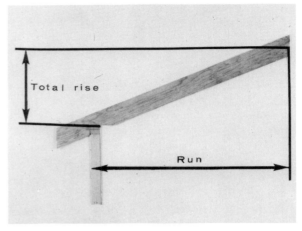

Some shed-roof rafters have a bird's-mouth at top and bottom of rafter; others have a bird's-mouth at the bottom end only, with top end cut plumb.

Begin by establishing the plate height of the highest wall with respect to the required roof pitch.

The difference in plate height is equal to the unit rise of rafter times the number of feet in run of rafter.

Dormer Roof

9-55. If your plans call for a gable dormer, proceed as follows. Reinforce the frame by doubling rafters A on both sides that support dormer walls. Also install double headers B at upper and lower ends of roof openings.

Lay out, cut, and install dormer frame on reinforced roof frame the same as pre-

viously described for previous wall and roof frames. Bottom of dormer studs are cut the same angle as for gable studs. Studs located 16 inches on centers will be progressively longer than the preceding one by the amount of rise for 16 inches of common roof run. Frame rough openings for dormer windows in the same way as described in Chapter 8 for window openings in wall frame. Since window headers carry little weight, two 2×4s fastened side by side usually suffice.

CAUTION: When finishing be sure to flash with nonrusting metal sheets between sides of dormer and roofing material. See Chapter 10 for instructions on making a flashing watertight.

rafter tails around the perimeter of the house. Miter one edge of each piece of facia to correspond to the pitch of the roof. Then locate the rough facia, miter edge continuing the roof lines, onto the rafter tails. Next drive two 16-penny nails through the face side of the rough facia into the end grain of each rafter tail. Here 2×6s were used because the rafters are 2×6s.

CAUTION: Some house plans call for 1-inch lumber for rough facia material. If your plans so stipulate, be sure to follow the architect's recommendations.

9-58. Before proceeding, be certain ceiling nailers are located over all wall cap plates on which to nail ceiling material later. Do not overlook partition wall cap plates. In the picture, A shows an example of a 2×4 fastened with 16-penny nails halfway on top plate to provide nailer where ceiling joists are lacking.

9-56. Using a tight line as a guide, check all rafter tails between each pair of adjacent corner rafters. Are any uneven? If so, mark those that extend beyond the line. Then saw the uneven tails in line and plumb on all sides of the roof.

9-57. Select enough construction-grade 2-inch lumber to serve as rough facia A for covering the

Roof Decking

9-59. Using a saw, cut 4×8-foot sheets of ⅝-inch plywood into edges adjoining the cornice plumb with the rafter tails. Then start laying the

roof decking at the eave or lower end of the rafters, allowing approximately 1 inch to extend over the cornice board that will be applied later to box the rafter ends. Using 8-penny nails at intervals of 6 inches, fasten the plywood sheets to the rafters.

Because roof planes join at different angles at the juncture of the ridge, hips, and valleys, use a saw to bevel the adjoining edges for a butt fit before nailing such areas of roof decking in place.

Roof Felting

9-60. To protect roof decking from the weather, install roofing felt.

Staple 30-pound roofing felt in even, horizontal strips, beginning at the eaves and laying toward the ridgeboard. Apply the staples about 12 inches apart along each edge and down the middle of each strip.

9-61. Overlap each strip approximately 3 inches. Using a linoleum knife, cut the

felt at hips and valley, overlapping at these points. Also lap the last strip over the ridge board, as shown by arrow.

9-62. If you do not plan to install roof shingles next, temporarily fasten lath near eaves around the perimeter of roof to protect the felt from the wind. Use three 1-inch nails per lath.

10

THE FIREPLACE AND THE CHIMNEY

In general, lightweight, modular concrete blocks were used for the masonry in the fireplace shown in the picture here. Blocks are easier and quicker to lay than bricks and serve the purpose just as well.

The blocks formed the base and were laid around a heavy metal Heatilator fireplace unit. Then the blocks were laid around sections of flue liners, mortared together, to the roof line. A furnace flue was also included in the basement. Three different widths of Indiana limestone were used to face the fireplace.

10-1. Outward appearances of fireplaces vary in accordance with the tastes of the different people who design them, but each fireplace requires sound construction from the base of the chimney to its completion above the roof.

10-2. Begin fireplace and chimney construction by driving a nail partway in each of the corners of the fireplace framework on the main floor. Using a plumb bob, drop lines from each corner to the basement floor, the four points indicating the four corners of the fireplace base. Using a piece of chalk and a straightedge, connect the four points. Note: in Chapter 5, "The Excavation," a fireplace footing pad was recommended to support the fireplace.

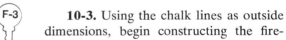

10-3. Using the chalk lines as outside dimensions, begin constructing the fire-

place masonry base. Use 8×8×16-inch blocks for the base.

As you lay the first course of blocks, place mortar the full width of the block on the concrete floor. (Place mortar on face shells only for succeeding courses.)

Build corners up three or four blocks high, using a level to check each block laid. The base must be kept level and plumb as you proceed. Make mortar joints ⅜ inch thick. CAUTION: Be sure to use a corner block with one flat end at corners, shown by black arrow.

frame. Then lay blocks up around it, being sure the frame is securely mortared in place.

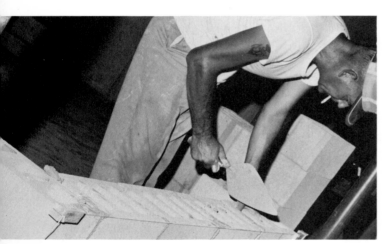

10-4. Stretch line between corners to lay blocks to. Then build wall between corners. Continue to build corners, then build walls between them until desired height is reached. Don't be disturbed if your devices for holding the line taut are different from the ones in the picture here. Almost every stonemason has his own pet devices, and all serve the same purpose.

 10-5. Install a 10×12-inch ash pit cleanout door directly underneath the middle of the proposed fireplace and near the basement floor. Position the ash-pit door-

10-6. Continue building the rectangular base to a point 8 inches below where the furnace smokepipe is to enter the flue, if your plans call for such a flue.

As you come up with the base, lay nine 4×8×16-inch blocks spaced as shown here. Then cover with 4×8×16-inch blocks laid flat. These serve as a foundation for a furnace flue. The number of blocks for the flue foundation will vary from job to job.

10-7. As you go up with the base, lay blocks around sections of rectangular flue liner. If you do not have a section of

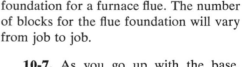
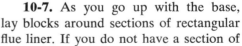

flue liner with a precut smokepipe opening, cut an opening in one of the regular sections, using a hammer and a chisel.

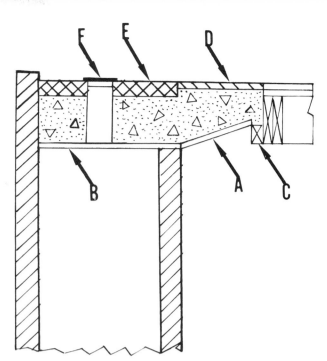

10-8. Position a smokepipe thimble in the base wall so that the smokepipe from the furnace will fit into the flue properly. If the thimble is too long, cut it to correct length before mortaring it in place.

Continue laying up the wall and furnace flue, placing a seal of mortar between the blocks and the thimble as you proceed to the point where the floor joists frame the opening in the floor.

10-9. At this point, your fireplace base with furnace flue should look similar to the picture here.

F-3

F-11

F-12

F-13

F-14

10-10. Construct and brace wood form A for pouring cantilevered concrete hearth base.

Bring back and two sides of base about one block above floor level. Notch blocks in rear of base so as to leave a 4-inch-wide by 5-inch-high space to provide a hold for poured concrete hearth and base for the firebrick. Then cut a piece of ⅝-inch plywood B to support poured concrete. 2×4 C spiked to floor joists helps to support hearth form. Later remove this 2×4.

The drawing shows concrete over block base and hearth form as it will be poured in the following step. Note that concrete under hearth D is thicker than concrete under firebricks E. This difference is necessary because the finished hearth is not as thick as the firebricks. Also, ash-pit dump F is shown as it will look when put into place. For clarity, the furnace flue is not shown.

10-11. Cut ½-inch reinforcement rods to fit inside form, not less than 6 inches apart. Next prepare a four-sided wood

form with outside dimensions the same as the outside dimensions of the ash-pit-dump frame. Note: Later when the concrete is hard and ash-pit-dump form is removed, cut hole in plywood so that ashes can fall to bottom of base.

Pour a mixture of concrete made of 1 part Portland cement, 2 parts clean sand, and 3 parts small rock into the form, troweling smooth and level. Be sure that surfaces of firebricks and finished hearth, when laid, will be flush with finished floor.

When concrete has hardened, use heat-resisting fireclay mortar, mixed thin as pancake batter, to lay the firebricks in place. Then remove accessible form material.

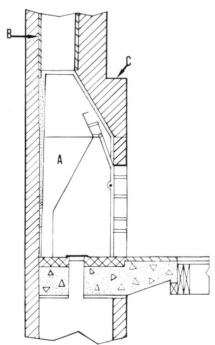

10-12. Locate the four inside points where fireplace chimney is to come through roof opening, followed by dropping plumb lines (similar to way in which they were dropped through the floor joists) to locate chimney opening.

Next position fireplace unit A in place. Now proceed with the laying of 4×8×16-inch blocks on two sides and rear of the fireplace, bringing them and the furnace flue to the height of the lintel as indicated in the instructions accompanying your

metal fireplace unit. Note: Use 4×8×16-inch blocks here and in remainder of chimney to the roof line. Also, pay close attention to the instructions for installing the lintel and the unit, including insulation and air intakes and outlets.

As you proceed with the chimney construction, join the sections of flue liners B at the joints with brick mortar, and then lay blocks around them. Also provide niche C for supporting mantel later. Be sure to face the fireplace with special finish or "face" bricks, which have an especially neat appearance. Of course, you may use stone if you desire.

Install ash-pit dump in opening. Then scatter a coating of sand over firebricks to prevent mortar from sticking to them as you proceed with the chimney. Again, for clarity, the furnace flue is not shown.

10-13. Continue laying 4×4×16-inch blocks toward the fireplace chimney opening in the roof, bringing them over by following the slope of the smoke chamber of the unit. If the hole for the chimney to pass through has not been cut in the roof yet, cut it now.

Also, gradually bring furnace flue (indicated by black arrows) over within 4 inches of fireplace flue. Begin by mitering the ends of the flue tile by not more than 30° from plumb. Then mortar it in place, followed by laying blocks around it. Fill space between the two flues with 4-inch blocks and mortar.

flue liners extending about 4 inches above the last course of bricks or stone. Then cut bricks or stone to form pillars for each corner.

Trowel in a topping of mortar on chimney top, beginning flush at outer edge and tapering upward to within 1 inch of flue liners as shown.

10-14. Continue laying blocks and flue liners until the chimney reaches the roof opening. If you have not yet installed roof decking, do it now.

Next begin laying the exposed part of the chimney, using bricks or stone. If your chimney comes through the roof at the ridge, cut 1-inch-deep grooves in the masonry adjacent to the ridge as shown. A stone saw was used for cutting the grooves in the picture here before the stones were laid.

10-15. Continue laying bricks or stone until the top of chimney is 2 feet above the roof ridge with

10-16. Have a 2¼-inch-thick stone slab cut to the length and width of the outside chimney dimensions. Then lay a mortar joint onto the top of each pillar. Now, with the aid of several helpers, position the outside corners of the slab flush with the outside edges of the corner pillars. Using a trowel, remove excess mortar that squeezed out of the joints.

10-17. This is the time to make the joint between the chimney and the roof watertight by installing a copper or other nonrusting metal flashing.

Make the flashing with four pieces of metal cut and bent to fit, one for each side of the chimney. Then overlap the corners two inches and solder the joints. Be sure top edges of flashings are bent at right angles so they can extend at least 1 inch into the joints. For clarity, the picture here shows only one side of chimney flashing. The following picture shows how to make the flashing between the roof ridge and chimney.

10-18. Begin making the flashing for roof ridge and chimney the same as in the previous step. Then cut and bend top edge A as shown. Bend bottom part B at lower edge of cut so as to fit over roof ridge. This forms a V in top edge. To correct this, cut, bend, and solder metal part C over V in edge A, making watertight joints. While fashioning flashing be sure it will fit into grooves cut into side of chimney as well as lie flat over roof ridge.

When top edges of the four pieces of flashing have been placed in their respective grooves and the corners have been soldered to form a solid flashing all around the chimney, caulk grooves with roofing compound to assure a watertight seal.

10-19. Place a layer of mortar over mantel support on fireplace. Then with the aid of a helper

pick up mantel and bring it down horizontally on top of mortar joint. With a trowel, carefully remove surplus mortar that squeezed out beyond joint.

10-20. Complete fireplace installation by laying hearth tile onto a bed of brick mortar.

11

THE EXTERIOR FINISHING

11-1. Now is the time to complete the exterior finish of your house. I recommend doing the following operations in order:

1. Building boxed cornice, if required
2. Applying asphalt roofing
3. Installing exterior door and window units
4. Applying exterior siding
5. Installing guttering

Building The Boxed Cornice

11-2. Begin construction of the boxed cornice by leveling across from rafter overhang to wall at the two ends of the eave. Next snap a chalk line between these points. Using two 8-penny box nails spaced 16 inches apart, fasten bottom end of 1×4 lookout ledger A to this line. Next cut 2×4 lookouts B to fit between lookout ledger board and rough facia board C.

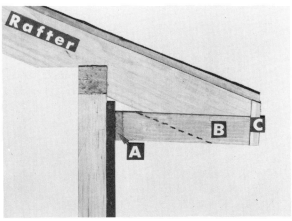

Beginning at center of house, position lookouts between rough facia and lookout ledger on 16-inch centers. Then, using two 16-penny nails, toenail inner ends to the ledger. Fasten outer ends by driving two 16-penny nails through face of rough facia into end grain of lookout.

11-3. Cut ¼-inch exterior plywood as plancier material A to fit frame on both sides of ventilating screen B and to extend ¼ inch beyond rough facia C. Starting in the middle, use 1-inch nails spaced 16 inches on center to fasten plancier material in place.

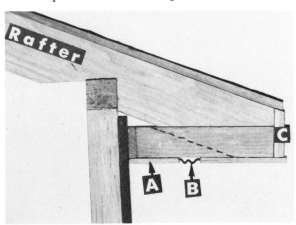

11-4. Select grade A 1×8 finish boards to serve as finish facia shown by black arrow in picture. Saw top edge of boards to the roof slope or pitch. Then plow a groove ¼ inch deep and wide enough to accept extended plancier edge shown by white arrow. Position facia board in place. Fasten by using two 8-penny galvanized box nails at 12-inch intervals.

or the roof decking are shown in picture.) Then spike regular lookout C alongside it and locate remaining lookouts on 16-inch centers as described in step 11-2.

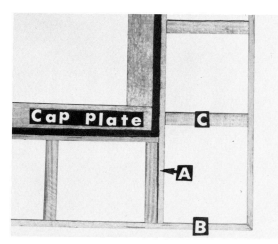

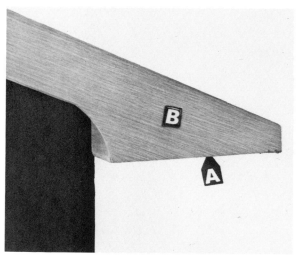

 11-5. If yours is a hip roof, extend side wall lookout ledger A across the overhang to end of rough end facia B. Next nail lookout C against ledger extensions, which provides backing for the plancier end.

Complete cornice job for the remaining sides of the house.

 11-6. If your house has a gable roof, extend ledger A a distance equal to gable overhang. Now cut lookout B to fit between end of ledger and underside of gable rafter. (For clarity no other roof rafters

11-7. Line the underside of the gable ends with soffit material. Next box in the eave. Then apply soffit material A to bottoms of lookouts and nail finish facia to rough facia as described in steps 11-3 and 11-4. Using 1-inch finish lumber, cut and fasten bargeboard B in place with 8-penny galvanized box nails, spaced 16 inches on centers.

Applying Asphalt Roofing

 11-8. If possible, use the same kind of metal starter strip as you plan for the guttering.

Using 1-inch nails spaced 16 inches apart in a zigzag pattern, fasten the roofing metal starter strips onto the edge of the roof. Overlap the metal joints about 2 inches. CAUTION: Drive nails only through the top of the metal strip. Do not drive nails through the metal overhanging the facia.

 Use 1-inch roofing nails for laying the asphalt roofing. Begin by nailing asphalt starter strip (same design as roofing tabs) shown by arrow along the eaves, spacing the nails about 12 inches apart.

11-10. Begin laying the first layer of strip shingles by using a part of a strip at the hip or at the rake if your roof is of the gable type. Using a sharp linoleum knife, cut the part of the first strip as shown by the arrow for a gable roof. Cut tab at an angle if yours is a hip roof.

Then nail the strip, slots down, in place, followed by using full-length strips to a valley or the opposite end of the roof, whichever is reached first. Nail according to instructions accompanying roofing tabs. Cut last shingle to fit.

11-11. Begin the second course of shingles with a full strip at the starting end of the roof.

11-9. If lath stripping was nailed to the roof decking, remove it. Be sure all nails are also removed.

Continue laying the roof with every other layer beginning with a cut shingle as you did in laying the first course.

Always be sure the center of each shingle lies directly above the corresponding slot of the shingle in the preceding course.

11-13. Use individual shingles of the same color and weight as the roofing shingles to cap ridge and hips if your roof has them.

Fold shingles over hip and ridge so that the roofing nails will be covered (as seen on shingle A) by following shingle B. Be sure to have a 5-inch exposure for each shingle as well as an overlap of 2 inches.

Use roofing plastic cement to make a waterproof cement lap joint.

Now use two roofing nails (shown by arrows) to the tab, placed 1-inch from the bottom edges and the same distance from the end which is to be overlapped with the following shingle.

11-14. A fireplace or furnace requires a chimney through the roof. If your plans call for a chimney, refer to Chapter 10, for instructions on chimney flashing.

11-12. If there is a valley in the roof the installation should appear as shown in the picture here. A indicates roofing felt application as described in Chapter 9.

Begin by bending a 10-inch-wide strip of aluminum B or other nonrusting metal in accordance with the roof-valley angle. Then place the metal material in place in roof valley. Hold metal in place with a few roofing nails driven near its edge into the roof decking.

Cut the end of the last shingle of each course parallel with and extending over the metal valley material to within 1 inch from the center line. Thus the valley material is kept open for correct drainage. C indicates roof mastic, which provides a weathertight seal between valley material and asphalt shingles D.

Installing Exterior Door And Window Units

11-15. Primed exterior door and window units wholesaled by Morgan-Wightman, 9910 Page Boulevard, St. Louis, Missouri 63166, were used in the houses illustrated in this book.

Lay packaged door unit on two sawbucks. Then remove nails and other material holding unit together during shipping.

CAUTION: Do not remove door from frame.

11-16. The part of the sill that projects beyond the casing should equal the distance from the face of the sill. If the sill extends farther, saw it off accordingly. Also, the side jambs should not project more than ¾ inch above the head jamb or below the sill.

11-17. Place door unit in the rough opening. If sill is not flush with finish floor dimension, use wedges and cleats to support the sill to this elevation.

11-18. Using level, check trim for plumb and straightness on the hinge side. Use shims, such as wood shingles, on the opposite side and on top to wedge it securely in the rough opening and to give solid backing at butts and strikes.

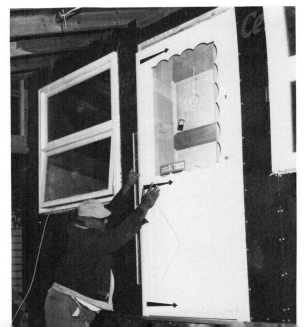

Door units from Morgan-Wightman come with 2⅛-inch holes drilled through door face A and in center of door edge B for latch. If your doors are not bored, follow directions on template and instruction sheet found in lockset box. I locate centers of lockset holes 36 inches above finished floor.

11-19. Using 8-penny finishing nails spaced 16 inches on center, fasten trim to wall.

Next nail through the jambs and shims. Do not nail through stop.

Cut away any projecting wedges flush with studs.

Countersink finishing nails, filling holes flush with wood putty.

11-20. Kwikset's "400" line locksets were used in the houses in this book. They are of rugged, reliable construction. Have locks keyed for a single key. This way one key will unlock all outside door locks.

11-21. Insert latch A in hole, keeping it parallel to face of door. Mark outline and remove latch.

Next chisel ⅛ inch deep or until latch face is flush with door edge.

Now insert latch and tighten screws.

11-22. Following instructions on template, mark template from edge of jamb and locate center line for screws.

Next drill latch bolt hole ½ inch deep and

square out with a chisel. This forms the pocket for latch bolt.

Now match screw holes on strike A with center line on jamb. Outline outside edge of strike. Then chisel out 1/16 inch so strike will fit flush with jamb.

Installing strike and tightening screws completes this step. (Adjustable tong B on strike permits bending in or out to eliminate too loose fit between door and door stop.)

11-25. The following three steps explain installing packaged window units.

Begin on the outside. Check frame size against opening size as you did for the exterior door frames.

Be sure to trim the ends of the sill flush with the outside of the casing. Then turn the frame over, casing down. Now trim the ends of the side jambs within ¾ inch from the sill and head jamb as you did in preparing the door frames. Then place the pre-assembled frame into the rough opening.

Place wedge-shaped blocks under sill to hold the top of frame plumb and to the correct height.

11-23. Insert exterior knob with spindle A into latch, making certain that stems B are positioned correctly through latch holes. Press flush against door. Note: For easier installation, depress latch bolt.

11-24. Install interior knob and nose A by placing on spindle and aligning screw guides with stems. Push flush against the door. Insert screws and tighten until lockset is firm.

11-26. After plumbing, check the frame for level. Then using 8-penny finishing nails spaced 16 inches on center and ¾ inch from the outside edge of the casing, fasten securely in place.

11-27. The installation of small window units requires the same careful plumbing, leveling, and installation procedures as large window units.

Applying Exterior Siding

11-28. My own new house, shown in the picture, is sided with Masonite Corporation's Prefinished Colorlok X-90 siding. Of all siding products on the market, I believe this is the best buy for the money. It is guaranteed for ten years not to crack, peel, blister, or check so as to require painting, and it has a 25-year hail-damage guarantee.

Begin by fastening special starter strip in place with 6-penny galvanized box nails after adjusting up to 1 inch down for course layout. Locating strip parallel to soffit and wall joint will enable the top siding board to be installed equal width for full length of house.

11-29. Using prefinished 8-foot inside corner strips, cut to proper length, fasten in place on all inside corners with galvanized 6-penny box nails spaced 8 inches apart along the flange.

11-30. Install first course of siding so that mounting strip fastened into the back of the siding fits over the edge of the starter strip. Then drive 8-penny galvanized box nails through the nail slots into the wall studs.

11-31. Position metal joint molding from the top to bottom between butt joints. A gap of 1/16 to 3/32 inch is required at the siding butt joints.

CAUTION: Do not force or spring siding into place.

11-32. Using prefinished metal outside corners, insert tabs of corner behind lower edge of siding and fasten corners at top only with 8-penny galvanized box nails.

11-33. Be sure wood trim around doors and windows is at least 1⅛ inches thick. Then saw siding to fit, allowing a 1/16-inch gap adjoining all trim. Now nail siding in place.

11-34. Measure and cut with hacksaw prefinished metal drip cap for tops of each window and door.

11-35. Fasten prefinished metal drip-cap pieces in place with 6-penny galvanized box nails.

 11-36. Complete siding job by caulking around doors and windows as well as inside corners and cracks. Matching colored caulking is available from Masonite Corporation.

 11-37. If your home design calls for a Western-style exterior, Masonite Ruf X-ninety hardboard exterior siding will

provide a deep-textured exterior that gives the appearance of a rough-sawn surface. Each panel is available either factory prime-coated or not prime-coated. Panels are 7/16 inch thick and 4 feet wide, and lengths run to 16 feet and have butt edges for use with battens.

Begin application of panels by snapping chalk lines lengthwise on 16-inch centers. (In this way, nails go through the panels and sheathing into the 2×4 wall studs.)

Next position panels, one at a time, plumb against the sheathing. Be sure to cut panels for fitting around doors and windows.

11-38. Fasten panels in place with 8-penny galvanized nails spaced 4 inches apart around all

panel edges and 8 inches apart at intermediate stud locations. Nail at least ⅜ inch from panel siding edges.

11-39. If 8-foot panels applied to your house fail to reach the soffit, use finish board as shown in picture here. The application of a 1×6 clear white pine frieze board makes for a neat appearance between top of panels and soffit.

 11-40. Apply corner trim boards (shown by white arrow) and batten strips (shown by black arrow) of your choice over all vertical joints. To assure tight joints, apply caulking before installing corner boards and batten strips. Also, caulk joints around windows and doors.

11-41. Complete siding job by applying two top coats of paint or stain (color of your choice). Be sure that all exposed edges of the siding are well painted.

Installing Guttering

 11-42. Do three things before starting the guttering job:

First, become acquainted with the box type fittings as shown in the picture. The fittings have the following names:

    A. Gutter
    B. Left end cap
    C. Strainer
    D. Drop outlet
    E. Slip joint connector
    F. Inside corner
    G. Valley shield
    H. Outside corner
    I. Spike and ferrule set
    J. Strap hanger
    K. Right end cap
    L. Facia bracket hanger
    M. T-bar hanger
    N. Regular elbow-60° angle
    O. Pipe strap
    P. Rainpipe
    Q. Side elbow-60° angle

Second, figure out just where to run the gutters, rainpipes (sometimes called downspouts), and other fittings.

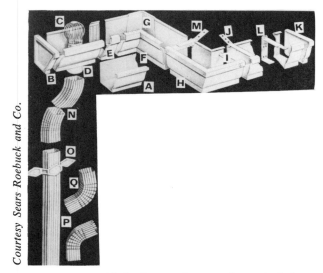

Courtesy Sears Roebuck and Co.

Join together slip-type gutters, corner pieces, end caps, and drop outlets after first having prepared them with waterproof sealant as recommended on your particular instruction sheet.

Check your house for levelness by driving a small shingle nail at each end of the roof line. Then stretch a chalk line between the nails and to this string attach a line level. If the roof is perfectly level, lower one end of the string in the direction that the drainwater should flow through the gutter. When proper drop (1/16 inch to a foot) has been reached, snap the line to the facia board. This line on the facia board serves as a guide line for securing the gutters. Note: Although some instructions call for gutters to be installed perfectly level, I have found that a slight slope toward the rainpipe opening is more satisfactory, and the appearance of the gutter line and roof line is not noticeably affected.

Install gutters, according to instructions, at the cornice line of the roof to collect water runoff and carry it to the downspouts, where it is in turn emptied into a drain tile or onto a splashguard.

Third, figure the number of fittings required, including size of gutter and rainpipes.

Guttering assembled with slip-joint connectors are recommended because a pair of tin snips, hacksaw, screwdriver, and hammer are the only tools required, and soldering joints is completely eliminated.

11-43. Because specific installation instructions vary slightly among guttering manufacturers and because instructions are furnished for each brand made for the do-it-yourself man, only general installation instructions follow.

Prepare to assemble gutters on level ground or on a driveway or on a sidewalk in groups of three 10-foot sections, two 16-foot sections, or two 20-foot sections unless a shorter run is required. (The assembling of two or more pieces of gutters is called a run.) Use a hacksaw for cutting a piece to proper length where a short piece of gutter is needed to complete a run. Be sure to make a straight cut.

11-44. If you do not wish to build scaffolds as shown in the previous picture, you can prepare an extension bracket for each of two ladders as shown in the picture here. With outer end of the

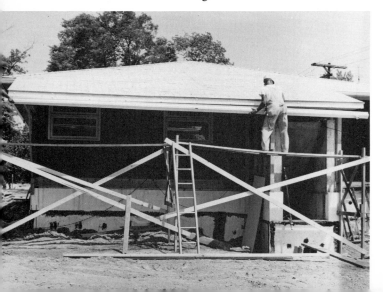

bracket resting against the outside wall, the ladder proper is free of the gutter.

Make the bracket from 1×4s or 1×6s that are free of knots. The length of the bracket will depend upon the width of the overhang, the width of the gutter, and the width of the ladder rails. Use 8-penny box nails for bracket assembly and for fastening bracket to ladder. Clinch all protruding nails.

11-45. As each side of the roof is guttered, make a water test. If the gutters are not draining toward the rainpipe outlet, now is the time to find out.

11-46. Next make up the rainpipe assemblies. Each assembly consists of a piece of rainpipe cut to proper length and fitted in place by friction to

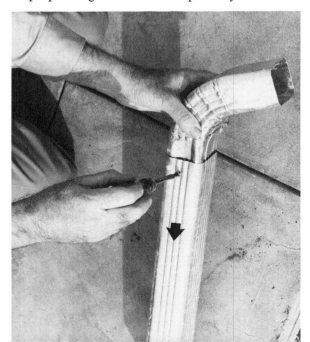

an elbow as shown in the picture. This in turn is fitted to a short piece of rainpipe and a second elbow. Cut the short piece of rainpipe connecting the two elbows exactly long enough to ensure that the main rainpipe fits snugly against the wall when the assembly is in place. Cut rainpipe to proper length with a hacksaw. Be sure to make straight cuts.

To make up rainpipe assembly properly, always insert each top section into top of the next section until it is firmly held by friction. (A metal screw, as shown in the picture, for each joint makes for a more rigid assembly.) If you keep the direction of the proposed water flow in mind, you will not experience any difficulty here. In the photo the elbow is being placed inside the drain pipe because the water flow will be in the direction of the arrow.

11-47. Secure the rainpipe assemblies against the wall with a minimum of two pipe straps or hooks on each rainpipe. Ornamental leader straps may be placed over rainpipe and leader hook if desired as shown in picture. Where walls are made of wood or have been sheathed with plywood, straps can be fastened with wood screws. Where walls are of masonry, first drill holes with a concrete bit. Then insert lead anchors. Now straps can be fastened with wood screws fastened into anchor holes.

Insert rainpipe into a tile that leads to an elevation lower than soil at foundation or to a shoe and splashguard to direct drainwater away from the foundation. Splashguards can be purchased from most hardware stores or from your favorite mail-order house.

11-49. Gutter guards prevent leaves, sticks, balls, evening papers, and birdnests from clogging gutters and rainpipes. Some guards consist of ⅓-inch or ¼-inch hardware-cloth sections, 2 feet long and 5 to 7 inches wide, and bound on four sides with metal stripping. Install the guard by slipping one side underneath the shingles and attaching the other side to the outside gutter edge with the spring clips provided. Gutter guards may be secured from your local tinner or hardware store, or ordered from your favorite mail-order house. This operation completes gutter installation.

11-48. If your roof has valleys, you can install a valley guard with two metal screws onto the inside of the outside gutter edge opposite each valley. During a heavy rainstorm, valley guards help to prevent fast-rushing water coming down the valleys from overshooting the gutter. You can make valley guards from pieces of metal bent at right angles as shown in the picture above. Finish to match gutters. Be sure you use the same metal here as used in your guttering system.

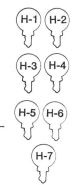

12

THE PLUMBING

12-1. Now is the time to install all pipes through the floors, walls, and ceiling for supplying fresh water and draining waste materials, and also to install the outlets for the plumbing fixtures as indicated on your house plans. Whether bathroom fixtures are located along a single wall or on several walls, plumbing layout principles are the same. The parts are as follows:

Supply System Parts

A. Stop and waste valve. Install one at low point of system.
B. Cold water main line. Cold water line serving two or more fixtures.
C. Hot water main line. Hot water line serving two or more fixtures.
D. Branch line to fixture. A line (cold or hot water) that serves one fixture only.

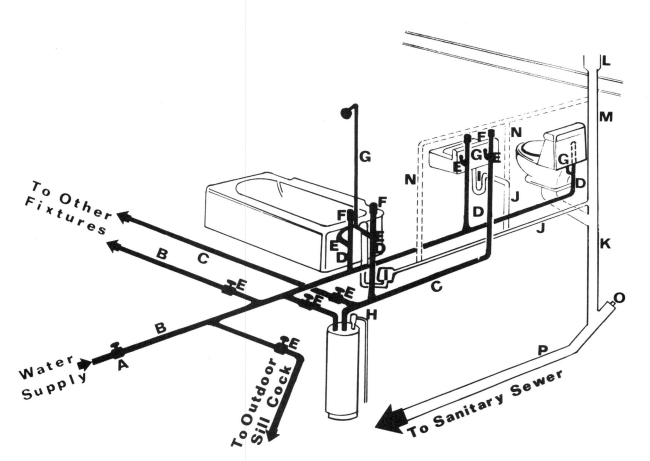

E. Shut-off valve. Install one in every branch line, and in main lines wherever cutoff is required.

F. Anti-hammer. Install one in every branch line terminating in a faucet.

G. Fixture supply line. A section of a branch line adapted to the special requirements of a particular fixture.

H. Safety valve. Combination pressure and temperature relief valve to be installed either in the hot outlet service line or directly in the hot water tank tapping.

Sewage And Drainage System Parts

I. Fixture drain. A section of branch drain adapted to the special requirements of a particular fixture. Be sure each has a trap built in or installed. Each trap must have a built-in or installed trap, which prevents gases from escaping into the house.

J. Branch drain. A line that serves as a drain for one fixture only.

K. Soil stack. Vertical pipe into which branch drains empty. Every installation requires at least one.

L. Vent increaser. Topmost length of stack larger in diameter than stack proper, required by some building codes.

M. Vent. Upper portion of a soil stack, which allows gases to escape to outside air.

N. Re-vent. A bypass for air and gases between a branch drain and the vent portion of a stack. Not required by some building codes.

O. Cleanout. Install one at every point where obstruction is most likely to appear. Always install one at the foot of each stack.

P. Building drain. All wastes must drain toward stack, thence through building drain to final disposal.

If your plans lack rough-in measurements for fixtures, you can obtain them from the dealer where the fixtures are purchased.

I recommend a copper drain system with a 3-inch soil stack and toilet drain and 1½-inch branch drain lines. For the cast-iron main drain line leading to the sanitary sewer, a minimum of a 4-inch line is recommended.

The houses in this book contain Crane Company copper supply and drain system parts as well as bathroom fixtures. I had Crane products installed in a previous house, and they were more trouble-free than other bathroom fixtures I had previously installed.

12-2. Completion of the house calls for much work at or near ceiling level. Since floor-to-ceiling heights generally vary among basements, utility rooms, living quarters, porches, and garages, adjustable mini-bucks to support a 2×8 make ceiling jobs more comfortable and easier.

Refer to Key C-4 for construction details on making a sawbuck without a tray. Then build two mini-bucks from scrap 2×4s and 1-inch material. Make them about 2 feet long and high enough to suit for the lowest ceiling work in the remainder of the house construction.

Next drill four ⅝-inch holes 1 inch deep in each of two 2×4s, cut the same length as the mini-bucks. Be sure all holes are exactly the same distance apart. Then glue ⅝-inch dowel pins in the holes, allowing an extension of 1½ inches as shown in the picture. Now drill two ⅝-inch holes centered in top edge of mini-bucks (shown by black arrows) to accommodate any pair of dowel pins mounted in either 2×4. With the short pieces of 2×4s, the mini-bucks, and the 2×8 walking board you have three different height possibilities to work from. Two dowel pins mounted in each of two 2×6s give you additional height, if needed.

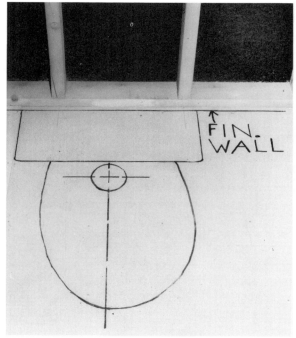

12-3. Begin installation by using a piece of chalk or pencil to locate roughing-in locations of such fixtures as toilet, lavatory, bathtub, shower if separate from bathtub, kitchen sink, and hot and cold water connections as well as drainpipe exits entering walls, floor, and ceiling. Do not overlook locating the main 3-inch soil stack where it is to go through the first floor.

12-4. If a hole was not provided for the 4-inch soil pipe to exit from basement, make one now a minimum of 1 foot below top of floor.

12-5. Next begin laying 4-inch cast-iron soil pipe with a minimum rise of ¼ inch per foot where it exits from basement to a point directly underneath main 3-inch soil stack location on first floor. Since the last pipe laid will most likely require cutting, it is advisable to lay it in conjunction with the following step. Also lay branch drain lines, if required, as you proceed. Be sure to provide for basement floor drain (shown here). Install a deep-seal trap in drain line to prevent backwater from flooding basement.

As you lay cast-iron soil pipe, cut out spaces in basement ground floor for cast-iron hubs so sections of drain pipe rest entirely on solid ground.

12-6. Connect a 4-inch cast-iron sanitary Y branch to a 4-inch cast-iron ⅛-bend, which you attach to a section of 4-inch cast-iron soil pipe cut to fit into drain line as laid in previous step.

Next position and fasten unit temporarily in place, being certain that the bottom of tee rests solidly on freshly poured concrete below finished floor level.

Then align the vertical outlet plumb and directly under the point where the 3-inch stack pipe will go through the first floor, thence up between the walls of bathroom partition on its way out through the roof.

Using a level, check main drain line and all branch drain lines, being sure there is a minimum of ¼-inch per foot drop all the way along each line.

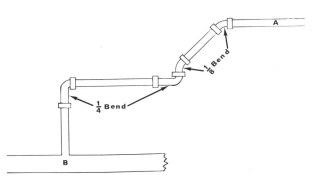

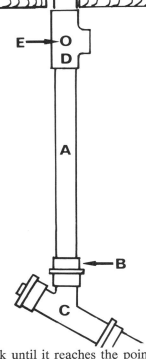

12-7. Next dig ditch from where main drain line is to exit from basement to sanitary sewer line. Never allow the general fall of the sewer line A leading away from the house to be less than ⅛ inch nor more than ¼ inch per foot. Where greater drop is required, such as in reaching a deep sanitary sewer line, begin laying 4-inch cast-iron pipe with a ¼-inch pitch per foot. Then make a combination of drops of 45 degrees with ⅛-bends and/or 90 degrees with ¼-bends until sanitary sewer line B is reached. Such an arrangement prevents drainwater from rushing away from solids where they may remain to block the line.

Generally, the water department reserves the right of how and by whom the connections between your property line and sewer line are made. Also, there is usually a charge to tap onto the sewer line.

12-8. Solder a section of 3-inch copper stack pipe A into a copper soil pipe adapter B. Then locate adapter into hub of Y branch C, using fastening method previously used for connecting cast-iron soil pipe.

Continue upward with 3-inch copper

stack until it reaches the point for soldering 3-inch sanitary tee D with two 1½-inch side-tapping E on each side, which takes care of the toilet, lavatory, and bathtub drains.

If your plans call for a double bathroom (one adjacent to the other), install a 3-inch double tee with two 1½-inch side openings instead of the tee described in the paragraph above.

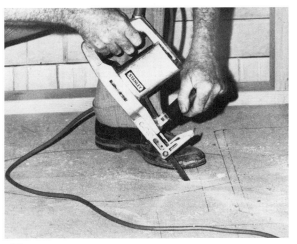

12-9. If your toilet is to drain through the floor, cut a hole through it. Start by drilling a hole on the inside of marked location made earlier from specification layout. Then saw out circle. I use a Stanley reciprocating power saw for such jobs.

If toilet drains through wall instead of through floor, cut hole in wall at proper location.

Cut a second hole at predetermined location if a second toilet is to be installed.

stalled. Place floor flange on top of floor with short piece of connecting pipe positioned in hub of toilet drain elbow located below floor. Solder together. CAUTION: Floor flange must rest squarely on floor as shown. If finish floor is not installed at this time, be sure to allow for it.

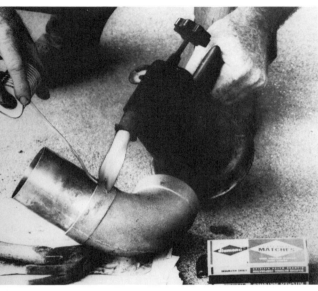

 12-10. Solder a piece of 3-inch copper pipe into 90° elbow. Then solder pipe into side opening of sanitary tee so ¼-bend opening is directly under hole in floor.

 12-11. Cut a piece of drainpipe to fit between the elbow for toilet connection and floor flange. Position floor flange down over pipe and solder, being certain that slots are positioned for properly accepting toilet bowl bolts later when stool is in-

12-12. From top of tee continue soldering soil-stack sections together up to and through the roof for a minimum distance of 6 inches.

Along the way, between attic floor and roof, solder in a 3-inch to 1½-inch reducing tee for attaching vent pipe from kitchen sink if required on your house plan. Also, check plumbing plans to see if more than one vent opening is required at this point. Reducing tees were not used in the houses in this book because a separate 1½-inch vent pipe, run through the ceiling, was used for venting kitchen sink.

Use a special lead flashing (shown in the picture) for making a watertight seal between pipe and roof. Extend shingles over the flashing on top and over two sides of flashing piece.

12-13. If yours is a cold climate in winter, keep frost that forms inside stack pipe from preventing proper ventilation by increasing size of

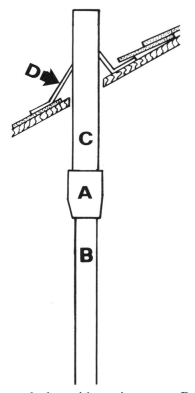

Start with a 1½-inch tee, copper to copper to inside threads where lavatory trap is to fasten to drain line C from bottom of tee downward through floor to one of the 1½-inch inlets of the 3-inch sanitary tee in soil stack A below floor level. Be sure all drain lines have a minimum drop of ¼ inch per foot.

From top hub of tee located at beginning of lavatory trap location, run a 1½-inch copper vent pipe B to 1½-inch sanitary tee vent opening located in soil stack A above floor level. Be sure vent lines gradually slope upward from lavatory trap location to soil-stack tee. Along the way install a 1½-inch tee (point B to the left in the picture) at a convenient location if bathtub vent pipe is to be attached to the same 1½-inch vent line.

If you plan a second lavatory, install those drain and vent lines next.

Finally, be sure all joints are well soldered before proceeding.

last section of pipe with an increaser. Beginning about 12 inches below roof line, solder 4×3-inch reducing coupling A onto 3-inch soil stack B. Then solder piece of 4-inch soil pipe C into reducing coupling. Be sure to install roof flashing D as described in previous step.

12-14. Next provide drain for the lavatory or lavatories if plans call for more than one as in the picture. If not previously located, mark locations on floor and cut holes where drain or vent pipes are to run below floor level.

In the installation illustrated, A is the 3-inch soil stack, B the vent lines, and C the drain lines, connecting to soil stack below floor level.

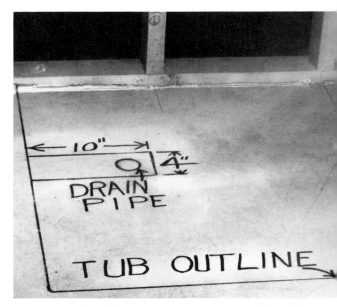

12-15. From measurements taken of tub drain hole, locate rectangle of tub outline on floor for drainage line passage. (Specifications in picture here are for a Crane tub.) Using a reciprocating saw, cut out rectangle.

Using strong pieces of rag, plug drain outlets and water-supply lines temporarily to prevent debris from getting in them.

Check for unused tee openings in soil stack and other drain and vent pipes. If open hubs are found, close by soldering in a short copper nipple, then soldering a copper cap onto the nipple.

 12-16. Next make up the drain line, including the trap. Solder one end of 1½-inch copper pipe A into elbow B. Solder opposite end of pipe into trap C. Next solder 1½-inch copper pipe D into remaining opening of elbow B. Solder 1½-inch copper adapter with outside threads E to opposite end of pipe. (Note: Cut pipe D long enough so that later you can fasten it with a slip-joint nut onto the tub drainpipe assembly.) Solder trap together so pipe opening on top side is in proper position for connecting drain line to main soil stack. Hold unit in proper position with copper strap, indicated by arrow. Solder 1½-inch drain line F into remaining opening in trap. Continue drain line F into 1½-inch outlet in sanitary tee located in main soil stack. Then solder joint.

 12-17. When vent and drain lines are installed for fixtures, do two things.

 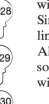 **12-18.** Beginning at service tap located in the water main, lay ¾-inch type K flexible copper tubing on solid bottom of ditch, bringing it through basement or foundation wall. If a 1-inch hole was not provided previously, make one with a masonry bit and drill or a star drill and hammer.

Next caulk hole between pipe and wall with a bituminous caulking compound. Since flexibility is important in laying the line, do not use cement for caulking. Also check entire service line for flexibility so that when backfill of dirt is made, it will not damage line.

12-19. Just inside basement wall, install a stop-and-waste valve with a drain on service side (shown by arrow), followed by a water faucet, which provides a convenient shutoff if fixtures or supply pipes need repair later. Also, faucet serves as a water supply as well as a quick means of draining the supply system in an emergency.

If you are building a seasonal house or a vacation house that will not be heated in the winter, be sure to locate the stop-and-waste valve below frost level.

12-20. Code permitting, use type L copper tubing for carrying water-supply lines aboveground throughout the house.

 H-31 From stop-and-waste valve, run a ¾-inch main, cold water line to hot water heater cold-water-line connection.

H32 Install union A and shut-off valve B just before cold-water-line heater connection. Note: Make all direct connections to heater with adapters, copper to outside threads. Also solder copper reducing tees at appropriate locations along the main line for supplying ½-inch branch cold water supply lines to fixtures requiring them. Be sure to include enough tees to supply a branch line to at least one outside water faucet.

H33

H34

H35 Near hot water connection on tank, solder union C into line. Also solder reducing tees at appropriate locations along main hot water line for supplying connecting ½-inch branch lines to fixtures requiring them.

H36 Connect temperature and relief valve D to ½-inch copper line that extends downward to about 6 inches over a floor drain. If more convenient, run line outside house. CAUTION: Opening in end of pipe from relief valve must always remain open.

H37

H38 Use adapters, copper to outside threads, for last couplings to which fixture pipes will later be attached to branch water-supply lines. Also, install anti-hammer devices in branch lines as close as possible to where fixtures fasten to branch lines.

H-39

Be sure all water supply lines are fastened securely with copper straps held in place with ¾-inch roofing nails.

H40

12-21. Install a branch cold water line to each outside faucet location, preferably one for each side of house. If you live in an area with freezing winter temperatures, install freezeless wall faucets like the one shown in the picture.

Toilet Installation

12-22. Not until finished walls are installed (see Chapter 14) should you install bathroom and kitchen plumbing fixtures. However, it is just as well to understand what you have ahead of you while you are doing the rough-in plumbing already described, so I am including information on fixture installation in this chapter.

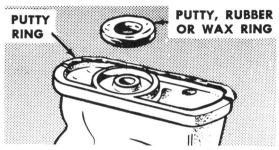

Courtesy Sears Roebuck and Co.

Begin with the toilet. If your toilet is a wall-hung type, it most likely is supported as a unit by metal hangers bolted to the wall studs. Here the toilet discharge is part of the hanger assembly. Use a gasket to provide a watertight fit between discharge and opening in soil stack.

On the other hand, if your toilet has a separate tank and bowl, turn the bowl bottom side up on the floor. Then build a putty ring about 1 inch high around outside rim. Next place a rubber or wax ring, specially designed for the purpose, around discharge openings.

12-23. Next position bowl carefully over flange bolts. Turning it slightly, as you find the proper location, will help the

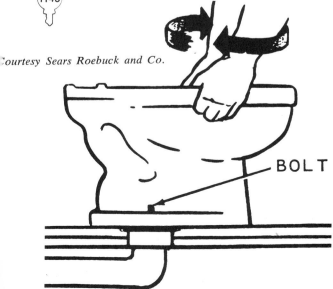

Courtesy Sears Roebuck and Co.

putty and wax ring make a watertight seal. Hold bowl firmly by tightening nuts. CAUTION: Overtightening the nuts may cause bowl to crack.

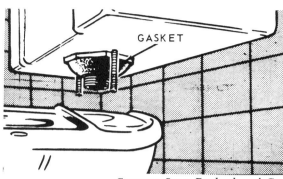

Courtesy Sears Roebuck and Co.

12-24. A toilet with a separate bowl naturally has a separate water tank. If this is your case, it may be necessary to screw a 1×6 board slightly less than the width of tank onto the wall studs where bowl will be held by two bolts. If board is required it may be necessary to notch studs so the face of the board will be flush with finished wall. Use a flush ell to fasten tank to bowl.

If tank rests on bowl as shown in the picture here, use a gasket and two bolts to make a watertight seal.

CAUTION: Never overtighten bolts.

12-25. There are two kinds of installation for bringing cold water to the tank. Either wall in-

Courtesy Sears Roebuck and Co.

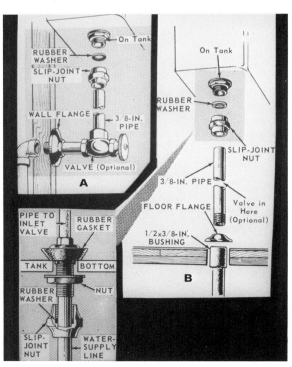

stallation A or floor installation B is acceptable. However, a wall installation makes the job of laying carpet or linoleum on the bathroom floor somewhat easier.

Complete toilet installation by attaching seat to bowl.

previously described for installing a toilet tank separate from its bowl.

Either floor or wall drain lines must contain a trap to prevent sewer gases from entering the house. Either wall type A or floor type B makes a satisfactory installation.

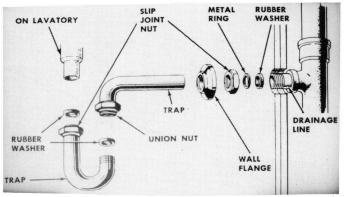

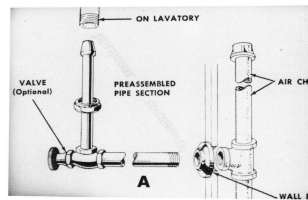

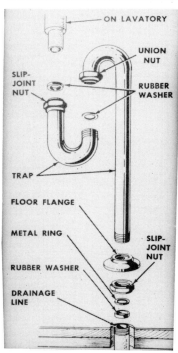

Courtesy Sears Roebuck and Co.

 12-26. If you are installing a lavatory that is not a part of a cabinet unit, support with hangers (supplied with bowl) attached to a 1×8 board recessed in notches cut into two wall studs at desired height. This is a similar operation to that

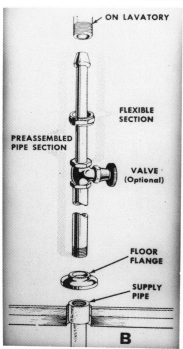

Courtesy Sears Roebuck and Co.

12-27. Next attach faucets to lavatory. Then connect faucets to proper cold and hot water supply lines. Illustration A above shows how to assemble a wall-type water supply line, while illustration B shows a floor-type installation. Although a shut-off valve is optional in each line, I recommend one in each hot and cold water line for greater convenience when later servicing faucets.

Complete lavatory installation by permanently fastening escutcheons and faucet handles in place.

Bathtub Installation

  12-28. Check the tub branch drain previously installed against the actual openings in the tub.

If yours is a cast-iron tub, temporarily set it in place. Then, using a level on floor of tub, be sure slope is toward drain before proceeding. Cast-iron tubs are not fastened to wall.

 12-29. With tub properly located, install drain operating mechanisms. Since each make is slightly different, follow instructions included in package. Then use slip-joint nut for connection to 1½-inch branch drain line.

Connect hot and cold water lines, each with an anti-hammer, to tub. If your plans call for a combination shower and tub installation, install shower mixing valve mechanism in accordance with instructions accompanying package.

When finished walls are completed, complete tub installation by fastening escutcheons and handles permanently in place.

12-30. Because bathtub pipes are always hidden in the wall behind the tub, be sure wall framing provides an opening large enough to install a service panel or door when you are completing finished walls.

Be certain that proper installation is made for your tub. When resting on the floor, steel tubs are held in position by flanges fastened with screws to 1×4 boards fastened with 8-penny nails at proper height across wall studs.

Some tubs are installed on special metal hangers, first nailed to studs at a predetermined height. Here adjustments can be made also so bottom of tub slopes toward drain opening.

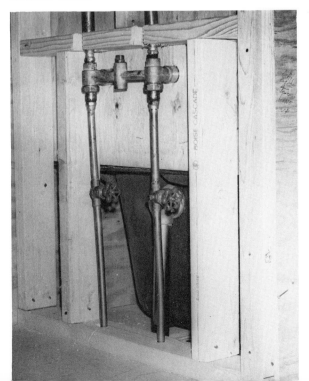

Shower Stall Installation

12-31. A Trintessa packaged shower (Fiat Products, Michael Court, Plainview, L.I., New York 11803) was installed in one of the houses in this book. The installation of this particular shower unit can be done by one man in one hour. This shower unit was selected also for two other reasons. There are no grout joints to crumble, crack open, or harbor grime. All vertical wall joints and base channels that fit over floor flanges are made of corrosion-free aluminum and factory-bonded to ensure permanent leakproof performance.

12-33. Install each side panel by tilting panel forward and seating bottom front portion over floor flange. Next lower panel and insert into back corner molding. Then fully seat panel down on flange and into back joint molding.

Begin by positioning shower floor over waste pipe. Level in two planes and shim where necessary. Lead-caulk wastepipe to drain.

12-32. Position back panel, lift and tilt slightly forward. Then lower until flange of shower floor engages with channel across bottom of panel.

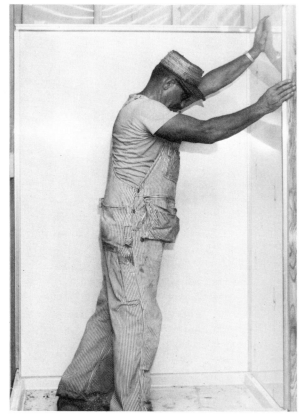

12-34. Slip back and side moldings over top edge of panels. Apply inside corner molding, starting at bottom, by forcing serrated leg between surface of wall panel and behind exposed side of flange of corner molding.

12-35. After cutting bottom frame 3/16 inch shorter than stall opening, but-

ter underside liberally with adhesive and set in place on threshold.

 Set wall jambs in place and fasten each with panhead sheet-metal screws.

Cut header ⅛ inch shorter than stall opening at the 72-inch height. Then straddle header over and onto wall jambs.

Mount two rollers onto each door with roundhead machine screws. Then hang doors on track. Fasten towel bar and brackets onto outside door.

Assemble and mount shower head to stall according to instructions in package. Then connect to hot and cold water lines.

Installing Sinks And Other Fixtures

Kitchen sinks are mounted in various ways, depending upon the kind of cabinet that holds them. Usually complete instructions are found in the package containing the sink. The drain installation and water-supply lines are the same as those previously described for the lavatory.

Connect the garbage-disposal drain into the sink drain line above the trap, which must be exactly the height specified in the instructions contained with each particular unit. I found this a relatively simple matter with a Whirlpool disposal unit.

Installing drain lines and water supply lines to laundry tubs, washing machines, and dishwashers is similar to connecting other appliances previously described in this chapter. For basement appliances you may wish to use ordinary pipe and fittings instead of chrome-plated ones. CAUTION: Always provide a trap in the drain line of every appliance, even though it may be located in the basement.

If you plan to install a refrigerator with an automatic ice-cube maker, be sure to install a cold water supply line to the refrigerator location.

13

WIRING AND FIXTURE INSTALLATION

dining room. The electric carving knife and electric heating units are designed to do the jobs easier and better.

That is why the use of electricity has tripled in the average home during the last twenty years. So it is a good idea to plan your electrical needs to meet both present and future needs. If you plan to use electric heat as recommended in this chapter, install nothing less than 200-ampere service. Otherwise, 100-ampere service is recommended.

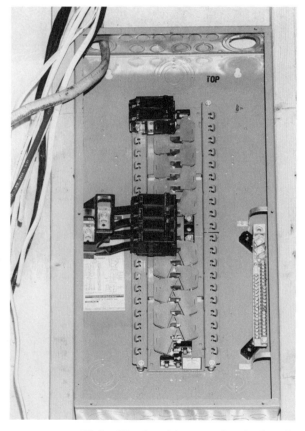

 13-1. With the myriads of lighting fixtures available today, the single light bulb at the end of a drop cord hanging from the ceiling is as outdated as the Model-T Ford.

The same is true in the electric appliance field. In some households, Grandpa's old carving knife for carving the Thanksgiving turkey seems as old-fashioned as his coal stove for heating the

 13-2. Check with your local electric service company for their recommendations concerning best meter location. Also, find out who furnishes the meter mounting box as well as how much of the outside wiring is your responsibility.

Next, use appropriate nails or screws to fasten service panel to inside wall as near as possible to meter mounting box location on outside of house.

The picture shows a 24-circuit panel recommended for 200-ampere service, mounted onto basement wall. Each cable hanging nearby represents an individual circuit to be connected later to proper circuit breaker. For illustrative purposes, a 230-volt circuit breaker is shown connected to two tabs at top of panel.

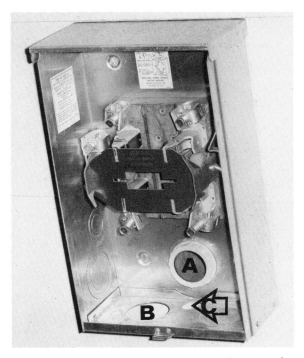

13-3. Remove cover and protective inner liner from meter mounting box. (Secure from local power company.)

For 200-ampere service, remove 2-inch knockout from rear. Then fasten 2-inch connector A in place.

Now remove 2-inch knockout B from bottom of box as well as knockout C for ½-inch conduit.

Next measure and cut hole through wall for conduit connector A to fit. Later service wires pass through this opening on their way from meter mounting box to service panel located inside house.

Put ¼-inch screws or bolts through mounting holes in box, and position and fasten box to wall.

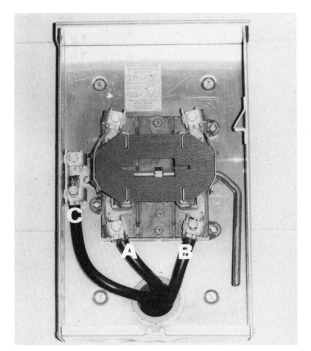

13-4. For 200-ampere installation, use three #3/0 wire cable, type RHW insulation.

Remove clamps from lay-in terminals of meter mounting box. Trim ½ inch of insulation from one end of black and red wires.

Lay conductors (black A, red B, and ground wire C) into "load" terminals located on lower part of box. Note: Ground wire need not be covered. Replace clamps and tighten to 250 inch-pounds (21 foot-pounds).

Next, work wires through conduit connector in rear of box to service panel. CAUTION: Check your local code. Generally, these wires are required to run through conduit all the way to service panel.

13-5. Connect black wire A of service cable to left terminal of service panel and red wire B to right terminal. (Note:

Rather than 3-wire cable, single black-covered wires are sometimes used. If this is your case, connect one black wire to the left terminal, the other to the right terminal, since each of these terminals will carry 115 volts of electricity.) Connect third or neutral wire C to ground or neutral strip.

Using your house electric plan as a guide, write number and description of each circuit in place provided in service panel, sometimes called a distribution box. If circuits are not designated on your house plans, proceed to step 13-8, which explains how to figure the circuits.

13-6. Dig hole about 6 inches deep at ground-rod location. Fill hole with water. Then with both

hands begin pushing 8-foot length of ½-inch copper ground rod into the mud at the desired location. Raise rod, allowing water to enter the small hole it has made. Now jog rod up and down, each time allowing it to go deeper into the ground as well as allowing the hole to refill with water. Continuing this process for ten or fifteen minutes will sink the rod completely, unless you strike a hard object, such as a rock.

When top of ground rod is 1 foot below grade, cut to length, then fasten ½-inch conduit A to small knockout hole in box with conduit connector B. Using conduit straps C every 4 feet, fasten conduit to wall.

Next fasten one end of #2 ground wire to solidly grounded neutral connection D in meter mounting box.

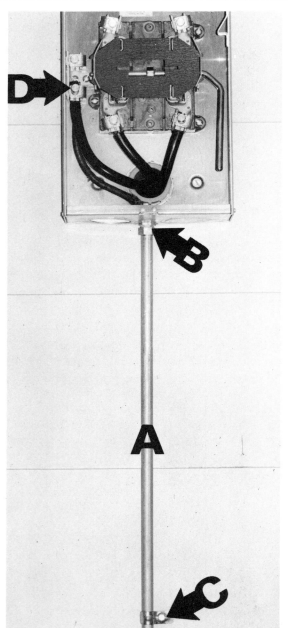

13-7. Run free end of ground wire through conduit to ground rod. Use special ground-rod clamp (shown by arrow) to fasten ground wire to ground rod.

The electric utility company will connect the underground service wires to the "line" locations inside the meter mounting box at the time of meter installation. Usually the customer furnishes the conduit and necessary connectors. Be sure to check with your electric utility company on this point.

13-8. The picture here is an example of a 115-volt, 20-ampere general-purpose circuit. Notice that the total wattage is

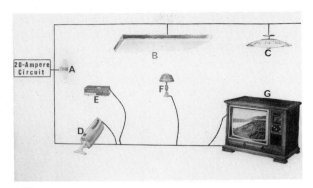

kept to less than the recommended maximum of 2400 watts:

A.	Wall light	100
B.	Fluorescent light	80
C.	Ceiling light	100
D.	Vacuum cleaner	400
E.	Radio	100
F.	Table light	100
G.	Television (b&w)	300
	Circuit total	1180

Unless already stated on the house plans, divide lighting and service outlets into branch circuits. Generally, a separate 20-ampere general-purpose circuit is recommended for every 500 square feet of floor space or a 15-ampere circuit for every 375 square feet. I recommend three 20-ampere circuits for dining room, kitchen, and laundry in addition to the lighting circuits, making up additional circuits. If shop tools or photographic darkroom appliances are called for in the plans, place each group on an additional circuit.

13-9. Now you are ready to install the switch, service outlet, ceiling light, and junction metal boxes for the 115-volt circuits. Check your wiring diagram for designated boxes for each particular circuit.

Begin with the switch box installation. Using 2-inch nails, fasten metal switch box hangers between the studs at designated locations. If hardboard is planned for the finished walls, fasten switch boxes temporarily onto hangers at this time. (Note: Position and fasten hangers so that when service boxes are fastened later, front of boxes will be flush with finished wall.)

Next fasten metal service outlet box hangers between studs and fasten service outlet boxes onto the hangers.

Use same type of box for mounting switches and service outlets.

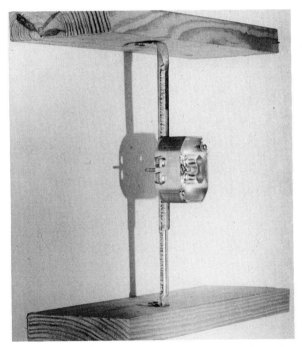

13-10. Next fasten the metal ceiling light hangers to ceiling joists and the ceiling light boxes to the hangers. Installations are the same as previously described for installation of service outlet boxes and hangers. Only the boxes themselves are of different shapes. Be sure bottom of box will be flush with finished ceiling.

Where ceiling tile is planned for ceiling, temporarily fasten hangers in place and ceiling light boxes onto hangers.

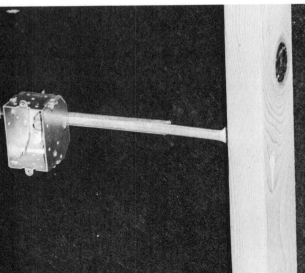

Be sure to install a junction box (same as ceiling light box) for making connection later to chime or doorbell transformer. If other junction boxes are called for on your plans, install them now.

Then do same for each switch box. Generally, cable is brought from service panel down through top and cap plates or up through bottom plate.

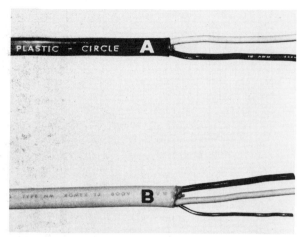

13-11. Two types of installation for wiring 115-volt circuits are discussed in this chapter. First, nonmetallic sheathed cable without ground wire (A) is illustrated and discussed. Second, non-metallic sheathed cable with ground wire (B) is illustrated and discussed. More and more local codes are requiring the second method of installation. Find out what your code requires, if you have one in your area.

The picture also shows two styles of cable covering. Some nonmetallic cables are manufactured with a white covering, while others come with a black covering. Either covering is acceptable.

13-12. Drill holes in studs, just large enough to clear cable, between adjoining outlet boxes along each circuit leading toward service panel.

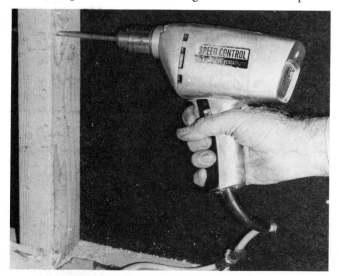

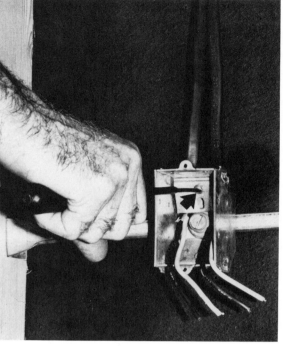

13-13. The picture shows a two-wire, 115-volt cable installation for a service outlet box.

Begin by stringing cable from service panel through holes drilled in studs to each outlet box along a particular circuit. Upon reaching each box, cut cable, allowing about 20 inches of excess to both cable coming to box and cable leaving box.

Using a pocket knife, strip 8 inches of cover from one end of each cable, leaving the insulated wires undamaged for making connections later. Next remove two knockout plates from box. Then insert cables through holes, screwing locknut tightly from inside of box as shown in picture. Be sure plate inside box holds covered cable to box. Stripped wires must not be held by plate to box. (Note: To avoid complications, pictures and text of 115-volt installations first deal with using cable without grounding wire, and then separately with using cable with grounding wire.)

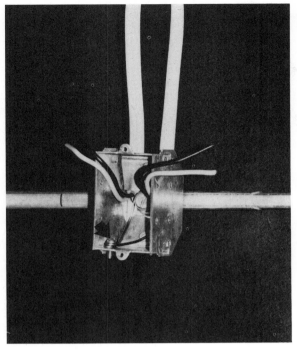

13-14. The picture shows a three-wire 115-volt cable installation for a service outlet box. With three-wire 115-volt cable, connect insulated wires as recommended in preceding step plus an additional step of grounding wire installation. Later when cables are connected to service panel, connect grounding wire (bare wire) to neutral strap in cabinet. Now, using an extra screw, connect the two ends of the bare wires to an unused hole in box, shown by arrow. Never use this screw for anything else but for grounding the bare wires.

13-15. Using an electrician's multipurpose tool or a sharp pocket knife, trim about 1 inch of insulation from ends of black and white wires for making connections to service outlets later.

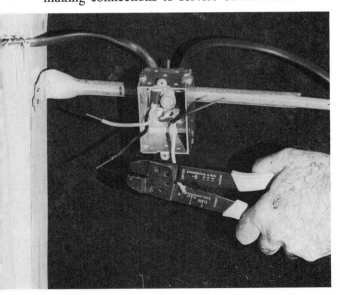

13-16. Bend wires accordion-style, as shown in the picture. If desired, push wires into box out of the way.

Complete wiring remainder of 115-volt service outlet circuits.

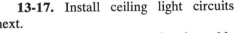

13-17. Install ceiling light circuits next.

Beginning at service panel, string cable to each outlet box in a particular circuit. Wiring is like that previously described for wiring service outlet boxes, with one exception.

A is electric feed cable. B is cable running from ceiling light box to single-pole switch. Twist together hot wire (black) from feed cable and white wire (arrow) of switch cable. Be sure to put tape or black paint on the white wire in switch cable. This indicates that white wire is *not* neutral, but hot. Do same thing at switch end of wire.

13-18. The picture shows a three-wire 115-volt cable installation for a ceiling light outlet box or a junction box. Here connect insulated wires as in preceding step, and also install grounding wire. Later when cables are connected to service panel, connect grounding wire to neutral strip inside cabinet. Using an extra screw, connect bare wires coming into and going out of box to extra hole in box, shown by black arrow. If a receptacle is to be installed in box, run an additional grounding wire (or a green insulated wire), shown by white arrow, from extra grounding screw to green terminal of the receptacle. This *extra* grounding wire is superfluous on one condition: if the receptacle is installed so that its mounting strap is in solid contact with box. An example is when a receptacle is installed in a surface-mounted box such as a handy-box located in a basement or workshop.

13-19. Next bring lighting wires to switch boxes.

I-24
I-25

Before proceeding, study the following three steps, showing how different switches are wired.

Begin with single-pole switch cable as shown in the picture here, which controls light from only one location. Expose 8 inches of insulated wires in addition to about 1 foot of excess cable. Make entrances to boxes and fastenings of cable in same way as described previously for service outlet boxes. Also, bend and push exposed wires back into boxes. CAUTION: In all switch installations, paint white wire black for about 2 inches at switch and fixture location. If black paint is not available, substitute a layer of black plastic electrician's tape.

I-25

13-20. The picture shows how to wire a single-pole switch and a light. Notice purpose of switch is to open or close circuit, as case may be, between line and

lamp. With two-wire cable, as shown here, the black wire is the hot wire and the neutral wire is white. With three-wire cable, the uninsulated wire is the grounding wire.

NOTE: Switches are shown here and in the following two steps so that you can properly wire the lighting circuits. It is best not to install the switches permanently until later when the lighting circuits, including switch wiring, have been tested.

13-21. Wire three-way switches as shown here. Connect black wires to dark terminals and white wires to light-colored terminals on lighting fixture.

13-22. Install four-way switch as indicated. Connect black wires to dark terminals and white wires to light-colored terminals on lighting fixture.

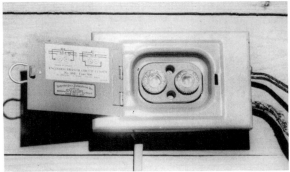

13-23. If you require electricity to adjoining buildings such as a tool shed or service areas such as barbecue pit, install underground cable laid on bottom of trench below frost line or a minimum depth of 18 inches. Lay cable loosely in a "snaky" fashion, and do not splice underground. Where cable comes out of ground, run cable through conduit with a bushing fastened to each end. Conduit should run from bottom of ditch to a minimum of 6 inches above ground level. Note: Size of cable depends upon wattage requirements. If cable is brought into a building, have it terminate at a junction box, circuit breaker, or service switch as shown in the picture here.

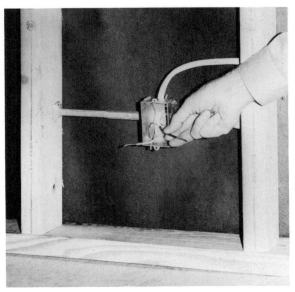

13-24. By now all 115-volt circuits should be completely wired. The picture here shows the last box in a three-wire 115-volt circuit.

Check circuits for any mistakes that might have occurred. CAUTION: Before proceeding, be certain that the electric power has not been connected to service panel.

As further preparation before testing the wiring thus far completed, spread apart the bare ends of the lighting fixture wires and service outlet wires that are to be fastened together. Be sure that bare ends are also free from contact with metal box or hanger. Also, twist together wires that will be permanently attached later, such as certain switch and ceiling light wires.

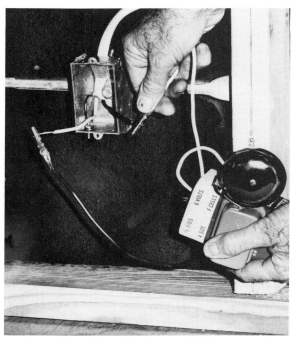

 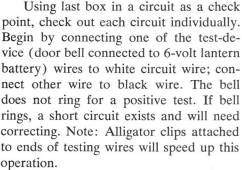

13-25. The picture shows a three-wire 115-volt circuit.

Using last box in a circuit as a check point, check out each circuit individually. Begin by connecting one of the test-device (door bell connected to 6-volt lantern battery) wires to white circuit wire; connect other wire to black wire. The bell does not ring for a positive test. If bell rings, a short circuit exists and will need correcting. Note: Alligator clips attached to ends of testing wires will speed up this operation.

Check out black and white wires of two-wire 115-volt circuits in the same manner.

13-26. The picture shows a three-wire 115-volt circuit.

Now make a low-voltage test of actual electricity flowing through each service outlet circuit.

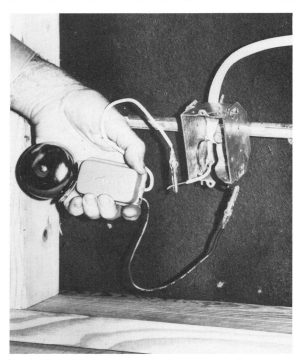

Begin by disconnecting bell from battery. Then connect one battery wire to white cable wire near service panel, and connect other wire to black cable wire of circuit.

Using bell at last box in circuit, connect one wire to black wire of service outlet box, and connect other wire to white circuit wire. Here the bell rings for a positive test.

With switch wires properly twisted together to indicate that switch is on, check lighting circuits individually as you did the service outlet circuits above.

Make check for two-wire 115-volt circuits in the same way.

 13-27. If conduit or two-wire non-metallic cable with grounding wire is used as in the picture here, make another test. Connect battery to black wire and grounding wire of cable near service panel. Then

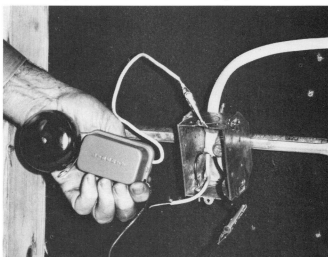

connect one bell wire to black wire at end of circuit, and connect other bell wire to metal box. The bell will ring if you have established a good ground throughout the circuit. Make the ground test for each three-wire circuit, being sure battery is wired to circuit being tested.

Note: This check cannot be made and should not be tried for two-wire 115-volt circuits.

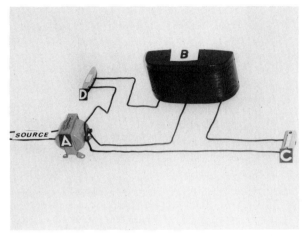

13-28. Next install front and back door chime or bell buzzer hookup as shown here. Locate step-down transformer A close to junction box provided previously. (This supplies source of 115-volt current to transformer.) Be sure power is *not* connected to circuit. Then connect primary side of transformer to 115-volt circuit (source) from junction box previously installed.

Next centrally locate chimes B or bell buzzer in house as well as locate a separate push button for front C and back D doors. Complete installation by connecting bell wire from chimes or bell buzzer and push buttons to secondary side of transformer, indicated by its two knurled head terminals. Hold bell wire in place with bell-wire staples, spaced about 3 feet apart.

13-29. Check chime or bell buzzer installation, using battery from testing device for the circuit. Pressing the front-door push button should produce a chime

sequence, while a single tone should sound when back-door push button makes contact. A bell buzzer should sound the same when either front door or back door push button is depressed. If operation fails, make the following checks:

Check the battery. It may be worn out, or it may not contain a high enough voltage.

Check out wiring against picture in previous step. Be sure all connections are clean and tight as well as being properly connected.

Check push buttons for lack of contact or corroded contact points.

Take transformer and chimes to electrical supplier for performance check if you cannot find the trouble.

13-30. In the electrical field there are literally dozens of available receptacles. Each calls for a different type of plug, because prongs are sized

and located on plug to fit only a particular outlet designed to do a particular job. The outlet shown is designed for a two-wire (with grounding wire) 115-volt circuit. Arrows point to grounding opening in outlet. Outlets for two-wire 115-volt circuits have only two openings similar to the two top openings above each arrow.

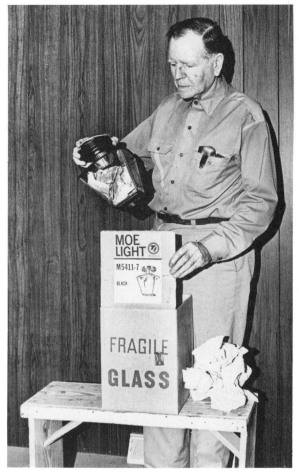

 13-31. Since the final portion of general wiring is done when finished walls and ceiling are completed, for the present you can skip steps 13-31 to 13-33.

Connect insulated wires to outlet (if not already completed). Using a screwdriver, mount outlet in outlet box with machine screws that come with outlet. Note oval mounting holes in outlet. These are provided so that it can be mounted vertically even though box is not installed perfectly vertical. Be sure wire connections on outlet are not touching inside of metal box. Next mount plate on switch with screw that comes with plate.

When all outlets and plates are in place, install switches and their respective plates in the same way.

13-32. Fixtures are designed to give many years of service. Because they are a very important

part of the room decor, they are protected in shipping with such materials as crushed paper and corrugated cardboard pads. Even so, they can be easily damaged during unpacking and installation if reasonable care is not exercised.

There are various mounting devices used for fastening fixtures to the electrical boxes. Instructions and mounting devices for a particular fixture are usually included in an envelope inside the fixture package.

13-33. If you prefer, soldered wire splices can be made rather than making splices with solderless connectors.

Using a blowtorch or a plumber's furnace, melt some solder in a plumber's ladle.

 Solder fixture (such as ceiling light) colored wires to similarly colored circuit wires extending out of ceiling outlet box. First be sure scraped ends of wires to be spliced are clean. Next apply a good cop-

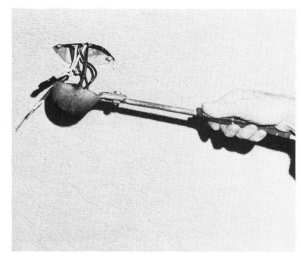

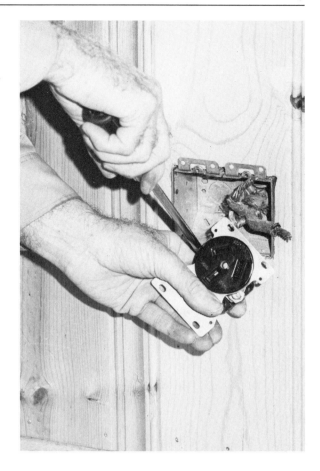

per flux to wires to be soldered together. Now bring ladle containing melted solder in contact with the wires just long enough for the solder to flow down into every little open space in the splice. With ladle removed, check to be sure a good soldered joint is made. The solder should be just thick enough to make a good bond between the wires. Be sure solder is not piled thick on splice, resembling a grape hanging from a stem. Complete soldering operation by covering joint with several rounds of plastic electrician's tape. The layer of insulating tape must be applied as thick as the original layer of insulation. CAUTION: To avoid burns be careful with the ladle containing melted solder.

13-34. Now install wiring for major appliances.

Begin with the electric range, making up a separate circuit. Install 50-ampere, 230-volt, heavy-duty, three-wire receptacle so it will be in back of range. Then run #6 with #8 neutral three-wire cable from receptacle to service panel circuit containing a 50-ampere circuit breaker or fuse. When range is installed, connect a three-wire cord, sometimes called a "pigtail," to its terminals. Other end of cord has a three-prong plug to fit receptacle. Frame of range must be grounded. Because of the nature of range construction, it is automatically grounded when pigtail cord is connected to range and receptacle.

Wire the electric clothes dryer like the range, using a pigtail cord like the one used for the electric range. Most electric dryers require a 30-ampere receptacle connected to a separate circuit of 230 volts. Their motors and lights require only 115 volts. However, if yours is a high-speed dryer rated at approximately 8500 watts, install a 230-volt #6 wire circuit with a 50-ampere receptacle.

The electric water heater is not a combination 115/230-volt appliance. Rather, it is a 230-volt appliance only. You do not need a separate disconnect switch if your service panel has circuit breakers, containing properly sized fuses on a pull-out block.

Make low-voltage tests of all major appliance circuits, just as you made them previously for 115-volt circuits (steps 13-24 to 13-26).

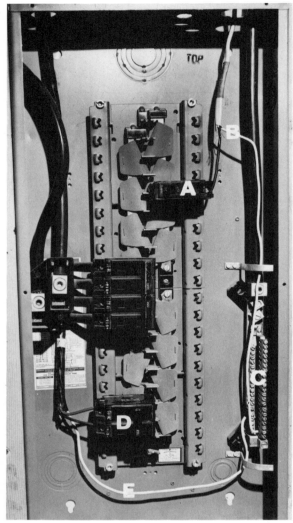

(115 volts each) connected to the two terminals on double-pole breaker D and grounding wire E connected to neutral strip C.

Be sure circuit breakers (or fuses if your service panel requires them) are stamped with the amperage rating required by each circuit.

To avoid confusion, only one circuit each is shown connected to service panel of two-wire 115 volts and three-wire 230 volts.

When all circuits test satisfactorily with low-voltage electricity and are properly connected inside service panel, make a final check. Be sure all circuits, including disconnect switch, are set on off positions. Then instruct electric utility company to install meter on outside of house and bring in incoming power lines.

Electric Heat Installation

13-36. Electric baseboard can surround your room with a wall of warmth, eliminating cold drafts. Electric baseboard offers a clean, quiet, draft-free system that has no moving parts and, therefore, requires no maintenance. When a home is properly insulated, the cost of heating electrically is about the same as the cost of using gas or oil. Electricity offers the added advantage of individual thermostat room-by-room control and elimination of

13-35. When all the circuits are installed and tested with low-voltage electricity, connect end wires of circuits properly to connectors inside service panel box. Because there are so many different types of service panels, follow the instructions for making connections that come with your particular service panel.

The picture here shows a two-wire 115-volt circuit with black wire connected to terminal on single-pole breaker A and white wire B connected to neutral strip C. With three-wire 115-volt circuits, connect black and white wires as pictured above. Then also connect uninsulated grounding wire to neutral strip.

Also, the picture shows a three-wire 230-volt circuit, with the two hot wires

Courtesy Markel Electric Products, Inc.

central furnace or boiler and ductwork or piping.

I recommend Markel electric baseboard perimeter heating systems (Markel Electric Products, Inc., Buffalo, N. Y.). The elements are designed for the life of the building, and the units may be mounted directly on finished floors even if wall-to-wall carpeting is added later. The units operate quietly because there is no metal contact between heating element and casing. Also, you have a choice of built-in or wall thermostats.

Baseboard heaters should always go along outside walls first. If necessary, they can also go along inside walls.

CAUTION: Do not try to figure the baseboard footage required for your job or the size of electric wiring for each circuit. Get the help of an expert! Generally, the electric utility company will have one of its engineers draw you specifications free of charge.

supply connections are made in end junction boxes. Do not change any wiring or attempt to connect power supply in center box on 8-foot and longer models.

Remove appropriate knockout for supply connection and insert nylon bushing. Then bring 3-wire supply cable through hole as shown in the picture.

Secure to wall or studs with the four screws supplied, being sure unit is level. Use builder's level to check.

Remove wire nut. Do not disturb permanent pressure-type connectors.

Connect power supply to identified leads and make connection to grounding screw provided in junction box.

13-38. To install built-in thermostat, remove front panel and junction-box cover at right side. Also, remove wire connectors in this junction box.

Align bracket-mounted accessory so that bracket tabs fit into the two slots in the baseboard partition and tighten screw.

If applicable, route the thermostat capillary tube (shown by arrow) through the slot provided at the lower inside edge of the partition. Then attach the thermostat bulb clip to the baseboard at hole located 4½ inches from junction box.

13-37. Install baseboard heaters after finished walls are completed (described in Chapter 14). Generally, supply lines come up through floor into bottom of units. If you plan to have supply lines come up or down between wall studding, install them now.

For single heater installation, remove front panel and junction box covers. All

Using solderless connectors, wire accessory according to wiring diagram on bracket. Connect wires to pigtails furnished, not to sealed terminals.

Remove oval knockout in junction-box cover, to accept accessory shaft. Then replace junction-box cover.

Assemble front panel.

Push on the thermostat knob and nameplate, engaging the nameplate in the slots provided in the front panel.

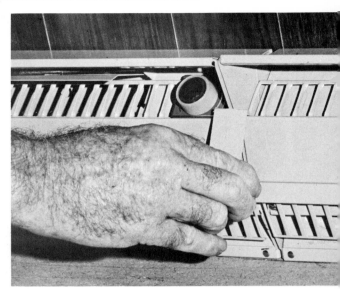

13-39. To install two heaters around inside corner, remove front panels of both heaters. Then remove junction-box covers.

Remove ½-inch knockouts in adjoining junction boxes of each heater.

Position inside corner.

Position heaters against corner. Secure in place.

Insert nylon bushings through end-plate knockout of baseboard into hole in corner section.

Make ground connection between units with the ground wire supplied with corner kit.

Remove wire connector and connect to appropriate leads.

Connect power supply and ground.

13-40. To join two heaters, remove front panels of both heaters and all junction box covers. Next remove appropriate knockouts.

Mount the heaters together and secure to wall with the eight screws provided. Allow ⅛-inch

space between heaters to allow for expansion. Insert chase nipples in knockouts and secure with a nut. Using a builder's level, be sure units are level.

Make ground connection between units with the ground wire supplied with kit.

Remove wire connector (wire nut) on leads in the two adjacent junction boxes.

Bring power supply into one of the two adjacent baseboard junction boxes, and wire the two baseboards in parallel and ground to grounding screw. If built-in thermostat is required, install it in right side of either heater.

Replace junction-box covers and front panels.

Use the two joining straps to cover joint between the two heaters.

Note: So long as power supply is brought into one of two or more baseboard junction boxes—that is, where only one thermostat is to be installed—units may be located in different parts of the room. All that is necessary is to wire the baseboards in parallel and ground.

13-41. When baseboard heaters are completely wired, check each room. Be sure thermostat is in off position. Then

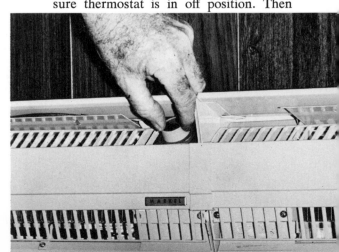

throw proper circuit breaker to on position in service box. If fuses are used instead of circuit breakers, be sure fuse is located properly and tightened. Next turn thermostat knob clockwise to last stop. When room reaches desired temperature, turn thermostat knob counterclockwise until heater goes off. You will hear a slight click. If room becomes either too cold or too hot, adjust thermostat to suit.

13-42. To install wall thermostat, begin by installing an R841 relay (manufactured by Honeywell, Minneapolis, Minnesota) designed for a two-wire 24-volt thermostat.

The R841 relay is silent and may be installed on the end of a baseboard heater (if space is provided) or in a utility room or basement. The picture shows the supply line being connected to the relay, which in turn is fastened with #8 ¾-inch roundhead screws to basement ceiling joist. Be sure to wire supply line to relay according to diagram on relay.

Later connect the two wires coming out of front of relay to wall thermostat. Always observe color codes, both in low and in line voltage.

13-43. Install a T87F wall thermostat (also manufactured by Honeywell) about 5 feet above floor on an inside wall where there is good natural air circulation. Drill a ½-inch hole through wall

for bringing two-wire low-voltage line to thermostat.

Using a builder's level locate backplate with "UP" line perfectly vertical. Then mount backplate to wall with screws furnished. After wiring, plug any free space to prevent drafts from affecting thermostat.

Next connect red wire from thermostat to red wire on relay and connect white wires together from thermostat to relay.

Move indicator on thermostat scale to 0.2 amp. This is the amperage rating found on the R841 relay.

Checking heating operation is similar to checking built-in baseboard thermostat as already described. To select the temperature control point, turn the dial until the desired point on the setting scale (top) is in line with stationary pointer.

The T87F is calibrated at the factory. If it seems desirable to recheck calibration, first be sure thermostat is accurately leveled. Then follow instructions for recalibration found in thermostat installation instructions.

Electric Air-Conditioning Installation

13-44. Central air-conditioning units are designed in different sizes and shapes

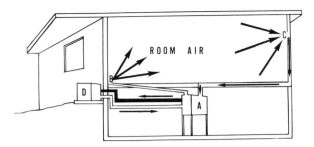

ROOM AIR

altered, if necessary, to fit the particular type of installation that you are making.

Measure, mark, and cut holes in floor just large enough so air-supply boot coming up from plenum will later fit snugly into opening.

13-46. Using four 1-inch roofing nails, install return-air metal duct framing near ceiling between wall studs. Later, finished wall fits around opening and air-conditioning grill covers edges.

Also, cut floor plate, and subfloor directly under it, inside the partition directly below metal duct framing. Later this provides a duct for the passage of return air.

13-47. Complete runs from cut floor plates to blower-coil location.

for basement, utility room, first floor, and attic locations and also for different climates.

The picture shows how central air-conditioning systems with air-cooled condensers operate. The air in the house is cooled and dehumidified by passing over blower coil A. This cooled air B is circulated through supply ducts to various parts of the house. As the air becomes warm, it moves through return ducts C and is eventually discharged from the house by means of condensing unit D, containing the compressor and the condenser.

If you are going to make the installation yourself, first study your own air-conditioning plan carefully. Before starting to cut or to locate the various parts of the unit, mark exactly where the beginning and end of the supply and return ducts go and mark the locations of the plenum, condenser, and compressor.

13-45. The following steps do not represent a set order in which installation must be done. Rather, they should serve as guidelines. Procedures should be

For this step, your plans may call for sheeted joist or direct sheeted metal ducts or a combination of the two. If opening cuts are required in the sheet metal, see step 13-52.

Fasten metal sheets to joists with 1-inch nails spaced 4 inches apart. Fasten direct sheeted metal ducts to floor joists every 3 or 4 feet by driving an 8-penny box nail on each side of duct through the top of drive clip into floor joist. While nailing, position duct tightly against floor joist so as not to disengage drive clips from the U-channels.

Note: It is only necessary to complete this step, because later finished walls and wall studs provide return-air duct from metal framing to cut floor plates. Generally, inside walls serve as return-air ducts and do not require insulation. If an outside wall does serve as a return-air duct, a 1-inch blanket-type insulation stapled to the outside wall is required, vapor barrier located next to the air flow.

SHORTENING A DUCT LENGTH

PUNCHING OUT NEW SNAPS

Courtesy Montgomery, Ward and Co.

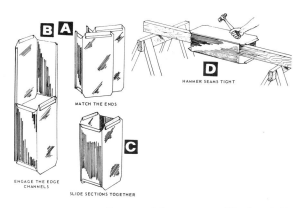

MATCH THE ENDS

HAMMER SEAMS TIGHT

ENGAGE THE EDGE CHANNELS

SLIDE SECTIONS TOGETHER

Courtesy Montgomery, Ward and Co.

13-48. Next install air-supply plenum from blower-coil location to where farthest air-supply round pipe takes off.

To form a duct length from two half-sections, place the two pieces on the floor with the S-hook end up as in A. Pick up one piece and engage its edge channels with the channels on the other piece as in B. Slide the two together C. Hang duct over a sturdy board suspended between two sawhorses so that seam lies flat on the board edge, then hammer each channel snug for a tight fit D.

13-49. To shorten a duct length, cut the two pieces before forming it. Always cut the end without the S-hook connector. Measure carefully, then cut both pieces to the same length with tin snips as in A. After cutting, pry up the edge channels to original form. Cut back corners of the new end and bend over edge to form a new connector channel. Use the cut-off end as a model. Smaller ducts may have snap-lock ends for making joints; always cut the snap end. To make new snaps, lay cut end of the duct on a piece of wood and punch with a cold chisel and hammer as shown in B. Hold chisel at 45° angle. Space snaps the same as on cut-off end.

13-50. Smaller ducts and fittings have snap-lock connections. Such pieces are joined by in-

Courtesy Montgomery, Ward and Co.

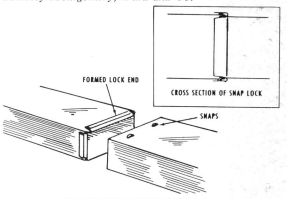

FORMED LOCK END

CROSS SECTION OF SNAP LOCK

SNAPS

SNAP LOCK CONNECTION

serting the snap end of one piece into the formed lock end of the next piece as shown in the picture here. If connected pieces must be separated again, pry up the flanges on the formed lock end with a screwdriver until snaps are released.

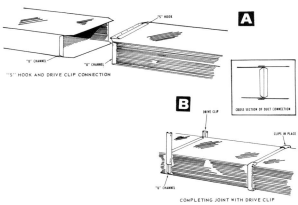

Courtesy Montgomery, Ward and Co.

13-51. Larger-size duct lengths and fittings are joined by S-hooks and drive clips. One end of each section or fitting has formed S-channels on the long edges and U-channels on the short edges for the drive clips as seen in A above. The other end has plain long edges and U-channels on the short edges. Join pieces by inserting a plain end into the S-channel of the next piece and sliding drive clips through the U-channels to lock the pieces together as in B. When the drive clips are on, bend ends down over duct to complete joint.

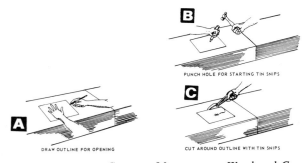

Courtesy Montgomery, Ward and Co.

13-52. Cut openings in plenum chambers, metal sheets, end caps, etc., where required to start branch pipe runs. Type of cut depends upon kind of takeoff or fitting required. Measure the fitting or make a template of the opening required and draw its outline accurately on the metal to be cut as shown in A. Punch through the sheet metal with a hammer and cold chisel or screwdriver blade, keeping within limits of the opening as pointed out in B. Insert tin snips and cut out to outline, then around the outline as indicated in C.

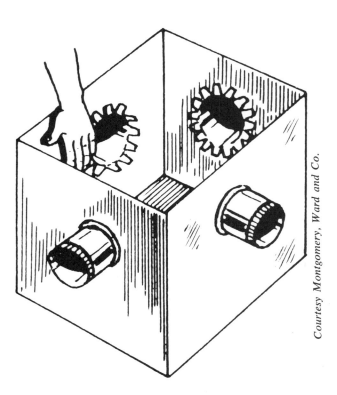

Courtesy Montgomery, Ward and Co.

TABS HOLD TAKE-OFF FITTING TO PLENUM

13-53. Insert each starting fitting into its opening in the plenum and attach permanently by bending over the metal tabs against the inside surface as shown in the picture.

Note: Some air-conditioning units have square-style plenums, while others have a rectangular style. The principle of attaching takeoff fittings is the same for either style.

13-54. When plenum is complete with takeoff fittings, fasten to ceiling joists as explained in step 13-47.

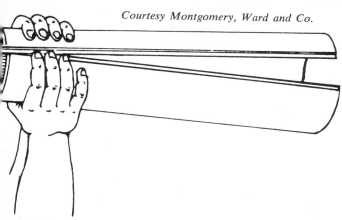

Courtesy Montgomery, Ward and Co.

LOCKING ROUND PIPE SEAM

13-55. Now you should be ready to install round-pipe supply ducts from plenum fittings to openings previously cut in floor next to outside walls.

For shipping purposes, round pipe is usually shipped nested with seams open. Fittings are usually formed ready to be installed.

Form the pipe by rounding it with your hands until the two seam edges meet and lock in place. Insert the tongue on one seam edge into the recess on the other seam edge. Start at one end of pipe and work down seam toward other end until seam snaps shut.

When filling out the end of a run you will most likely need to cut a pipe. Mark uncrimped end, being sure to allow enough extra length for the cut end to slip over crimped end of adjoining pipe, up to the bead. With pipe down as flat as possible, cut line with tin snips across pipe. Using a screwdriver, pry open the snap-lock seam edge where snips squeezed it closed and form the pipe as explained in the preceding step.

13-56. Join pipe lengths to fittings (usually a boot located below floor opening and a take-off fitting located at plenum). Line up seams for best

appearance, pushing lengths and fittings together as far as possible to assure a tight joint.

Note: Always install piping so that crimped pipe ends point away from plenum. For greater rigidity, secure each joint and fitting with three sheet-metal screws evenly spaced around joint.

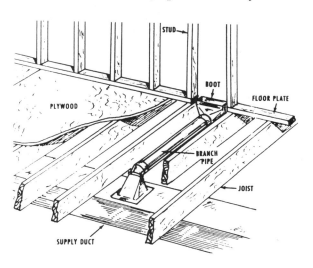

Courtesy Montgomery, Ward and Co.

13-57. Slide free end of pipe over plenum take-off fitting. Position boot on opposite end snugly into floor opening.

13-58. Secure boxes or boots from ends farthest from plenum to subfloor with 1-inch nails.

13-59. To keep long runs of supply pipes from sagging, nail wood supporting blocks or cross members even with bottom edge of joists.

CAUTION: It is important that plenum chambers and air conditioned ducts in non-conditioned spaces such as crawl spaces, attics, etc. be insulated. If such are not pre-insulated, use 1-inch fiberglass insulation with a vapor barrier. The vapor-seal prevents condensation of moisture within insulation material on the cool ducts. Also, supply ducts located in basement areas should be insulated.

13-60. Position blower coil with sheet-metal adapters to connect with cool air-supply plenum and sheeted joist or sheeted return-air duct. Then

make proper connections according to specifications on your plan. Be sure connections are perfectly tight so as not to lose cool air.

The picture shows a metal stand made at a local welding shop to support the blower coil so that it does not have to be suspended from the basement ceiling joists. With this type of installation, fewer vibrations reach the upstairs living quarters, making for quieter operation. Be sure to supply a drain for carrying water removed from the warm air to open floor drain or sump for disposal. CAUTION: Never connect to closed plumbing system.

13-61. Provide a 4-inch concrete base, slightly larger than the condensing unit and above-grade. When concrete is hard, position condensing unit on base, being sure that condenser is level. Allow a minimum of 12 inches of space between unit and house.

Plan the routing of the pre-charged tubing with quick-connect couplings between compressor and condenser. Drill necessary holes in wall to permit passage of tubing. Then uncoil both lengths of tubing and lay them out along the planned route. Now consult the instruction book furnished with your equipment, which tells you how to make the bends and how to connect the couplings for your particular system.

You will complete installation by screwing grills over return air holes in walls close to ceiling. Note: You should not make these two installations until finished walls are complete.

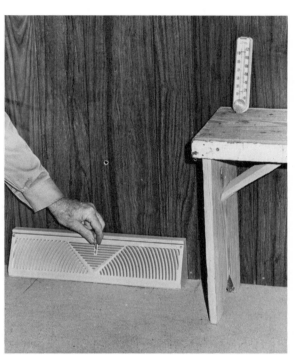

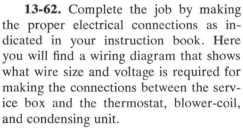

13-62. Complete the job by making the proper electrical connections as indicated in your instruction book. Here you will find a wiring diagram that shows what wire size and voltage is required for making the connections between the service box and the thermostat, blower-coil, and condensing unit.

13-63. Later, using screws supplied, you will fasten air-supply diffusers by screwing back plate to wall and bottom strip to floor. Be sure there is no air loss between boot at end of supply pipe and diffuser.

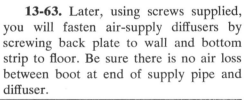

13-64. Set thermostat. Then throw air-conditioning breaker (or install fuse) in service box. If system operates satisfactorily, balance system. Place an accurate thermometer in each room, with the exception of room containing the thermostat fitted with a thermometer. Then by trial and error, adjust each damper on the air-supply diffusers until the temperature in each room is satisfactory. There is a chance that a few additional adjustments will be required from time to time to give complete comfort in every room of the house.

Central Vacuum System Installation

13-65. While installing the electrical wiring in your new house, why not install a whisper-quiet cleaning system? It requires no motor or tank to drag around, no cord to manipulate, no allergy-filled dustbag, and it lets you snooze in peace while the housework is efficiently being done around you.

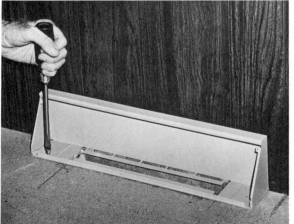

Photos for Steps 13-65 and 13-66, 13-69 to 13-75, and 13-77 courtesy Whirlpool Corp.

Drawings and pictures in this section of the chapter show a Whirlpool Jack-Vac Central Vacuum System installation manufactured by Whirlpool Corporation, Benton Harbor, Michigan.

13-66. The picture shows fabrication procedures and schematic layout of conveying system. These tubing conveying system lines may be installed under or between floor joists, in partitions, on face of walls, in attic or crawl space, on columns or in floor slab, and underground.

As you install keep in mind that the procedure is generally faster and simpler if you start from the farthest-away valve and continue back toward the power unit. Take care to see that flow through angled part of branch fitting is always toward the power unit. Seal connections with Pliobond or special tape provided with unit. Support both horizontal and vertical lines firmly with suitable hangers, straps, or clamps. Fasten these to walls, studding or joists.

13-67. If you plan to use the central vacuum system in a garage or other building separate from the house, lay main tubing line (shown by arrow) 3 feet underground surrounded by 2 inches of concrete with two ½-inch reinforcement rods located below tubing.

Instead of low-voltage control, I used standard on-off three-way switches in one of the houses in this book (one inside the house, the other inside the garage). Plastic cable is three-wire #12, recommended for underground installation.

13-68. Mount power unit on the wall at a convenient height for emptying the dirt collector. Power unit should be located at main floor or basement level to take advantage of gravity. Transmission lines carrying dirt upward should never be higher than one story.

If you did not previously provide for a hole in the wall to accommodate outside exhaust connection, provide one now. When power unit is fastened to wall, make exhaust connections and

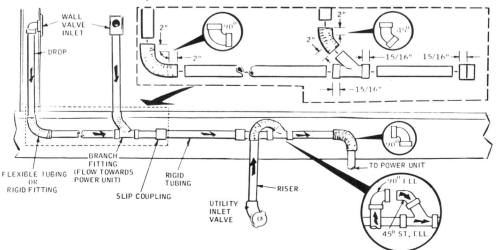

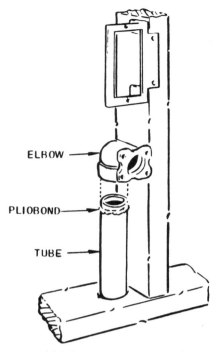

bring separate 115-volt electric circuit to power unit for connecting later.

13-69. Determine location for each wall valve required so 25-foot cleaning hose will give complete coverage to all areas to be cleaned. Height is optional, but 16 to 24 inches from floor is recommended.

Nail valve mounting plate to stud at desired height for each valve. Then mount plate to either right or left side of wall stud.

Drill hole through floor or ceiling plate. Center hole in the 2×4 plate to align with the exhaust or belled side of the 90° elbow of valve assembly.

13-70. Cut a piece of rigid tubing to proper length. Then put it through hole in plate and connect elbow to tubing, using Pliobond to seal joint.

13-71. Assemble O-ring and mounting bracket (long tab at top and flanges extended forward) to elbow, using the four screws through the slotted holes in bracket. Make sure O-ring is properly seated before adjusting for alignment with stud. Tighten screws completely. Use perforated strapping, hangers, or clamps to support the tubing.

Screw bracket to plate.

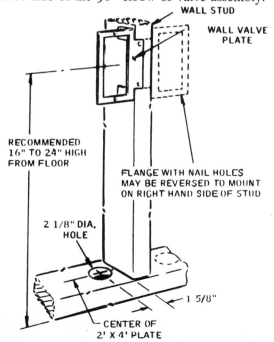

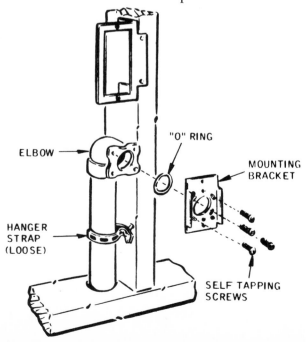

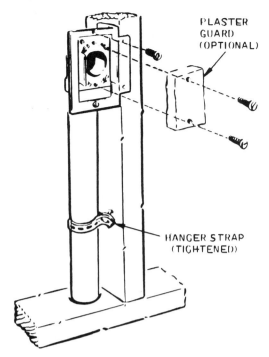

PLASTER GUARD (OPTIONAL)

HANGER STRAP (TIGHTENED)

13-72. If wall is to be covered with paneling, recess bracket until flush with stud. If wall is to be plastered, screw plaster guard to valve bracket to keep plaster out of elbow and to form opening for later installation of wall valve. After plaster has hardened, remove guard.

13-73. Power can be supplied either one of two ways—standard on-off switch or low-voltage control.

The picture here shows the wiring diagram for standard on-off switch. Locate the remote switch for the power unit close to the storage closet for the hose and cleaning tools. User can turn the system on when hose and tools are taken out and turn it off when the cleaning accessories are returned to storage. Three-way switches (wiring of

three-way switches is shown in this chapter, step 13-21) of the proper capacity may be used if two operational points are desired.

If you decide to use a low-voltage control system, doorbell (24-volt) wire is required to connect each inlet valve that is to be activated to the transverter-relay assembly. This assembly is in a convenience box that may be mounted to the power unit mounting bracket or on joists, wall, or studding close to the power unit.

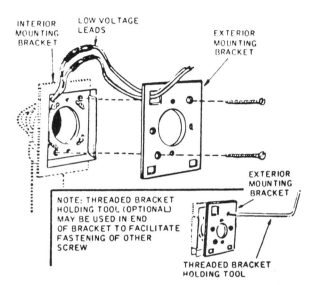

INTERIOR MOUNTING BRACKET LOW VOLTAGE LEADS EXTERIOR MOUNTING BRACKET

EXTERIOR MOUNTING BRACKET

NOTE: THREADED BRACKET HOLDING TOOL (OPTIONAL) MAY BE USED IN END OF BRACKET TO FACILITATE FASTENING OF OTHER SCREW

THREADED BRACKET HOLDING TOOL

13-74. If low-voltage control is desired, place low-voltage wires through rectangular opening in exterior mounting bracket. If low-voltage control is not being considered, disregard these wires.

Insert the long machine screws through countersunk holes in exterior mounting bracket and thread into matching tapped holes in interior mounting bracket. Tighten screws until the wall is gripped securely between the brackets.

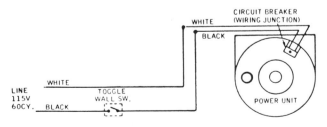

WHITE CIRCUIT BREAKER (WIRING JUNCTION)
BLACK
LINE 115V 60CY. WHITE TOGGLE WALL SW. BLACK POWER UNIT

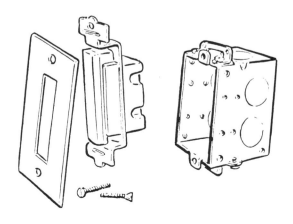

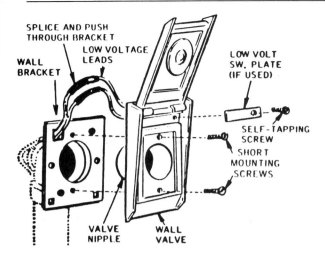

13-75. Assemble low-voltage switch plate (if used) to wall valve base. Splice the low-voltage leads together (if used). Insert valve nipple into opening in the mounting brackets; use care to feed low-voltage wires back into opening. Secure wall valve in position, using the two short machine screws.

13-76. Refer to the illustration in step 13-66, then connect tubing from wall valves to horizontal runs, connecting end of run into intake of power unit. Connect exhaust to exterior vent if you have not already done so.

Connect separate 115-volt electric circuit to power unit. If you need help with the electrical part of the installation, refer to the early part of this chapter.

13-77. Check out the system. Look for tubing connections overlooked, and make sure the electrical system is correctly wired.

Now make a check with the power turned on. The picture shows one way to make a check without the use of attachments. Whirlpool's Jack-Vac has a heavy-duty power unit that whisks away the contents of a dirty ashtray forever. No messy dust bag, unruly electrical cord, or heavy cleaning unit—only a pliable hose and wand.

Home Security System Installation

13-78. Of all deterrents known to housebreakers, two are detested more than any—loud noise and light. Thomas Industries, Inc., of Louisville, Kentucky, has developed a home security system that provides both loud noise and light along with many other features that discourage thieves if they try to break in.

Courtesy Thomas Industries, Inc.

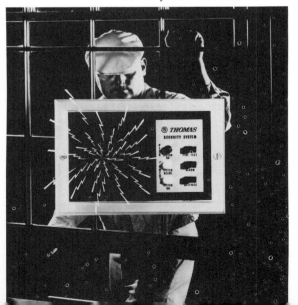

Also available with the Thomas system is an optional smoke detector. Since more deaths are caused from smoke inhalation than from burns, this is a most worthwhile addition.

Courtesy Thomas Industries, Inc.

13-79. Follow the wiring diagram accompanying the Thomas home security system. You will find this easy to do if you heed the general wiring instructions previously given in this chapter.

Begin by mounting an electrical box high on the front of the house for the wiring of the flashing light and signal. Mount it so the light can be seen by neighbors if a window or door switch has been tripped.

13-80. Next mount an electrical box for the switch that will trigger the system when tampered with. This installation was made in an attached garage by the back door of the home, because it was handy here for the outside authorized-entry key-operated door switch that enables the system to be turned on after the occupant has left the house and deactivated before entering.

Courtesy Thomas Industries, Inc.

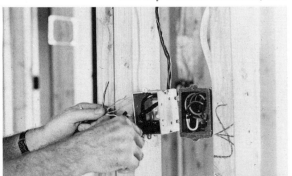

Courtesy Thomas Industries, Inc.

13-81. A remote control box is another recommended accessory. With this unit, you can activate the system from the master bedroom or any other room of your choice. A panic button is also available so that you can trip the alarm from the bedroom, for example. This accessory requires the mounting of two electrical boxes as shown.

Courtesy Thomas Industries, Inc.

13-82. The system also provides a home fire alert (a different-toned signal from that for forced entry) when small heat sensors are placed on the ceiling in the kitchen and other fire-prone areas. Now is the time to bring the necessary wiring to these points. Install the heat sensors as the ceiling is being installed.

when the system is in operation. Note: Should forced entry be attempted, the raucous signal emitting from the master control unit cannot be shut off by closing the door or window. It must be shut off at the master or remote control unit.

Courtesy Thomas Industries, Inc.

13-83. Bring the necessary low-voltage wires to one of the jamb locations of each exterior door. When finishing the interior of the house, mount a simple pressure or magnetic switch, which you build into a doorjamb. It trips the system when opened (if activated).

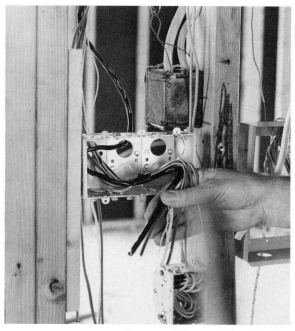

Courtesy Thomas Industries, Inc.

13-85. Provide wiring and electrical boxes for the master control box.

13-86. The deluxe Thomas Home Security System provides both fire and forced-entry alert. With the top switch

Courtesy Thomas Industries, Inc.

Courtesy Thomas Industries, Inc.

13-84. The same switches are installed in window sills or side frames, so provide wiring for them now. The shape of the pressure switch allows the window to slide up or down over it

placed at on, the red lifetime light glows, indicating the fire sensors are activated.

The second or middle switch is an exclusive feature of the Thomas system and allows you to test the security system to make sure that all the controlled openings are closed without danger of the system alarm going off. When turned to on, the white light glows if all openings are closed. If a door or window, for ex-ample, has been left open, the small signal light does not come on, and a check can be made to see where the forgotten opening is located.

The bottom switch activates the signal system, and the house is protected through its window and door switches. This is the switch that you must turn off if the signal alarm is tripped.

14

INSULATION AND INTERIOR FINISHING

and varnishing—can be the most thrilling part of the whole building project. Also, this is the time to provide for the built-ins, such as cabinets and large appliances, particularly if they require a nook of special dimensions like the electric stove in the picture.

While finishing the interior, I installed Whirlpool washer and dryer, electric range, electric disposal unit, dishwasher, and refrigerator with an automatic ice maker.

Ceiling Tile Installation

 14-2. Beginning at one end of room, use stapler to fasten end of polyethylene along edge of ceiling. Next stretch polyethylene lightly and fasten to bottom of

 Photo courtesy Whirlpool Corp.

 14-1. Interior finishing—installing finished floors, walls, and ceilings, fastening lighting and plumbing fixtures in place, putting on the hardware, and painting

ceiling joists. Shoot staples at distances of about 3 to 4 feet, since polyethylene will be held firmly in place later with furring strips.

 14-3. Before applying furring strips, figure their spacing so the border tiles at the end walls will be the same width on opposite sides. Also, avoid having to cut ceiling tiles around the perimeter of ceiling less than 3 inches wide plus the width of wall-ceiling molding.

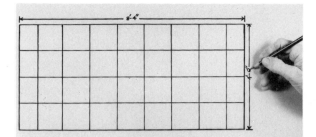

First measure length and width of ceiling. If the measurements are in multiples of 12 inches and you are using 12-inch tiles, there is no problem. Each border tile will be the same size, requiring only one small tongue edge to be removed. For dimensions that are not in multiples of 12 inches, cut tiles for those borders so each tile equals half the odd inches of ceiling width plus 6 inches. Apply the same principle when cutting ceiling end border tiles.

As a practice exercise, figure the required blocks for a hall ceiling that is 8 feet 4 inches long and 4 feet wide.

Perhaps you have already discovered that 28 full 12-inch tiles and eight 8-inch tiles are required.

14-4. To see if ceiling joists are level, stretch a cord from one end ceiling joist to opposite end ceiling joist where furring strips are to be fastened. Where joists are not level, nail a wood shim of required thickness in place. If bottom of joist protrudes, plane off excess wood.

Starting where ceiling joins wall, fasten 1×3

or 1×4 furring strips (as required from previous step) with two 8-penny box nails to bottoms of ceiling joists.

14-5. Keeping fingers off finish face of tile as much as possible, press it against ceiling strips. Then butt against adjoining tile.

14-6. When the two adjoining seams of tiles are perfectly closed, fasten to furring boards with 9/16-inch staples, four to each 12×12-inch tile, six to each 12×24-inch or 16×16-inch tile.

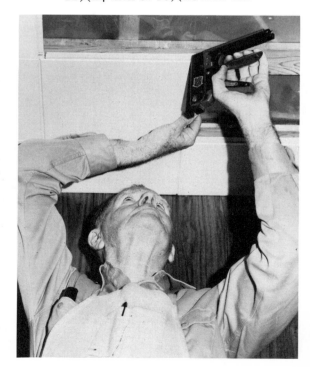

Insulation

14-7. I used Borg-Warner ALFOL insulation in my own home. ALFOL does not have or need a thick bulky layer of fibrous material. Since there is much less

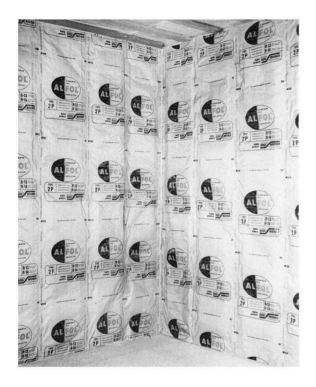

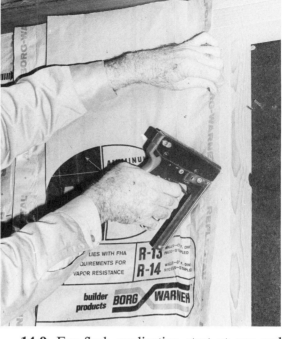

14-9. For flush application start at one end, stapling the side of the insulation to the framing member, following the handy guideline. Place staples about 8 inches apart. Staple until entire length is secured.

material to handle, it is ideal for a one-man installation job. It requires less labor, less equipment, less storage space, and less time.

14-8. Begin with the walls. Cut or tear unexpanded blanket to length of the area to be insulated. Allow 4 inches to 6 inches extra to permit sealing at the ends.

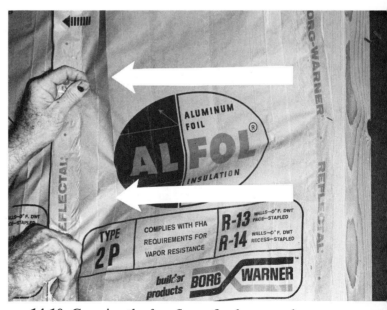

14-10. Grasping the free flange firmly, expand blanket to full width. This action automatically spaces the aluminum-foil layers.

14-11. Keeping blanket stretched taut, staple free flange to the face of next framing member. Staple entire length.

14-13. When outlet and switch boxes are encountered, cut the foil blanket to fit around them snugly.

14-12. Staple the ends of the blanket at the floor and ceiling members to complete the insulation seal.

14-14. If you prefer you can do the following insulation steps later. Before applying ALFOL around windows and exterior doors, loosely tuck any commercially available bulk insulation in the small spaces between the window and door frames and the wall stud framing.

14-15. Air currents have a way of forming between top and bottom of floor joists after floor installation has been made. To prevent this take a 3-inch insulation batt of just about any commercially available bulk insulation and stuff it up against the header and sill plate and the subflooring between the floor joists. Do this around the perimeter of the house.

14-16. To insulate crawl space or basement ceiling, staple the flanges to bottom of ceiling joists in the same way as previously described for applying ALFOL flush to wall studding.

CAUTION: Do not insulate crawl space or basement ceiling until after pipes and diagonal bridging have been applied.

14-17. Finish ceiling as described later in this chapter, then complete insulating job. You can employ a commercial firm to blow an 8-inch layer of conventional bulk wool in the attic, or you can purchase insulation material in bags. Then pour it between the attic joists, level it, and the job is completed.

Hardboard Panel Installation

14-18. I recommend Masonite hardboard panels because they combine so many desirable physical characteristics in a single material. Masonite hardboards have no knots, and no grain to rise or check or to otherwise interrupt the smooth uniformity of the panels. They won't

Courtesy Masonite Corp.

split, splinter, or crack, they will resist dents, they can't rust or corrode, they are exceptionally resistant to moisture, mildew, and termites, and they are easily worked with ordinary carpenter's tools.

The picture shows a boy's quarters. This is only one example of what a little imagination can produce with Masonite Living Wall. This is a prefinished hardboard paneling with inconspicuous slots in the panel grooves to hold adjustable shelves and picture hooks.

 14-19. Begin application of hardboard by using 1-inch nails spaced 16 inches apart to fasten inside corner molding to corner studs.

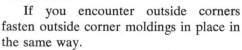 If you encounter outside corners fasten outside corner moldings in place in the same way.

14-20. Although installing hardboard panels can be a one-man job, the work is quicker and easier with a helper.

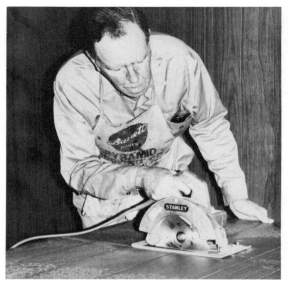

 14-21. Here I use a power saw equipped with a carbide-tipped blade to cut hardboard panels. A carbide-tipped blade will last much longer than a regular blade without resharpening.

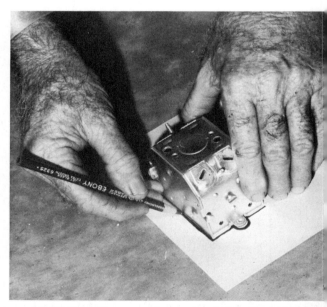

14-22. The first step in cutting holes in panel for electrical outlet or switch boxes is to make a template representing the box.

Place an outlet box on a piece of heavy cardboard as shown above. Then mark around outside edge of box. Cutting out the line forms template.

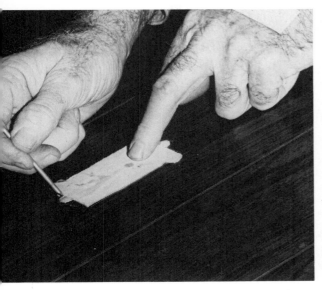

14-23. Place template on panel at proper location, then mark around it. A nail marks well on dark-colored panels, and a pencil on light-colored panels.

14-24. Next drill four ½-inch holes within template outline. The two center holes provide openings in panel for "ears" on outlet or switch box. The other two holes are for the sawblade. CAUTION: Back up panel with a piece of scrap lumber so the drill doesn't make a ragged hole on the back of the panel.

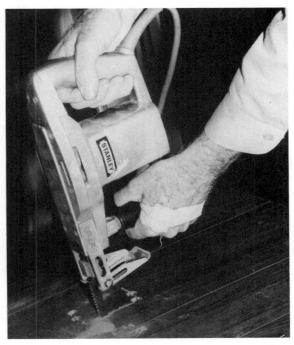

14-25. Next saw panel along template outline.

14-26. There are two methods of applying hardboard panels. One way is by nailing at 4-inch intervals at joints and along edges and 8-inch intervals at intermediate supports. The Masonite Corporation manufactures color-matched nails, one color for panel faces, a second color for nailing in grooves. Each colored panel requires a different set of colored nails. When nails are driven flush, the heads can hardly be detected, making for a professional-looking job.

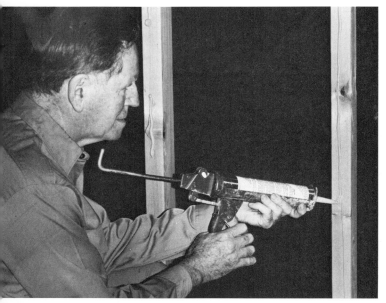

14-27. Gluing panels to open wall studding is a second method of applying hardboard panels.

Apply Royalcote General Purpose Adhesive in a continuous ribbon ⅛ inch thick to studding, furring, or other surface where panel edges are to be bonded. Apply an intermittent ribbon (3-inch bead, then 6-inch open space) to intermediate bonding points. Adhesive and room temperature should be between 60° and 100° F. during application.

Press panels immediately into position. Install two nails at the top of the panel to maintain panel position. With uniform hand pressure press panels firmly into contact with adhesive bead.

14-28. Continue bonding the next four or five panels as previously described. After fifteen or twenty minutes, reapply pressure, using a padded

block of wood and a hammer or mallet to all areas to be bonded to provide a final set.

To remove excess adhesive from panel joints use naphtha or white gasoline as soon as possible.

14-29. If you have masonry walls either above or below grade, you can apply hardboard panels.

Begin by locating a vapor barrier A such as polyethylene next to the masonry wall.

Next use 2×2s as a furring framework B with uprights spaced 16 inches on centers.

Install panels either with nails or adhesive as previously described.

CAUTION: Leave ¼-inch space between bottom of panel and floor. This will be covered later when you apply base molding.

14-30. Edging molding has many uses in hardboard-panel installation. The picture here shows

how I used it in my own house where panel boards join a built-in fireplace.

If you have need for edging molding, first miter corners with a hacksaw. Then nail in place as previously described for nailing inside corner moldings.

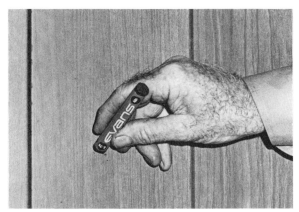

14-31. No matter how careful one is, a few nail holes, scratches, or mars seem to appear when the job is completed. If you have this experience cover them by using a puttystick. The putty dries fast and hard without leaving a messy residue.

Now return to the wiring chapter and complete steps 13-31 to 13-33.

Plank Wall Panel Installation

14-32. Prepare wall studs for fastening knotty-pine, oak, or cedar planks by

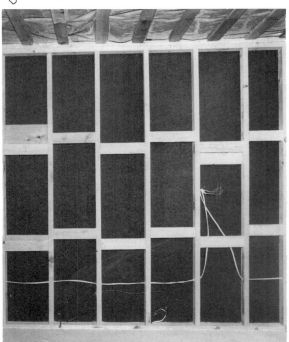

staggering 2×4 cross members between wall studs as shown above. Fasten cross members in place with two 16-penny common nails driven through a corresponding wall stud into the end grain of the cross member. Wall studs pictured here are spaced 16 inches on centers. However, they may be spaced as far as 4 feet on centers if preferred.

14-33. Using a stapler, fasten roll-type insulation at top of wall as previously described in insulation steps. Be sure to weave insulation in and out behind the cross members. Staple insulation tightly to studs at points just above and just below where cross members meet studs. This makes for a complete weatherproof wall seal between floor and ceiling.

14-34. For vertical paneling locate first plank, groove edge, in a corner. Be sure board is perfectly vertical, then face-nail at very top and bottom. Later these nails will be covered by trim boards.

Next fasten board to cross members by tongue-nailing (similar to toenailing), using 6-penny finishing nails. Drive nails almost all the way, then to avoid marring, set nail with nail set.

Complete job by lining up following boards with previous ones, being sure to bring tongue-and-groove joints up snug, but not too tight.

Electric Pressing Unit Installation

14-35. If you plan to install an electric pressing unit in the framing as shown in step 8-15, now is a good time to do it. Cut finished wall material so that it fits flush around 2×4 framing. If you have not provided for electrical connections, bring a 115-volt line to pigtails as provided in bottom of wireway. Make entrance into knockouts provided in top or bottom of wireway through left-hand vent hole.

Position unit in opening level and plumb. Then fasten in place with 8-penny finishing nails spaced 16 inches on centers around outside molding of unit. Countersink nails, filling holes to match finish.

Laying Hardwood Floors

14-36. Plan to lay the flooring over subfloor at right angles to the floor joists. Begin by laying 15-pound asphalt-saturated felt paper A over subfloor with 4-inch laps. Then position beginning strip of flooring B (groove edge toward wall) ½ inch from wall C, both sides and ends. This allows for expansion. With strip perfectly straight, fasten in place with 10-penny finishing nails (spaced 10 inches apart), face-nailed straight down through center of board. Later countersink these nails and fill holes before finishing the floor. Always use the piece cut off at the end of one strip of flooring to start the next strip, provided the piece is at least 6 inches long and does not come within 6 inches of the butt end of the previous piece.

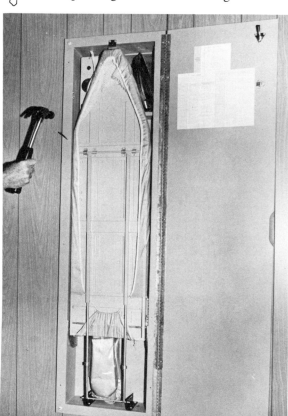

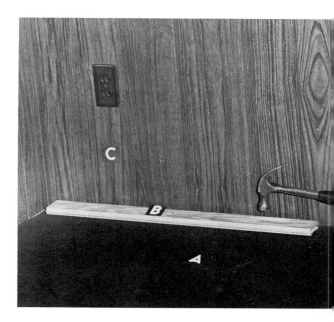

Various types of harmonizing moldings are available for most patterns. The picture here shows corner molding A, division strip B, and cap molding C.

Marlite panels can be installed either vertically or horizontally with appropriate moldings along the edges.

 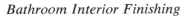

14-37. Holding nails diagonally and spaced 12 to 16 inches apart, blind-nail by toenailing subsequent strips. As each board is fastened be sure it fits snugly against previous board and that end joints are tight and square. If you want the ultimate in fastening hardwood floors, use threaded nails applied with a special floor-nailing tool. Regardless of how you nail, be sure hammer head is not damaging surface of board as you drive nails home. Using an ordinary nail set during the last few hammer blows helps to avoid a damaged flooring surface. To push successive boards tightly up to previous boards, place a scrap piece over the tongue that is being installed. Then hit edge of scrap with a hammer until boards are tight. Some carpenters wait until they have laid four or five boards before using this tightening-up procedure. Also, as you lay the floor be sure that end joints in adjacent strips are at least 6 inches apart.

Bathroom Interior Finishing

14-38. Marlite decorator patterns (manufactured by Marsh, Masonite Division, Dover, Ohio) are recommended for moist areas. Panels come in sizes of 4×6 feet and 4×8 feet and are 1/8 inch thick.

14-39. Apply top panel first. Measure, then cut panel (face side up with a fine-toothed saw) to size, being sure to cut openings for plumbing pipes, electrical fixtures, and end of tub. Now measure and cut bottom panel.

Next try panels in position to make certain of proper fit. Then install edge molding at the 4-foot level so that when top and bottom panels are finally slipped behind molding lips about ⅛ inch of space is left so that expansion and contraction of sheet is possible without buckling.

14-40. Using a Marlite comb spreader, apply a thin coating of adhesive in ridges over entire back of panel except for about 1 inch at edges. Then apply a light, smooth coating of adhesive to the wall area where panel is to be applied. (If furring strips are used on studs instead of solid material, mark location of furring strips on back of sheets. Then apply adhesive only on these locations as well as the furring strips themselves.)

While adhesive is drying, cover all seams where there is any possibility of direct moisture penetration with a waterproof caulking compound that is resistant to hardening, crackling, and shrinkage. Such caulking can be secured from your local lumber dealer.

Now press top panel firmly in place to assure good contact, being sure it is slipped behind edge molding, leaving

about ⅛ inch of space at bottom. Since the adhesive grips quickly, careful application is necessary. Press panel firmly in place. To ensure good bonding over entire panel, use a rubber hammer and padded 2×2 as recommended previously in step 14-28.

Interior Finishing of Darkrooms, Sewing Rooms, And Recreation Rooms

14-41. There are many similarities in the interior wall finishing of photographic darkrooms, sewing rooms, and recreation rooms. I find that Marlite products add a touch of distinction to such rooms, and they can be quickly and professionally installed by the average home builder.

Darkrooms do not require gruesome black interior finishing. Since colored interiors do not reflect light in a lightproof room, walls, ceilings, and floors may be just as colorful as the photographer desires. The picture shows 4×8-foot pegboard installed above space designed for a future photographic darkroom cabinet along with 4×8-foot by ¼ inch thick satin-finish square-edged panels being applied. Matching moldings should be used throughout wall finishing. For installation procedures of panels and moldings, see steps 14-38 to 14-40.

You can install ceiling tile or Marlite ceiling blocks as previously described. Doors, doorjambs, casings, and other trim can be installed and finished as described later in this chapter.

Doorjamb And Swinging-Door Installations

14-42. Use three milled pieces, called jambs, of finish material to make the frame, consisting of two side jambs and the top or head jamb.

Rip and plane to a width equal to the width of wall studs plus the width of the thickness of each adjoining finished wall.

Cut head jamb width of door plus depth of rabbet located in side jambs (shown by black arrow) plus ⅛ inch to allow for door clearance.

Beginning at bottom end of rabbet located near the top of each jamb, measure and cut side jambs length of door plus 9/16 inch.

CAUTION: If threshold is used, check its height. Some thresholds require more than ½-inch clearance.

14-43. Note direction of door swing. Then measure down 7 inches from the end rabbet and up 11 inches from bottom of jamb for the top and bottom hinge positions.

Using a knife or a sharp hard lead pencil, mark the length and width of the hinge gains from the hinge leaves onto the face of the jamb adjoining the edge from which the door is to swing. For 3½-inch butt hinges this is 1⅛ inches. Mark the depth equal to the thickness of the leaves.

Next locate and mark the length, width, and depth of a third hinge gain midway between the top and bottom hinge locations. Using a wood chisel, remove wood within hinge gain areas.

14-44. Place ends of head jamb in rabbet on side jambs. Then, using three 8-penny finishing nails for each side, fasten side jambs to head jamb.

14-45. Subtract the outside width of the frame from the inside width of the rough door opening. Then figure one-half the answer. Next cut five blocks about 3½ inches wide by about ¼ inch less than the frame width by one-half the width difference as found above.

Next fasten the five blocks on center to the trimmer stud located on the hinge side of the rough door opening. Begin by nailing first block directly under trimmer. Nail second block at floor level only when plumb with top block. If not plumb, trim bottom block or shim behind it, as the case might be, until both blocks are absolutely plumb. (Top and bottom blocks indicated by black arrows in picture.)

Nail the three remaining blocks on the trimmer stud at hinge locations, being sure they are plumb with top and bottom blocks.

14-46. If a threshold is to be used, cut it exactly the length of the inside width of door frame at the top. If a threshold is not used, cut a length of 1×6 to temporarily take its place.

Set frame in door opening with the hinge jamb against the blocks. Then place threshold or 1×6 on floor between jambs. Check head jamb with level. If not perfectly level, make it so by shortening the bottom end of one side jamb.

Using 8-penny finishing nails spaced about 16 inches apart, fasten hinge jamb, plumb on sides

and face. Be sure nails are placed in such a way as to be concealed later when door stop molding is nailed to face of jambs.

Now split a shingle lengthwise into pieces about 3 inches wide. Then using pairs as wedges, wedge and fasten lock jamb so that it is plumb and parallel to hinge jamb. One pair of wedges should be located just behind the lock position (36 inches above finished floor line.) Nail in place.

CAUTION: Do not fasten door casings to frame at this point. Fastening them *after* door is hung makes it possible to make minor adjustments to door jambs if door is binding slightly when in closed position.

14-47. Next prepare door for hanging. If you do not have a woodworker's vise to fasten to a sawhorse, make a door jack from pieces of 1×6 material nailed together as pictured here. Notch and pad jack as shown at A. This protects door edge while working on it. Nail door guides B to

base with space slightly wider than door width. Be sure base length C from directly below padded notch to end is as long as door, usually 6 feet 8 inches.

Check door for length, width, and squareness. Inside doors should have a clearance of ⅛ inch at top, 1/16 inch on each side, and ½ inch at bottom.

Nail jack temporarily to floor. Then position door. Using a jointer or jack plane, dress door edges as needed. To prevent door from striking jamb on inside corner as it closes, bevel lock edge about ⅛ inch toward closing side.

of hinge leaf as described previously. Fasten hinges to door with screws accompanying them.

14-48. Next fasten hinges to jamb. Half-surface butt hinges are shown in these illustrations.

Put each hinge leaf in position and mark the center of the screw holes with a center punch or nail. Then, using screws accompanying hinges, fasten each hinge leaf in place on jamb.

14-49. Position door in opening. Then block and wedge it to the correct height, being sure each side and top has the correct clearance. Mark the outline of the half-surface butt hinge leaves on the door with a knife. Mark the screw holes with a center punch or a nail. If butt hinges are used, mark gain outline, chiseling to depth

14-50. Check door for proper assembly. It should remain in any position placed between fully closed and fully open. It should swing freely and close without binding. If it does not operate

properly, the hinges may need some adjusting and/or a slight dressing may be required.

Photo courtesy Kwikset Sales and Service Co.

14-51. If you have not installed locksets or latch sets, do it now. Install latch sets where door is not to be locked from either side. Where doors are to be locked, follow installation instructions as given for installing locksets on exterior doors in steps 11-20 to 11-24.

Sliding-Door And Hardware Installations

14-52. Sliding doors are popular with many home builders. They do not require floor space

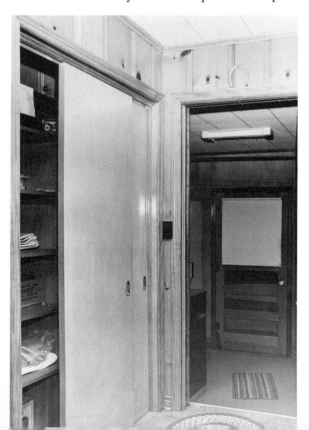

for opening and shutting. They do not detract from the room decor when open. This type of door with pocket (either of wood or metal) requires regular 2×4 wall thickness. The picture here shows how two sliding doors may be placed in a corner without blocking entranceway of either one.

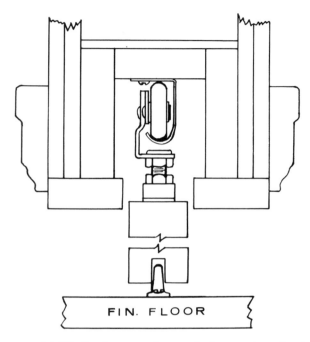

FIN. FLOOR

14-53. Study manufacturer's instruction sheet accompanying sliding-door pocket. Then install pocket, later to be covered with regular interior wall covering. Rollers, track, and screws and bolts are included with the pocket. Two or three by-passing sliding doors make it possible to have a large opening between two rooms and still provide privacy when needed.

14-54. Select a door sized to fit pocket. Mark locations on door for flush pull A and edge pull B 36 inches from finished floor to centers of pulls.

Note: Flush pulls are installed on both sides of door. Using a drill and wood chisel, mortise out just enough wood so pulls will fit flush with door surface.

Install pulls permanently after door is finished.

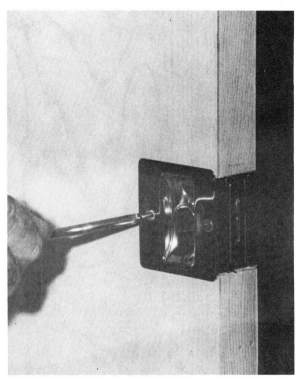

reversing lock assembly are included in sliding-door lockset package.

14-57. Mark and mortise strike on jamb to correspond to lock position on door. Then drill ⅞-inch-diameter hole ½-inch deep in center of mortise.

14-55. Kwikset's sliding-door locksets were used in the houses in this book on several interior sliding doors, including the bathroom door. With such installations, sliding doors can be latched from one side of door. Also, the locksets have built-in pulls for opening and closing door.

Begin installing Kwikset sliding-door locksets by cutting a single notch 1¾ inches wide by 2¼ inches high. Locate notch same height from finished floor line as recommended for locksets in Chapter 11, THE EXTERIOR FINISHING.

14-56. Slip pull into position. Then fasten machine screws. Note: Complete instructions for

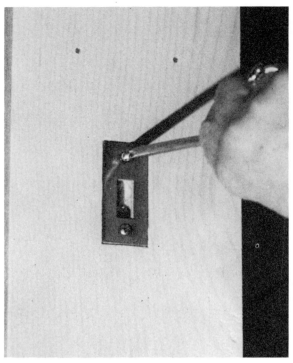

14-58. Screw strike plate into position, using ⅝-inch #6 flathead wood screws, which accompany sliding-door locksets.

Casing And Other Trim Installations

14-59. Since casings should not overlap edges of the door jambs, gauge a light pencil or nail line on edge of jambs, 3/16 inch back from face. Then lay off the

lengths for the side and top casings, allowing enough material for the mitered joints discussed in the following step. Check bottom ends of casings for squareness. Now place one of the side casings in position on a side jamb. Mark a point on the casing where it touches the gauge line located on the edge of the top jamb. This point indicates the short end of the miter cut to be made. Next position and mark opposite casing in same manner. CAUTION: Be sure to locate thin edges of casings on the door jamb, not thick edges.

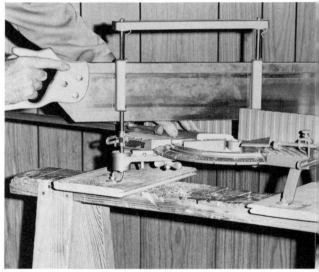

14-60. Using the miter box and saw, cut 45° miters on top end of each of the two side casings. Be sure short end of the miter cut coincides with the pencil mark made in the previous step.

14-61. Nail one casing in place about halfway up from floor, being sure edge of casing barely covers gauge mark. Then

fasten casing to jamb with 4-penny casing or finishing nails; along the outer edge, use 6-penny casing or finishing nails, nailing into stud. Space nails about 14 inches apart.

Next mark and cut 45° miters on each end of top casing, using gauge marks located on side jambs as guidelines.

14-62. Position top casing tightly against fastened side casing. When joint fits perfectly, nail top of side casing in place as well as part of top casing where it joins side casing.

Now position second side casing in place. When joint fits perfectly, nail side casing and remainder of top casing in place.

14-63. If doors are already hung, measure and cut 45° miters for joints, fit, and nail door stops in place with 4-penny finishing nails. If doors are not hung, stops should be tacked in place

from edge of casing about the door thickness plus ⅛ inch.

Complete jamb trim job by countersinking finishing nails in casings and door stops, filling holes with putty stick, color to match trim.

14-64. Cut and fasten window casings in place in the same way as door casings. Caradco windows were used in the houses in this book. Since no apron or stool is required for these windows, casings are fastened completely around the window, each end mitered to a 45° angle. If your windows are not of this style, skip this step.

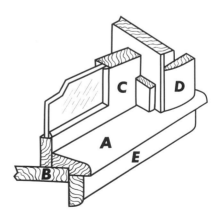

14-65. The drawing shows the style of a double-hung window requiring stool A and apron E as well as casings.

First cut stool A to length. This is the

distance between proposed outside edge of casing locations plus 1 inch. Next cut stool to width by ripping a piece from the tapered part so that the remainder is 1/16 inch less than the distance from outer edge of stool to bottom rail of lower sash C. (Note: Distance between stool, when nailed in place, and bottom sash should be about 1/16 inch.) Now notch out each end of the tapered part of stool so that it will extend ½ inch beyond proposed casing locations and almost touch bottom sash.

Position stool over window sill B. With ends fitting against wall surface and projecting part almost touching lower sash, fasten stool to window sill with 6-penny finishing nails.

Second, cut and fasten window casings D in place in the same way as door casing, except window casings rest on stool.

Third, fasten apron E in place by first cutting it to length, which is equal to the distance between outside of casings. Position under stool and against wall, fastening in place with 6-penny finishing nails. By slanting nails upward, you can pull apron tightly against bottom of stool.

Countersink nails in stool, casings, and apron.

14-66. Where external corners of molding meet between ceiling and walls, miter as you did in cutting door and window casings. Where internal corners meet, use a coped joint.

Using 4-penny finishing nails spaced about 16 inches apart, fasten a piece of cove molding to both ceiling and wall from one side of room to the other. Then countersink nail heads, filling nail holes with colored putty stick. If more than one

piece is required, join together, using 45° mitered joints.

Begin coping operation by placing vertical side of second piece of molding against back of miter box. This is the same position that it will be placed in against the wall. Next saw a 45° miter cut near end of molding.

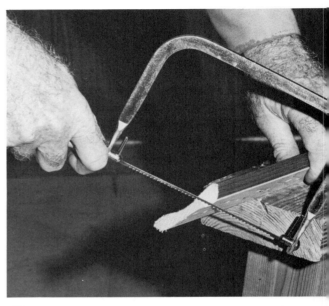

14-67. Continue coping operation by placing vertical side of molding down on top of a sawhorse. Then, using a coping saw, make a right cut on the waste side of the line formed by the miter cut. Note: Slightly undercut coped end so that front edge will butt tightly against adjacent molding. If coped joint is not exactly correct, true up with a pocket knife. Then fasten molding in place.

14-68. Begin baseboard installation by locating and marking wall stud locations on the floor with a light pencil mark. Miter external joints. Cope internal joints by first squaring both ends of a piece of baseboard to correct length of room.

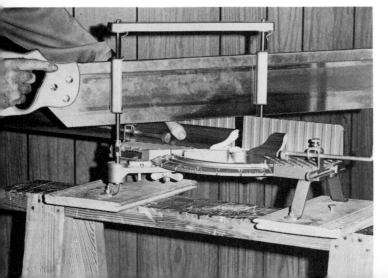

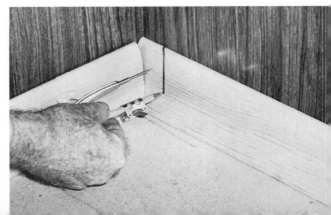

Then fasten in place with two 6-penny finishing nails at each stud location. Place lower nails so that base shoe or carpet strip will later hide them. (If baseboard requires piecing along a wall, join together with a 45° joint at one of the stud locations.) Hold a second piece of baseboard (slightly longer than adjacent wall) firmly against face of baseboard as you scribe the end as shown in the picture here. Using a coping saw, make a vertical cut along the scribed line, undercutting slightly for making a tight butt joint. Then position and nail in place, being sure butt ends of baseboards also form a square joint against door casings. Countersink nails, filling holes with putty stick to match color of trim.

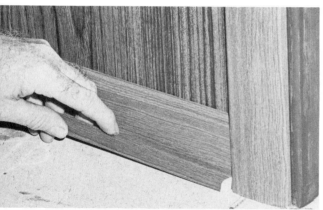

14-69. Miter external joints of base shoe or carpet strip and cope internal joints similar to coping cove molding as mentioned previously. Then, using 4-penny finishing nails, fasten directly to hardwood floor. Where wall-to-wall carpet is part of the decor, nail base shoe in place following carpet installation.

Base shoe will extend out from door casings, so miter end of base shoe for making neat joints. If prefinished base shoe is used, finish cut to match.

Countersink nails, filling holes with putty stick to match trim color.

14-70. Begin the staining and varnishing operation by sanding trim members with number o sandpaper to remove sharp corners, slivers, dirt, etc. Then re-move all traces of dust with a clean cloth or a vacuum cleaner. A sealing stain is recommended over an oil stain for matching trim members with the wall colors. Before using, be sure to stir sealing stain for obtaining uniform color. Apply a thin coat with a clean brush, brushing out well. A good-quality varnish brush is recommended. Select a brush width to suit the job at hand. Generally, a 2½-inch or 3-inch width serves as a single all-purpose sealing stain and varnish brush. Since there is no wiping as in oil stains, the depth of color during application will be the final color.

When sealing stain is thoroughly dry, rub lightly with grade 6-0 sandpaper or grade oo steel wool to remove any slight roughness, being careful not to rub through the finish. Dust thoroughly. Then finish with semi-gloss or satin-finish varnish. Probably two coats of varnish will be required. If so, use grade 6-0 sandpaper or grade oo steel wool to remove slight roughness that occurs between coats. Rub final coat lightly with grade oooo steel wool for securing finish effect. CAUTION: Never rub stained or varnished surfaces until they are thoroughly dry. Generally, this takes 24 hours.

For giving a natural finish, apply a clear seal to the trim instead of a sealing stain. Sand lightly as recommended for sanding sealing stain above. Then follow varnishing suggestions as recommended previously.

At the end of the sealing stain or varnishing session, clean the brush thoroughly with paint thinner or turpentine.

dents, and flaws in the wood are not completely filled.

Thoroughly mix the paint or enamel for uniform consistency. Then apply one or two coats as it comes in the can, spreading each coat evenly over the surface. As the job progresses, watch for runs, keeping them stroked out before they harden. Note: Use grade 6-o sandpaper on undercoat and in between coats of paint or enamel for removing roughness. Do not sand or use steel wool on final coat.

At the end of each painting or enameling session, clean the brush in either paint thinner or turpentine.

Completing The Odds And Ends

14-72. When you think your home is complete, don't be too hasty to move in. Rather, make a final check on the little things that usually require doing before the house is really finished.

Make a punch list. This list shows exactly what is needed in the entire house, inside and outside from the top of the roof to the bottom of the basement. Such

14-71. Prepare the trim for painting or enameling exactly as recommended in the previous step for preparing trim for sealing stain.

Purchase a top-quality interior paint or interior semi-gloss enamel. Then follow the manufacturer's instructions. Generally, an undercoat is required as the first coat. When it is thoroughly dry, fill in any nail holes, dents, or flaws in the wood with plastic wood. Next sand the wood and plastic wood filler smooth with number o sandpaper. Do not apply so much pressure as to expose the bare wood. Apply plastic wood again if the holes,

a list includes all unfinished items, damaged places during construction, and overlooked items and their locations in or out of the house. In your examination, make a notation of such items as noticeable dents in walls, floors, trim, and ceilings, unfilled nail holes, scratches on finished surfaces, uncaulked bathtub, sinks, lavatories, and shower stalls, broken furnishings, such as a broken leg on a lavatory, loose paneling, a nail missing here, a screw there, broken plumbing and lighting fixtures, etc.

Above all, check the working drawings and specifications to see if anything is actually missing. For instance, don't be surprised if you find no drain in the laundry area, or that the electric water heater is in place and properly connected to the water pipes but there is no 230-volt electric line provided for heating the water. The best of home builders may end up with such items on his punch list.

PART II | KEYS TO BETTER BUILDING

THE
EXCAVATION

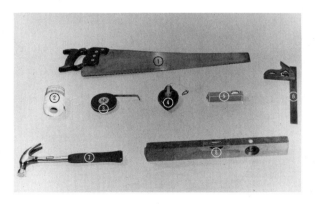

A-1. Other than power equipment or a shovel as mentioned in **A-3,** you will need the eight basic tools shown in the group photograph here and described below.

1. Hand saws come in several varieties. Here you need a crosscut saw for cutting boards across the grain. The crosscut saw has 8, 11, or 12 teeth per inch. Naturally, the more teeth per inch, the finer the cut. This is the reason most carpenters use an 11- or 12-point saw for finish work, such as cutting door and window trim boards, and an 8-point saw for rougher cutting.

2. You will need a lightweight cord made of nylon.

3. For accuracy, use a 50-foot steel tape rather than a cloth tape for measuring dimensions more than 3 feet in length. If you are purchasing a tape, select one with special markings indicated every 16 inches, 32 inches, 48 inches, etc. Such markings will save time later on, come framing time where 2×4s, 2×6s, etc. are laid out on 16-inch centers.

4. A combination chalk line and plumb bob consists of a weight attached to a heavily chalked string. It is a tool used to obtain a vertical line. CAUTION: Plan to plumb on a calm day, if possible. Wind tends to push lightweight plumb bobs to one side, creating an error as the line moves out of plumb.

5. Locating benchmarks and completing other building layout jobs can be done quickly and accurately with a building level or transit. Such instruments are quite expensive when purchased to do only a single building job. On the other hand, one can be rented rather cheaply. A hand sighting level costs approximately $3.50. If the builder is extremely accurate in his work, it can be used quite effectively for laying out drainage ditches, foundations, contour plowing, grading, fences, water levels, and gardens.

6. A combination square consists of a steel blade (marked off in fractions of inches) set at right angles to the inside face of a wood or metal stock. Use a combination square for checking squareness of edges and sides of boards. Also, use it as a guide in marking a board "square" prior to sawing.

7. Carpenter hammers come in different sizes. If you plan to use a single hammer for the building job, select one weighing 16 ounces.

8. A level has a rectangular body of wood or metal. A glass tube, partially filled with a non-freezing liquid, is recessed in its side and near the end. Use a level in bringing your work to a horizontal or vertical position, which is in-

dicated when the small bubble in the tube is exactly centered.

Look at the picture. Notice that the side and end tubes are at right angles. When the bubble of the side tube is at the center, the level is in a vertical position. On the other hand, when the bubble of the edge tube is at the center, the level is in a horizontal position. For all-round building needs select one 24 inches long, if you wish to purchase only a single level.

A-2. Use the following table and the reading material in the excavation section of this book to determine material needs at this point.

EXCAVATION MATERIALS

Name	Description
Corner stakes and excavation stakes	Scrap lumber
Nails	6-penny box
Batter boards	1 × 4-inch lumber 6 feet long
Batter-board stakes	Scrap lumber

A-3. A strong determination, a rugged back, and a shovel will remove dirt. But you can do the job easier and better by employing an operator of a tractor with a bulldozer blade attached.

A-4. If you have come across the word "benchmark" in your reading, perhaps you wondered what it meant. A benchmark is simply a known point of elevation. On city, state, and federal projects a surveyor establishes the benchmark as a definite height above sea level. Generally, in residential work the benchmark is arbitrarily established at 100.00. Thus, 100.00+ is above the benchmark, while 100.00— is below. Benchmarks throughout the area are related.

Check your house plans for floor elevation. If given, this is a given point above an established benchmark. For instance, suppose your plans call for a 102.75+ feet for the finish floor level. This would mean 2¾ feet higher than the benchmark, if the arbitrary elevation of 100.00 was chosen for the benchmark.

A-5. Generally, local regulations specify the minimum distance permitted in locating a house from the front and side lot lines. If you are not familiar at this point with local building code requirements, STOP CONSTRUCTION until you find out. Also, be sure that your lot was originally surveyed by a licensed surveyor. Also check the protective conveyances. If they exist, a copy of this document should be on record in the county courthouse. Your real-estate salesman should be familiar with such regulations and should advise you accordingly.

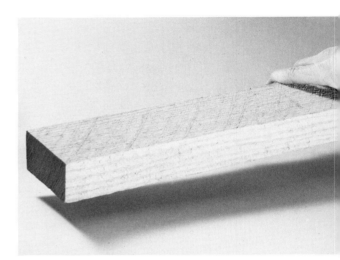

A-6. Finished boards referred to as 1 inch thick are not necessarily so. Generally, such boards are only ¾ inch thick. The difference results when the boards are planed at the mill. Also, the widths are generally short of their stated dimensions for the same reason. The board shown in the picture is a piece of 2×4 in the rough exactly as it was sawed at the mill. It is actually 2 inches thick and 4 inches wide. Since the ends of boards are not planed, such dimensions are exact or a bit longer than stated.

ACTUAL SIZES OF FRAMING LUMBER

Stated size	Actual size
2×4	1½ × 3½
2×6	1½ × 5½
2×8	1½ × 7¼
2×10	1½ × 9¼
2×12	1½ × 11¼

A-7. Mark guidelines accurately in preparation for sawing. Then do not cut on them. Rather,

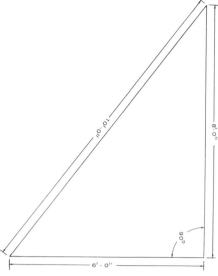

angle opposite the hypotenuse (longest side) a 90° or right angle.

A-10. Always doublecheck your measurements before going to the next step.

cut to the side into the waste stock. Since the thickness of the saw blade cuts through waste stock, the finished piece of wood is the exact length desired.

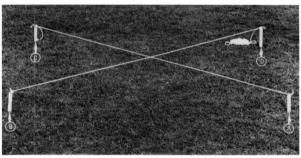

A-11. You can test the layout thus far by measuring the diagonals AC and BD with a steel tape. The corners are square only if the diagonals are equal in length.

Recheck to be certain the distances between nails AB, BC, CD, and DA correspond to the distances indicated on the house plans.

A-12. If your building plans call for an irregularly shaped house, lay it out from a large rectangle also. Lay out the offsets and wings later in the building program.

A-8. Using a combination square, pencil, and handsaw, mark and cut ends of boards as indicated for making the lap joint.

A-9. Using the layout square method is called the 6-8-10 rule. It is based on the fact that a triangle whose legs (sides) are exactly 6, 8, and 10 feet long, is a right-angle triangle, with the

A-13. Also, this is the time to establish your grade elevations. A rule of thumb is to keep your grade lines somewhat in harmony with adjoining properties and street-curb elevations if you are building in an improved area. You will want to be certain that surface water from your property does not drain on your neighbors' properties and vice versa. Keeping this consideration in mind, the slope of the finished yard from the house is a personal matter, but a grade or slope of 1 percent is considered good practice by many house architects. This means the ground would drop one foot for each 100 lineal feet. To ensure a drier basement, plan the first 3 to 4 feet next to the house for a drop of from 3 to 5 percent; then continue with a 1-percent grade.

A-14. If stake is too long after being driven firmly into the ground, square and cut to desired length with a handsaw.

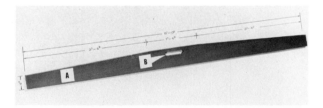

A-15. If your level is not long enough to reach from one stake to another, place a straightedge underneath the level.

You can make a straightedge from an 8-foot length of straight-grained 1⅛×6 white pine. If the two edges are not exactly straight and parallel, use a carpenter's plane to make them so. Now taper the board and cut a handle for ease of handling. Then paint the board with two coats of your outside color choice. Painting the board is essential as it helps to prevent warping.

A plane is a finishing tool used by carpenters for smoothing boards or other surfaces made of wood. It is made up of a stock and a cutting edge called an iron. There are a number of planes, ranging in size from a small block plane to a large jointer plane. Each one serves the skilled craftsman in a special way. Those planes to be used in planing with the grain are called bench planes, while those used to plane across the grain are called block planes. If you want an all-purpose plane for general carpenter work, purchase a jack plane (14 to 16 inches in length). A jack plane

properly sharpened can be used for jobs ordinarily done with a smooth plane (5½ to 12 inches in length) or a jointer plane (28 to 30 inches in length).

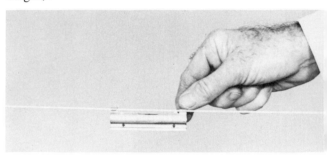

A-16. Prepare the sewer trench by stretching a nylon cord between two stakes. Drive one stake firmly into the ground next to the building foundation and 8 inches out from one of the trench side lines. Drive a second stake next to and above the sanitary sewer tap location and 8 inches out from the same trench side line. Since the line must be level, the length of the stakes will depend upon the elevation between them. Generally, the low point of the line should be about 1 foot above the ground before digging begins.

Now hang the line level, as shown in the picture, on the cord midway between the two stakes. Slowly raise or lower the cord, as the case might be, on the stake near the sanitary sewer tap until the cord is perfectly level.

Next measure the distance between the two stakes. After figuring slope per foot, lower and fasten the cord near the sanitary sewer accordingly. Thus, if your distance is 50 feet between the foundation and the sewer tap and you desire a slope of ¼ inch per foot, you would lower one end of the cord 12½ inches.

Now dig the trench near the foundation to the required depth. Then cut a stake, so when held in a perpendicular position, it is exactly the same length as the distance between the cord and the bottom with the measuring stake as you dig. Use a straightedge and a carpenter's level along the bottom of the ditch, when it is completed, as a final check for proper slope.

A-18. Building tradesmen use a combination chalk line and plumb bob or an ordinary plumb bob (a line or cord weighted at one end) to determine verticality. Sometimes a carpenter's level is used in a vertical position for the same purpose.

A-19. Use the leveling instrument and your rod to find out when the ground floor is exactly deep enough at all given points.

A-17. Before digging any ditch or excavation be sure of location of gas and water pipes and underground electric lines if they exist.

The picture shows the effect created by one backhoe operator who accidently dug into a water line.

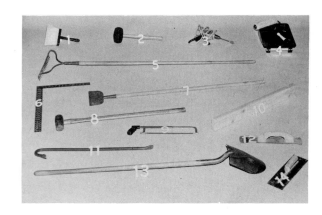

B

THE
FOUNDATION
AND
THE
BASEMENT
FLOOR

B-1. Some of the tools called for in constructing a foundation are shown in Key A-1. In addition, you will need the tools discussed below and shown in the photograph.

1. If your plans call for cement paint to be applied to either the outside or inside of the concrete walls, use an 8-inch whitewash brush for making the application.

2. For smoother walls, tap the inside of the outside forms with a mechanic's rubber hammer as concrete is being poured.

3. An electric drill with a proper bit makes holes in wood easily and quickly, but a hand-operated brace and bit serves the building needs just as well if you don't mind using a little elbow grease. Often electric power is lacking at the site and you will need a set of auger bits and a brace.

4. A paint roller and a tray are handy for applying oil to the forms before their erection.

5. Use a garden rake for spreading concrete within forms of footing size or larger. The rake is a much better tool for such a job than a shovel.

6. Many people refer to the framing square as a "steel" square. This is not accurate, because all types of squares may be obtained entirely of steel. This square is used especially for house framing and is correctly called a framing square. Select a framing square 16×24 inches. The longer arm of the square is called the body, while the shorter arm is called the tongue. The point at which the tongue and body meet on the outside edge is called the heel.

7. Working a flattened hoe or lawn edger up and down the sides of the forms as the concrete is being poured tends to make for smooth, even finished walls.

8. An 8- or 10-pound sledge hammer, whichever size you can handle best, is a convenient tool for driving stakes, especially if the ground is hard.

9. Hacksaws are used primarily for cutting metal. As with most saws, the blades come with different size teeth. For cutting conduit, select a blade with 32 teeth per inch.

10. A heavy straightedge, such as a 2×4, is used to strike off or smooth freshly poured concrete.

11. Wrecking bars come in various sizes. The one pictured is 30 inches long. This is a handy tool for pulling spike nails and prying framing lumber apart to correct mistakes.

12. Floats are made of either wood or metal. A float helps to push down coarse rock and to bring fine material, such as mortar, to the surface before using the cement finisher's trowel.

13. Shovels come in various sizes and shapes. The long-handled shovel pictured above is ideally suited for digging footing trenches and most other small excavation jobs involved in building a house.

14. A cement finisher's trowel consists of a slightly curved metal blade with a handle. It is used to produce the finish effect on a concrete surface.

B-2. Now is the time to figure how much and what kinds of materials you need for the basement job. Use the following material list as a guide in estimating your needs. The list is intended for a house with a basement; if your building project does not include a basement, eliminate the items you will not need.

FOUNDATION AND BASEMENT FLOOR MATERIALS

Name	Description
Footing stakes	1×2, length to suit
2×4 footing form	Length to suit
Concrete	Mixture and amount to suit
Basement prefabricated wall forms	Number to suit
Nails	¾-inch; 6-penny, 8-penny, and 16-penny box; and 1-inch concrete nails, amount to suit
Electric conduit	Size and amount to suit
Electric outlet and switch boxes	Number to suit
Wall form filler box material	1-inch lumber, width and length to suit, amount to suit
Form oil	Amount to suit
Wall ties and spreaders	Number to suit
Wall form pipe	Plastic or metal in sizes to suit
Anchor bolts, nuts, and washers	½-inch thick and 12 inches long, number to suit
Field tile	Number to suit
Asphalt building paper	15-pound weight
Basement wall waterproof coating	Amount to suit
Crushed stone	¾-inch minimum diameter
Basement wall door and window frames	Number to suit
Polyethylene	4-mil, amount to suit
Wood or steel girders	Sizes and number to suit
Steel bearing posts for girders	Sizes and number to suit
Reinforcement wire	#10 grid (6-inch squares), amount to cover floor area prior to concreting
Plastic pipe and fittings for seep-water drainage under concrete floor if desired	3 3-inch in 10-foot lengths, amount to suit
Plumbing drain system under concrete floor	See plumbing chapter
2×8s for basement entrance steps if required	Lengths to suit
2-inch lumber for concrete porch floors if required	Sizes to suit
Bell tile to carry foundation seep water to storm sewer	4-inch diameter, number of feet to suit

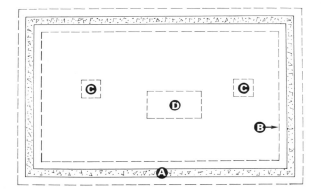

B-3. Generally, concrete construction above ground, such as wall A, are indicated by solid lines. Such construction as footings B, footing pads C, and chimney base D are shown with dotted lines.

B-4. Doublecheck by using leveling instrument and helper to check elevation of the four wall corners.

B-5. The length times the width times the depth of the footing equals the volume of concrete required. In one of the houses in this book these figures were: 140 feet long × 16 inches wide × 8 inches deep (chimney and footing pads included) = 124.44⅔ cubic feet. Concrete is ordered by the cubic *yard* or fraction thereof, and there are 27 cubic feet in a cubic yard. 124.44⅔ cubic feet

÷ 27 = 4.6+ cubic yards. Therefore, 4¾ cubic yards of 1:3:5 concrete (the first number represents the proportion of cement; the second sand; and the third gravel or rock.) were ordered for the footing job. It is always best to plan for a little more concrete than is actually needed.

B-6. For best results, select a time to pour concrete when the temperature is between 40° and 80° F.

B-7. If you prefer to mix your own concrete rather than use ready-mix, here is how:

Mix in the proportion of 1 sack of cement to 3 cubic feet of sand to 5 cubic feet of gravel (not larger than 1½ inches) to 6 gallons of water. CAUTION: Always mix the sand, cement, and gravel thoroughly while dry for each batch of concrete. Then add the water as you continue to mix until concrete is ready to pour.

The mixture described above is satisfactory for footings and foundation walls but not for basement walls. Remember that the strength, watertightness, and durability of concrete are at their best when the correct amount of clean water is used in the mixing process. If the water is fit to drink, it is fit to use in mixing concrete.

B-8. You can mix concrete in a large mixing box with the aid of a garden hoe. Make a mixing box that will accommodate the amount of concrete desired for each batch. Two boards, ends cut at an angle, with a sheet of 28-gauge galvanized iron nailed on the bottom edges made the small-batch mixing box pictured here. For mixing large batches of concrete, a 6×8-foot box approximately 8 inches deep with the bottom covered with 1-inch lumber or galvanized iron is generally satisfactory.

If you plan to mix concrete for several large jobs, consider buying or renting a small power mixer, either electric or gasoline.

B-9. Be sure you have at least one able-bodied helper. Also, check the form layout for durability. Then have your shovel, deep-tray wheelbarrow, and other required tools on the spot, ready for the truck the moment it arrives.

B-10. Want some free patio blocks or stepping blocks? If so, provide a few easy-to-make 2×4 forms placed on level ground in an out-of-the-way place, dimensioned according to your own requirements. The stepping blocks I made measure 14×14 inches, and they were poured each time the ready-mix truck contained more concrete than was required for a particular job.

B-11. If you value your time or plan to hire the work done, it is not realistic to build forms from plywood using 2×4 material as framing.

It is more economical either to rent prefabricated forms and set them up yourself or hire the owner to do it for you. Be sure to use forms that use keys and wedges to hold the structure firmly in place while the concrete is being poured.

B-12. The illustration shows how forms are held together with keys and wedges.

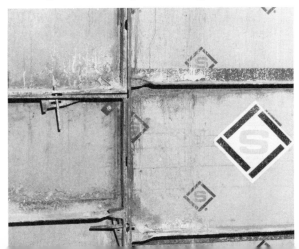

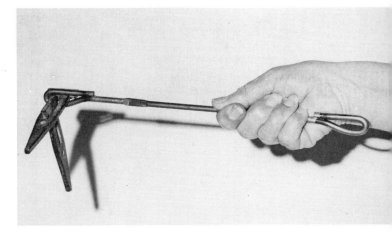

B-13. Tierods with triangular wedges driven tightly through slotted keys hold the forms the required distance apart, making for an accurate vertical and horizontal installation.

The 2-foot-wide prefabricated forms used in the three houses in this book had tierod spacing holes located 8 inches from the top and bottom and 6 inches from each side of a completed 8-foot section. Then the remaining vertical holes were spaced 20 inches apart.

B-14. Do not use conduit with bakelite or porcelain outlet or switch boxes.

Cut the conduit to length with a hacksaw. Then, using a file, ream the cut ends inside and taper. If bends are required, use a conduit bender.

Fit conduit to boxes by fitting the threadless end of a connector over the conduit. Next, insert the connector through the box knockout. Then tighten the locknut.

CAUTION: Do not pull wires through the

conduit at this time. Also, it is a good idea to stuff newspaper tightly inside the boxes. This prevents cement seepage from filling the boxes.

RECOMMENDED CONDUIT SELECTION

Conduit size	Size of wires carried
½-inch	4 #14 or 3 #12
¾-inch	4 #10 or #12; 3 #8
1¼-inch	4 #6; 3 #2, #3, or #4
1½-inch	3 #1
2-inch	4 #1/0 or 3 #3/0

B-15. For each utility-pipe opening, locate a form pipe in the wall forms with an i.d. (inside diameter) slightly larger than the o.d. (outside diameter) of the intended service pipe. The form pipes remain in place to become a permanent part of the basement wall.

B-16. Here is the information you need if you prefer to mix your own concrete for the walls rather than purchase ready-mix delivered by truck:

Mix in the proportion of 1 sack of cement to 2 cubic feet of sand to 3 cubic feet of gravel (not larger than 1½-inch) to 5 gallons of clean water. Mix in the same manner as described previously for mixing concrete. This mix applies whenever watertight concrete is desired.

B-17. For smooth walls be sure a vibrator is supplied by the ready-mix company if it has one. If a vibrator is unavailable, work a flattened hoe or a lawn edger up and down between the concrete and the side walls as the pouring operation continues. Also, as you work the flattened hoe, have your helper alternately tap the inside, then the outside forms with a rubber hammer as the concrete is being poured.

B-18. All through the pouring operation, check for even distribution of the concrete. Pour the horizontal layers no more than 6 to 12 inches thick, with the deposits at no greater than 6-foot intervals.

B-19. Check your house plans for the floor-joist layout, since each anchor bolt must be located between joists.

B-20. For areas where basements are known to be wet, use a 6-inch fiber roof-coating brush

to coat the outside of the basement walls with an asbestos mastic.

B-21. Upon delivery, stack field tile out of the way to protect it from breakage.

B-22. Now is the time to make a decision: you can plan to pour the basement floor now, or you can skip these steps and pour the floor later. It is a good idea to pour the floor after the house is under roof if the weather is apt to be rainy or too cold.

CAUTION: This is not the time to try your hand at concrete finishing for the first time. Unless you are experienced in finishing large concrete areas do not take on the role of a concrete finisher for the basement floor job. Rather, engage a more experienced person to wield the trowel and assume the role of a helper.

B-23. Be sure to dig ditches in a straight line so as to bypass footing pads.

B-24. The number of screeds required depends upon the skill of the concrete finisher and his helper. On a basement floor up to 32 feet wide, many skilled workers prepare only one screed. This is placed down the center of the area. Then they snap chalk lines parallel to the screed on each side wall. When the concrete is poured, they work the concrete level with a 2×4 placed edgewise, with one end on top of the screed and the other end worked along the top of the line snapped on the sidewall. Less experienced men prefer to spread concrete between two parallel screeds located 8 to 10 feet apart. This type of operation eliminates the lines snapped on the sidewalls.

B-25. If you prefer to mix your own concrete for your basement floor rather than purchase ready-mix, use the same mix as described previously in this chapter for basement walls.

B-26. Know exactly where you want the concrete placed before it begins to set and harden. Also be prepared to handle it as soon as possible. During cold weather, speed is not as important, since concrete does not set as quickly as in hot weather, when sometimes it sets in as little as 20 minutes. A cardinal principle in concrete finishing is this: The more concrete has set and the more you disturb it, the more its strength is lost.

B-27. Tamping concrete helps to eliminate air pockets and tends to bring the finer materials to the top.

B-28. Water may stand on the surface following the striking-off operation. Concrete finishers refer to this as "bleeding." If bleeding occurs, rest until the water disappears. Under no circumstance pour powdered cement or a mixture of dry cement and sand on the surface to absorb the water. This would cause the finished floor to form dust, and it will not withstand normal wear.

B-29. Striking-off action levels off the high places, carrying the concrete to the low spots. As the striking-off operation proceeds, shovel concrete into the remaining low places.

B-30. Waiting until the slab completely supports your weight is much too late for floating and troweling. If you wish, use platforms, such as 2×2-foot squares of 5/8-inch plywood, placed on the slab as stepping blocks so that places impossible to reach from off the slab can be floated or troweled.

B-31. For basement floors in the houses pictured in this book, a troweling machine was used. Even so, some hand finishing around drains and floor edges was necessary for securing a professional finish job.

B-32. The period of time between completing the floating job and the beginning of the troweling operation may be as little as 20 minutes during warm, humid weather or more than an hour during cold, dry weather.

The rule of thumb for the exact time to begin troweling is this: It is time to begin the final finish operation when you can pass your trowel in an arc over the surface without its digging in or causing the concrete to bleed. Watch the finishing operation carefully. Under no condition allow the concrete to "get away from you." Nothing is more heart-sickening than to live with a basement floor that was not properly finished.

B-33. From this point until the floor is finished, keep the pouring of concrete ahead of the final finishing operation. Here timing between the two is of utmost importance.

B-34. When the area between two screeds has been poured, leveled, and floated, remove the iron pipe nearest the wall. Next, drive the remaining stakes flush with the rock floor. Then, fill the void left by the pipe and stakes with fresh concrete, leveling it with a float.

Now use the iron pipe again, along with new stakes and nails, to form a new screed 8 to 10 feet from and parallel to the remaining screed. This becomes the second area to concrete.

Finally, complete the operation of building screeds and pouring, floating, and finishing concrete until the floor is completed. CAUTION: Be certain all pipes have been removed and their stakes driven flush with the rock floor before the concrete floor is completely finished.

B-35. In the three houses shown in the book, one week was allowed for the floors to harden before the step forms were built.

B-36. Generally, a convenient relationship between riser and run totals 17 inches, where the riser height is a minimum of 6 inches and a maximum of 7 inches as indicated in the table.

Riser (inches)	Run (inches)
6	11
6⅛	10⅞
6¼	10¾
6⅜	10⅝
6½	10½
6⅝	10⅜
6¾	10¼
6⅞	10⅛
7	10

B-37. If you lack confidence in pouring concrete in the step forms as described, pattern them after those in the picture here for a more sturdy set.

Select two 2×4 stringers A about 3 feet longer than the proposed distance between the top and bottom step. Next cut risers B as described in section 6-46. Using 16-penny nails, fasten these to short pieces of 2×4 cleats C. Then nail cleats to stringers A, equal distance apart for designed step tread, being certain bottom of riser is level with top of next lowest riser. Using 8-penny box nails, fasten a 1×4 brace D to each 2×4 cleat and stringer, to complete form.

If convenient, brace form by placing a 2×4 from lower end of each stringer to opposite wall. Otherwise, use 2×4 bracing E.

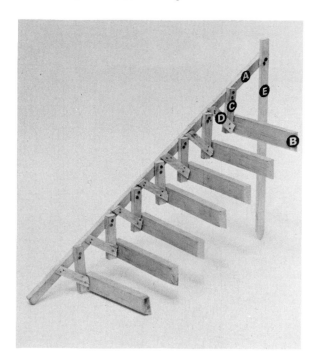

To show clearer detail, stringer A, cleats C, and braces D are not shown on right side of form.

B-38. Be sure complete angle cut on bottom of risers is free of concrete. This helps make for a smooth joint between the back of the run and the bottom of the corresponding riser.

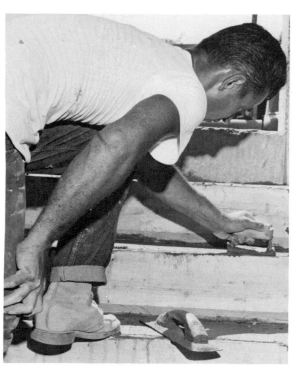

B-39. To prevent a rough edge where riser joins run, use a concrete edger at the time of finishing the step runs. Here the finisher alternates between the edger and the finishing trowel shown on the lower step.

B-40. Here the concrete finisher is using a darby—a large smoothing tool without a float's long handle—instead of a float because he can reach all the porch area while standing on the ground.

C

FRAMING: SILLS AND FLOORS

C-1. Most of the tools called for in framing the sills and floors have been previously explained. The four additional tools in the picture here are also called for during the framing operation.

1. This is a 28-ounce hammer made by Stanley Tools. Since it is 12 ounces heavier than the normal carpenter's hammer, it hits harder and is ideal for fastening together 2-inch lumber. It can be used for all framing operations from floor to roof.

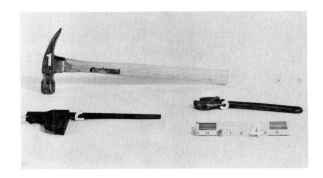

2. The combination square is rightfully a combination tool. It has a movable head that can be made to slide along the blade and clamp at any required location, and combined with the square it is a level and a miter.

3 and 4. The wrench and rule are common tools usually found in home tool kits.

C-2. The following list of materials is given as a guide for framing the sill and floor parts of your house. Use it as a checklist in estimating exact needs from your house plans.

SILL AND FLOOR FRAMING MATERIALS

Name	Description
Sills	2 × 8s
Headers	2 × 10s
Joists	2 × 10s
Bridging	1 × 4s
Subfloor	⅝-inch interior-grade plywood in 4 × 8-foot sheets
Nails	6-, 8-, 16-, and 20-penny box and 8-penny finishing, 6-penny resin-coated.
Stairs	2 × 12s, length to suit
	Riser and tread material

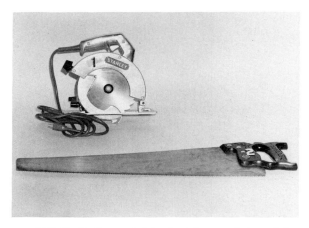

C-3. Both the portable electric saw (1) and the 8-point handsaw (2) are handy tools to have on the job for the entire carpentry operation. Of course, an electric saw is of no use unless you have electricity on the site.

C-4. Before beginning floor-cutting operations, make two sawhorses. Only one, as shown in the picture, requires a tray bottom. Light enough to move from place to place on the job as a portable workbench, the tray is handy for holding nails and small tools.

Pairs of sawhorses should vary in length, height, and spread of legs because they are cus-tom-built to suit the needs of specific builders. Here are the materials I used to build a horse for building the houses in this book:

One 2×6 3 feet long for the beam; four 2×4s 29¼ inches long (cut from a 10-foot 2×4) for the legs; two 1×4s 13½ inches long and two 1×4s 10 inches long (cut from an 8-foot 1×4) to serve as leg bracing as well as sides of the tray; a 12×21⅜-inch piece ⅝-inch plywood for the tray bottom; 16 8-penny box nails, and 28 6-penny box nails.

Begin by cutting four 2×4 legs A equal in length. Cut both top 1 and bottom 2 at the same angle. The spread you desire for the legs deter-mines the angle of cut. At any rate, these angles must be parallel to the floor when the legs are mounted later in place on beam B.

Next mark and cut leg angles indicated by arrow 3. Here again the amount of leg spread desired determines the angle of cut. The spread of legs on the inside in the picture measures 11 inches at the bottom. Begin cut 3 in top of legs in the center and cut to a depth of 1½ inches, the thickness of beam B. CAUTION: Be sure angle cut is in right direction so that when legs are assembled to beam, angles 1 and 2 will be parallel to the floor. Next make cut 4 in legs the same angle as cuts 1 and 2. Top of legs should now look like the detail shown in picture.

Now measure in 3 inches from ends of beam B, marking off cuts 3½ inches wide (width of a 2×4 leg) on both sides of each end. Saw cuts equal distance on top and bottom of beam to a depth equal to the top widths of legs A (13/16-inch in picture detail).

Using four 8-penny box nails for top of each leg, fasten legs in place to beam.

Next cut 1×4 braces C to fit as pictured.

CAUTION: Be sure brace height is such that plywood bottom will fit snugly at bottom edges of bracing. Here bracing may be raised or lowered if builder decides to alter tray size. Using three 6-penny box nails, fasten end of each long brace to a corresponding 2×4 leg. Locate short braces tightly against inside of two corresponding legs and between two long braces. Drive two 6-penny box nails through sides of long braces into end grain of each short brace.

Complete project by sawing ends of plywood tray bottom D square. Then rip the two sides at same angle as legs. Next locate bottom of tray parallel to bottom of braces. Now nail in place with 6-penny box nails, three on each side and one on each end.

In constructing your second sawhorse, you don't have to build a tray bottom, unless you think two such tool containers will be useful.

C-5. Blocks may be as wide as 2×4s or as wide as the headers themselves.

C-6. The blocks help provide support for the walls later. The headers laid out for attaching floor joists require no blocks, since here the joists themselves provide the partial support for walls located later. This is the reason the workman in the picture in step 7-9 is not fastening blocks in place to the header nearest him. Rather, he is preparing to mark joist locations.

C-7. Allowing for plumbing and heating openings now will save both time and framing material later on. Also you are likely to have a more substantial structure for your efforts.

C-8. If your toilet is to be placed against the stack wall, frame a minimum joist clearance of 16 inches. If your toilet is to be placed away from the stack wall, frame opening with single headers so as not to require cutting of joist when soil pipes are installed.

C-9. If the rear wall of your fireplace is located outside the house wall proper, you will not need a well for the fireplace.

C-10. Space the widths between double joists, called for under partitions, the width of a 2×4. This allows the partition studs to come directly over a space, leaving room for pipes and other equipment to pass between joists, if necessary.

C-11. If your house plans call for headers supporting more than four tail beams, support ends in metal joist hangers.

C-12. The picture shows one 2×4 toenailed to another 2×4. The arrow points to the proper way to toenail one piece of wood to another. Toenailing requires nails driven in pairs. Therefore, there are two corresponding nails to be driven on the opposite side of the 2×4.

C-13. It would take a small book to explain stair building completely. The kind of stairs shown in steps 7-25 to 7-27 is called the straight flight. It contains no turns or landings. The straight flight is made up of three straight stringers on which treads and risers are fastened. Because this set of stairs is built between two walls, it is called a housed stairs.

C-14. For a finish effect, use tread material with a nose (semicircular design) along one outside edge as seen in the picture in step 7-27.

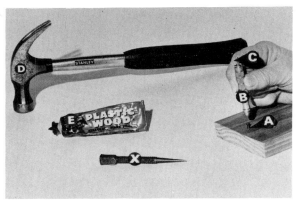

C-15. Nail sets are designed to drive heads of brads or finishing nails below the surface of wood, after which the holes are filled with wood filler.

The fingers in the picture hold a self-centering nail set about to be used to set a finishing nail. The conventional nail set is indicated with an X.

Stanley Tools, manufactures both conventional and self-centering nail sets. I recommend a self-centering nail set because it eliminates any chance of marring wood surfaces, which can sometimes happen when one uses a conventional nail set. Like traditional nail sets, self-centering nail sets come in different sizes for different sized finishing nails or brads. Be sure to use the set designed for the size finishing nails or brads that you plan to set.

Drive finishing nail A into wood until head protrudes ⅛ inch.

Then place sleeve B of self-centering set over nail head.

Next strike plunger C with hammer D to set nail in wood (plunger retracts automatically) slightly below the surface.

Finish by filling hole with wood filler E.

FRAMING: STUDDING AND SHEATHING

D-1. No additional tools are required for studding and sheathing beyond those recommended in Key C-1.

D-2. The following list of materials is given to assist in estimating studding and sheathing needs as required by your house plans:

D-3. Lengths of 12 and 16 feet make for easy wall raising later. While positioning plates be sure joints of sole and top plates are staggered.

D-4. Because studs are laid out ("laid out" means marking the position of each wall stud on the sole and top plates, which comes in a later step) on 16-inch centers, 12- and 16-foot 2×4s work out with a minimum of waste.

D-5. If you are unfamiliar with dimensions of corner studs and partition studs, read ahead in this chapter where actual steps for their construction are given.

D-6. The construction of the frame will be simpler and more accurate if you cut all pieces accurately first. As you proceed to cut and assemble individual parts of the frame, check your plans for exact specifications.

STUDDING AND SHEATHING MATERIALS

Name	Description
Plates (sole, top, and cap)	2×4s 12 feet long
	2×4s 16 feet long
Wall studs	2×4s 8 feet long unless different stud lengths are required
Special studs	Sometimes special studs wider than 2×4s are called for
Window and door header boards	2×4 minimum width
Header board shims	Laths or strips of ½-inch plywood
Wall bracing between studs if required	2×4s (short pieces)
Temporary stud bracing	1-inch lumber 12 to 14 feet long
Sheathing material	4×8-foot sheets of ⅝-inch plywood or insulating board, depending upon specifications accompanying house plans
Building paper if plywood sheathing is required	15-pound
Nails	6-, 8-, 16-, and 20-penny
	1-inch roofing nails for fastening building paper to plywood sheathing if used
	1-inch common nails for fastening lath material or plywood strips to header boards

HEADER MATERIALS

Lumber size (always use two pieces on edge)	Length required	
	Interior-wall openings	Exterior-wall openings
2 × 4s	3-foot maximum	3½-foot maximum
2 × 6s	5½-foot maximum	6½-foot maximum
2 × 8s	6½-foot maximum	8½-foot maximum
2 × 10s	9½-foot maximum	11-foot maximum
2 × 12s	11½-foot maximum	12½-foot maximum

D-7. Locate headers on edge to provide maximum strength. Use the above table only if your house plans are not clear on this point of construction.

D-8. I recommend using factory-made exterior and interior door units (I use those manufactured by Morgan-Wightman, St. Louis, Missouri 63166) rather than making door frames and fitting doors to them yourself. Factory assembly assures tight miters, correct mortising and boring for locks, and precision assembly of all parts. Packaged door units consist of weatherstrip (where needed), mortised hinges, door frame, door, and necessary trim, all assembled and ready to fasten in place. From rough opening to completely hung door takes only a fraction of the time necessary to prepare and hang a door by conventional methods, and the cost for all this is so reasonable that the builder cannot afford to take time to make the units himself.

If your plans call for sliding doors, be sure to study the packing slip found in each package. Knowing the specifications are most important, because some sliding doors require the combined widths of the doors plus 1 inch, while others require the combined width of the doors plus 2 inches.

D-9. Whether you rough-frame for double-hung windows, casement-type windows, awning windows, or picture windows, I recommend CARADCO packaged units such as wholesaled by Morgan-Wightman.

D-10. Additional operations to think about for special framing are built-in medicine cabinet, bathtub and lavatory, and soil stacks for bathrooms. If a cast-iron soil stack is called for, use 2 × 8s for wall framing, because a cast-iron hub requires a 6¼-inch opening. On the other hand, a 3-inch copper soil stack fits easily within 2 × 4 wall studs.

D-11. If enough help is available, it is possible to frame an entire side of a house, then raise it in place. It is much easier, however, to alternate 12- and 16-foot 2 × 4s for the sole and top plate. This makes the assembled frame easy to raise for two men.

D-12. If a broom closet or clothes closet is short and located in a protected area, it may be framed with 2-inch material. Such framing, of course, provides slightly more closet space.

D-13. In sighting top plates, you may find some with a crown, causing the top of the wall frame to bulge inward or outward, depending upon the direction of crown. Generally, this can be remedied by applying a cap plate with a similar crown in the opposite direction from the top plate crown. When the two are pulled together as they are nailed, the original crown usually disappears.

D-14. In addition to plywood sheathing, some builders use lumber applied diagonally or horizontally to the studding. Other builders use 25/32-inch insulating board sheathing, applying it in 4 × 8-foot panels. Still other builders use gypsum-board sheathing, made of a core of gypsum between two faces of water-repelling paper.

All three types of sheathing serve four purposes. They cover the frame, furnish a base for exterior trim, such as stone, brick or wood or hardboard siding, stiffen the building (giving more protection against wind pressure), and help provide insulation.

E

FRAMING: CEILING JOISTS, RAFTERS, ROOF DECKING, AND ROOF FELTING

Name	Description
Ceiling joists	2 × 8s
Ceiling joist bridging	2 × 8s
Common rafters	2 × 6s
Ridgeboard	2 × 8
Temporary rafter bracing	1-inch lumber
Collar beams	1 × 6s
Hip rafters	2 × 8s
Hip jack rafters	2 × 6s
Valley rafters	2 × 8s
Valley jack rafters	2 × 6s
Nails	1-inch
	8-, 10-, and 16-penny
Plywood sheathing material	⅝-inch plywood in 4 × 8 foot sheets
Roof felting	30-lb.
Staple gun and staples	
Laths or scrap lumber	

E-3. A shows a rectangular roof with the same slope or pitch on four sides. Notice that a ridge is formed at the top of the roof. This is called a hip roof. If a house is square the roof will come to a point as shown in B. The three houses in the illustrations in this book are rectangular and have hip roofs with gable intersecting roofs.

C shows a roof with one side of a single surface raised above the other. It is called a shed roof.

E-1. A stapler and a linoleum knife are the only tools required in addition to those recommended in Key C-1 for the framing jobs called for in this chapter.

E-2. Use the following list of materials as a guide in estimating your needs for this section of the framing operation:

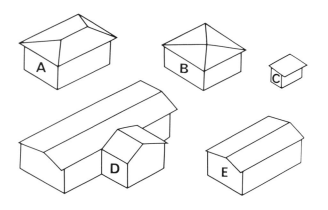

It is simple in design and construction and is used for some porches, sheds, or wherever roof appearance is not uppermost in the mind of the builder.

D shows a gable roof with an intersecting gable roof. A gable roof has two surfaces coming together, forming a ridge with gables at each end. Sometimes an intersecting roof is of hip design rather than gable.

If you want to build a house that is simple to design and comparatively inexpensive to construct, consider a simple gable roof as shown in E.

E-4. The following definitions tell how the structural members of a hip roof with an intersecting gable roof are involved in picture shown in step 9-1.

A. Wall plates, consisting of top and cap plates, that support the roof frame, were completed in Chapter 8.

B and C. Ceiling joists are fastened to the wall top plates. The main purpose of ceiling joists is to furnish a frame on which to fasten ceiling material later on. Generally, ceiling joists run across the narrow dimensions of the house. This, however, is not always true. Some joists may run in one direction and some in another direction. Stub ceiling joists, explained in step 9-3 are an example.

D. Ceiling nailers are generally 2-inch lumber nailed to cap plate so they extend as an overhang to which ceiling material is fastened later.

E. The major ridge is the ridge of the main roof.

F. A common rafter extends at right angles from the plate to the ridge.

G. A main ridge brace is a support for the common rafters. It is located between the cap plate of a partition wall and the ridge board.

H. A hip rafter extends from the corner of a wall plate to the ridge at an angle of 45° to the plate, and it forms the intersection of two adjacent roof slopes.

I. Jack rafters are of two kinds. A hip jack rafter extends from a plate to a hip rafter.

J. A valley rafter is one that connects two intersecting slopes of a roof at the valley. A supporting valley rafter extends from a plate to a hip rafter at right angles.

K. A short valley rafter extends from a plate to the supporting valley rafter.

L. A valley jack rafter extends from a ridge to a valley.

M. A cripple jack rafter extends from a hip to a valley. A cripple jack never reaches the plate or the ridge.

N. The minor ridge is the ridge of the intersecting roof.

O. In a house with a gable roof, the triangular area of the end wall that extends from the top of the wall cap plate to the rafters is called the gable. The two end 2×4 rafters are called gable rafters.

P. The rough facia board is 2-inch lumber nailed to the bottoms of the rafters extending around the perimeter of the house.

Q. A gable stud extends from top of wall cap plate to gable rafters.

E-5. Be sure there is an equal distance on each side of major ridge location on top plates and ends of house unless your plans call for different dimensions.

E-6. Joist sizes are recommended for ceiling loads only. If you plan to use attic space, then use ceiling joists the same size as floor joists. If ceiling joists are to carry any roof load, increase their width by 2 inches.

E-7. Before you cut the outer end of the joists, check two pieces of information: the pitch of roof A as shown on your house plans, and the height of the back of rafter B above plate.

E-8. As shown in the picture above, the span is the dimension of the house. Here two common rafters cover this distance. The run is that part of the span covered by one of the pair. A 12-inch

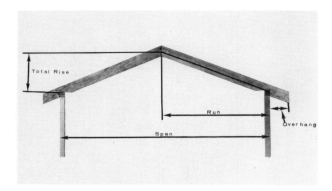

portion of the run of a rafter is referred to as the unit run. Because the run of a rafter is one-half the span of the building, the unit span is twice the unit run or 24 inches. The vertical distance from where the two common rafters meet to a point on the plate below is known as the total rise of the roof or rafter.

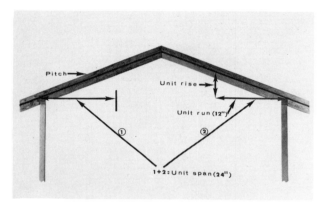

E-9. The unit rise is the rise in inches that the common rafter extends in a vertical direction for every foot of unit run. The pitch is the angle or slope of the roof from the ridge to the plate. The pitch is the ratio of the total rise of the roof to the total width of the house or total span.

If you need to find the pitch of your roof, divide the rise by the span.

If you need to find the rise of your roof, multiply the pitch by the span.

E-10. Bottom end of rafter is constructed by making vertical or plumb cut A. So the rafters

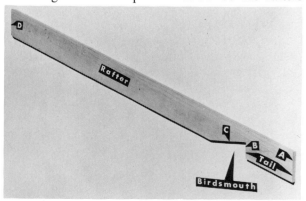

will rest firmly on the wall plate, a triangular section is cut from the bottom edge, called the bird's-mouth. It is constructed by sawing vertical cut B, called the plumb cut, and horizontal cut C, called the seat cut. The section between vertical cuts A and B is called the rafter tail. The top end D of each common rafter is cut vertically so that rafters located opposite each other meet in a straight line. Notice that cuts A, B, and D are all vertical or plumb cuts.

E-11. The depth of vertical cut in the bird's-mouth is governed by the strength required to carry the overhang. The greater the overhang, the greater is the thickness required of the rafter at this point. Generally, a 2½-inch vertical cut leaves a seat or horizontal cut in the bird's-mouth of sufficient size for fastening the rafter firmly to the plate.

The length of the vertical cut in the bird's-mouth affects the height of the rafter but will not alter the pitch of the roof.

E-12. Use a ridgeboard rather than have pairs of common rafters meet together at the top end. Not only does a ridgeboard make it easy to keep the top line of the roof straight, it also provides support and a nailer for roof sheathing between rafters.

The ridge of a gable roof is the length of the house plus the length of the two overhangs at the gable locations. The ridge of a hip roof is shorter than the length of the house, and its construction is fully explained later in Chapter 9.

When two rafters are separated at the top by a ridgeboard, the two lines meet in the center of the ridge, shown by point B. The distances between AB and CB are called the line lengths of the rafters. However, the rafter actually terminates at point D. Therefore, the distances AD and CD are called the true lengths. The short distance

BD, measured at right angles to the plumb or vertical cut, is called shortening. This is the location of the true ends of the rafters. As can be seen in the picture, the common rafters are shortened by half the ridge thickness.

Lines AB and CB are called measuring lines.

E-13. Use the framing square for calculating length of rafters used in the types of roofs described in this chapter. Examine the rafter table on the square, face side up. The numbers seen on the top edge of the blade represent unit rises of 2 to 18 inches per foot. Since 5 is the unit rise in the roofs of the three houses illustrated in this book, it is used as an example in this chapter wherever the unit rise number is required. Check the unit rise number called for on your house plans. If it is not 5, be sure to substitute your unit rise number each time 5 is used in the illustrations.

E-14. If ridgeboard is made up of two or more boards, be certain joints come halfway on a rafter joint.

E-15. Remember the unit run of 17 inches is as important a factor when laying out hip rafters as the unit run 12 inches is when laying out common rafters. Again, consult your framing square. Here is how the number 17 is found: The unit run of a hip rafter is the diagonal of a 12-inch square because the unit run of the common rafter is 12 inches (as seen on the square). Mathematically, the diagonal is 16.97 instead of 17, but for practical purposes 17 is used. Therefore, for every unit of common rafter run of 12 inches, the hip rafter has a unit run of 17 inches.

In future framing operations, other numbers are called for. Again check these against those on your square whenever such numbers are required.

E-16. Because hip rafters are located at the intersection of two slopes of a hip roof, each one is required to receive the ends of roof sheathing from both slopes. Providing two surfaces on the top edge makes it possible for the hip to receive the ends better. This step is called backing the hip.

E-17. If your plans call for an intersecting roof with a span the same as the span of the main roof, the ridge of both roofs A and C will meet on the same level as shown in the picture here. The common rafters of the main roof and those of the intersecting roof will have the same run. Therefore, construct both valley rafters B the same, with one exception, as described in step 9-38 for constructing the supporting valley rafter. The one exception is that here you make double side cuts to fit against both ridges A and C. The shortening is equal to half the 45° thickness of ridge as shown at D.

E-18. In a house with a gable roof, the triangular area of the end wall that extends from top of wall plate to the rafters is called the gable.

E-19. Sometimes plans call for gable dormers for the purpose of bringing more natural light inside the roof area and/or increasing attic floor space.

E-20. Building felt of 30-pound weight is 36 inches wide, and each roll contains 216 square feet. To find the number of rolls required, divide your total roof area by 216. To this number add enough felt to allow for the overlap on each layer applied to the roof.

E-21. Before laying the roofing felt, check the roof sheathing for projecting nailheads, which must be hammered home to prevent roof leakage later on.

E-22. This is a two-man job, one to unroll and one to do the stapling. Notice that while unrolling, the felt has a tendency to work toward the eaves. Use the parallel lines on the previously laid strip or sheathing board joints (if close by) as guidelines for straight laying.

F

THE FIREPLACE AND THE CHIMNEY

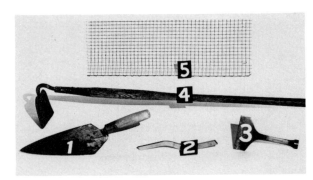

F-1. In addition to some of the basic carpenter's tools mentioned previously, the following masonry tools are required for building a fireplace and chimney:

1. The bricklayer's trowel is the largest of the trowels used in laying masonry.
2. Jointer tools come in different shapes, depending upon the shape of the joint desired. They are not required unless other than flush joints are desired on facing brick or stone joints.
3. Brick set, sometimes called a chisel, is especially designed for cutting blocks, stone, or bricks.
4. Mixing hoe has two holes in the blade. The garden hoe shown in the picture above makes a good substitute when the home builder is planning to do only a small amount of masonry work.
5. Wire screen (¼-inch grid) is used for separating usable sand from small rocks and stones.

F-2. Use the following table as a guideline in estimating the material for a fireplace:

MATERIALS FOR A TRADITIONAL FIREPLACE

Name	Description
Lumber	Mortar box sides
Mortar box bottom	30-gauge galvanized iron
Lumber	1×2-inch for sand screen frame
Wire screen	¼-inch mesh for sand screen
Nails	4-penny box
Mortar	Premixed or 1 part Portland cement to 1 part hydrated lime to 4 parts clean sand mixed with water
Blocks (lightweight concrete)	8×8×16-inch for base
	4×8×16-inch from floor line to roof line
Bricks	Face bricks (or stone) for chimney and front of fireplace
	Firebricks for hearth
Ash-pit door	Metal door located at bottom of chimney
Thimble	Fire-resistant liner for smokestack opening into chimney

Name	Description
Insulating material	Insulation between chimney and wood framing (generally included with metal fireplace unit)
Form material	For holding cement poured in hearth
Reinforcement rods	¼-inch in diameter
Ash-pit dump	Metal door located in hearth
Concrete	1 part Portland cement to 2 parts clean sand to 3 parts small rock mixed with water
Fire clay	Special clay used for laying fire bricks
Fireplace unit	Metal unit installed directly over hearth
Lintel	Angle iron located over fireplace opening
Flashing	Metal chimney flashing made of nonrusting metal
Chimney top	Stone or concrete slab to keep rain and snow from entering chimney
Mortar color (if desired)	Dry powder, color of your choice
Tin	1/32-inch-thick piece of tin for making guides to hold line level
Nylon cord	Cord used as a guide for laying masonry
Gunny sack	A cloth sack used to hold grain
Sawdust	Secure from local sawmill
Silicone sealer	Clear liquid used to waterproof masonry exposed to weather above ground level

F-3. If you have laid blocks satisfactorily on previous jobs, you can build your own fireplace and chimney without any difficulty. If your block-laying experience is limited, two choices are open: to hire yourself out as a helper to a professional block layer, or to practice as you lay up the fireplace base. If you start the fireplace base and don't like what you see, there is always the encouraging fact that nothing but a little time is lost. In fact, you can practice by laying up, then tearing down the first three or four courses until you feel proficient to complete the job. As you tear down your practice work, all that is needed is to clean the blocks of mortar before starting over again.

Laying blocks is not a "play-it-by-eye" way of piling block upon block with a layer of mortar placed in between. Rather, it is an orderly procedure of eight steps, requiring patience, accuracy, and a sense of pride in doing a job well. I will describe each step in detail.

FIRST STEP. Add clean water to factory-mixed ingredients of a prepared mortar mix purchased in bags from your lumber yard, or prepare your own mortar, which is much cheaper and just as good.

Prepare mortar by mixing 1 part Portland cement to 1 part hydrated lime to 4 parts clean sand mixed with clean water. You can mix mortar

in the bed of a wheel-barrow, or you can make a mixing box by constructing the sides from 1-inch boards, cutting them sled-runner style as noted in the picture and as described previously in Key B-8.

A mason's helper uses a regular mixing hoe, which has large holes in the blade, or a mixing machine to mix mortar. However, a garden hoe makes a good substitute.

Begin by screening the sand constantly so that you won't have to remove small rocks and stones from the mortar. Screen the sand by shoveling it against a screen.

Make a screen by nailing ¼-inch wire screen to a wood frame. Use only the sand that passes through the screen.

To save steps between the mortar box and the job, place small amounts of mortar on a small mortarboard. You can make a mortarboard by using a piece of ½-inch or thicker plywood about 24×30 inches.

Before adding water, use the hoe to mix the dry ingredients of sand, hydrated lime, and cement thoroughly. If you desire colored joints for the fireplace face bricks or stone, mix a dry, artificially colored powder with the other dry ingredients. Be certain to follow the manufacturer's instructions as to the exact amount of coloring material to use. To assure consistent colored joints, always use the same amount of dry ingredients for each succeeding mix.

Now add small amounts of water to produce a plastic, workable mix. The mortar is ready for use when it slips easily, without running from the trowel. Mix only as much mortar as you can use in a couple of hours.

The second, third, fourth, and fifth steps are basic in laying blocks. They must be mastered. Practice them before proceeding to the actual building of the fireplace base. The photographs illustrating these steps were selected at random to show specific procedures in block laying and do not necessarily represent a systematic development of a project from beginning to end.

SECOND STEP. Practice the process of placing the mortar with the bricklayer's trowel by picking it up and "throwing" it until you become proficient in the operation.

Hold the trowel loosely but firmly with the thumb pressed against the ferrule shown by arrow. From this point on, always pick up a bricklayer's trowel in this manner. This position is absolutely

necessary for correctly turning the trowel during the throwing operation. Holding the trowel correctly, practice on the mortarboard until you can pick up a trowelful of mortar and spread it evenly.

The four sequential action pictures show how the mortar spread is accomplished. For clarity, actual throwing of mortar is not shown in the first three pictures.

Beginning of turn. Position trowel face up, point down, on outside edge of face shell as mortar begins to leave trowel.

Continue the turn, moving the trowel along and down the side of the face shells, depositing mortar on top of them. Picture shows trowel at about a 30° angle.

Continue the gradual forward and downward movement as well as the turning of the trowel. Picture shows trowel at approximately a 60° angle.

Completing the turn, the trowel should reach a vertical or plumb position along the side of the face shells. At this position all mortar held by the trowel should have been deposited on the face shells of the block course.

When enough mortar has been spread for the laying of two or three blocks, spread same amount of mortar on opposite face shells of block course.

THIRD STEP. "Butter" or place mortar on end of block.

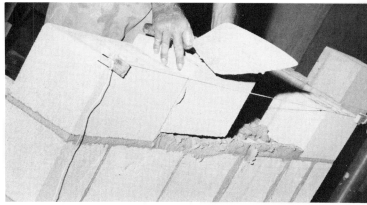

FOURTH STEP. Lay each block by placing, shoving, tapping, and cutting off mortar.

Press block downward and shove toward adjoining block so as to press the mortar up into end joint.

Here the joint is ⅜ inch thick.

This is the way your spread mortar should appear on both face shells of block course.

If the block is not forced home by shoving, tap it in place with the stick of the trowel. It is better to give the block a few hearty taps rather than several lighter ones.

The mortar may begin to set up before you use a complete batch. In this event, add a small amount of water to the remaining mortar in the mixing box. Always keep the mortar to a consistency where it slips from the trowel as described previously.

FIFTH STEP. Flush jointing. Hold the trowel as shown. Then cut off excess mortar for buttering the end of the block.

CAUTION: Never leave a block until the end joint is completely filled. You may need to add some mortar from the mortarboard.

SIXTH STEP. After you have mastered the previous steps you are ready to try your hand at actually laying up the fireplace base.

Start by laying up two corners of the base. Make joint gauge to assure uniform thickness of

joints for corners. Paint marks ⅜ inch wide at exact mortar locations on a narrow board. Spaces between painted joints must be exactly the height of your blocks. Uniform corner joints are a must, because corners must be level with each other as they are being built.

Begin by laying blocks in the first course in both directions from each of two opposite corners.

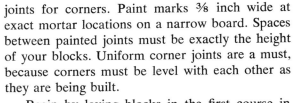

Note how blocks interlock at the corners. After laying the first course, build up corners three or four blocks high. Use the level constantly so that each corner goes up level and plumb. Use the joint gauge to be certain all joints are of uniform thickness. Be sure that blocks interlock at the corners and that corner blocks are the ones with one flat end at corners.

SEVENTH STEP. Cutting blocks. As you lay blocks in the next step from each corner toward each other corner, the last block in each course is called the closure block. This comes somewhere

about midway between the two corners. Blocks are made in half sizes as well as full-length blocks, but sometimes neither size is just right for the closure. If you rent a masonry saw, you can make your cuts with it. You can also cut a block by scoring both sides with a stone set, then breaking cleanly along the score lines by striking the set a single, hard blow.

EIGHTH STEP. Aligning blocks in each course with a stretched line. As you lay blocks between corners, align them to a stretched nylon line for securing level joints. Begin by cutting two small pieces of heavy tin or galvanized iron 1/32 inch thick, and cut and shape it as shown in the picture. These vary in size from mason to mason.

The country match in the picture gives you an idea of satisfactory dimensions. To avoid cut fingers, round sharp corners with a file or grindstone.

Using the pieces of metal as guides, stretch a line over them from the outside of two opposite corners, making it fast. Be sure top of line is on the same plane as the top of blocks. The guides assure the line being placed 1/32 inch outside top edge of the blocks. Remember this space well. It must be maintained at all times, as it is your guide space for laying blocks in a straight and level line. This is one style of line guide. Almost every mason uses a style of his own choosing.

Continue base with a series of laying three courses of blocks followed by filling in between them.

F-4. If you enjoy laying blocks, you will find stone masonry challenging.

Although stonelaying is similar to laying blocks, there are certain special aspects of it that should be considered before starting the job.

Ashlar stone is used often to face a fireplace, in building a chimney above the roof line, or in home building in general. Stone can be purchased either square-faced or cut-faced as shown in the picture.

It is best to use a stone saw rather than a stone set for cutting to size. However, a stone set can be used to cut stone, just as described previously for cutting concrete blocks.

Notice that the stone in the picture is laid in broken courses or in random lengths. Generally, there is no definite pattern, but you can get a good idea of how to lay up pleasing wall designs from looking at the picture.

Keep the horizontal joints 4 feet or less in length, making both vertical and horizontal joints ½ inch wide. In the picture, three different thicknesses of stone are used, namely 2¼, 5, and 8¾ inches. Also, the joints are raked. If you prefer, you can lay stone in regular courses, with horizontal joints.

In laying stone in broken courses, break the vertical joints of each course with the joints of the course below, making the lap 4 inches or more. This is necessary to secure a good bond between the individual stones.

Raked joints set apart each stone from the other, creating a very pleasing appearance. Begin to rake joints only when the mortar is hard enough to be dented by the thumb nail.

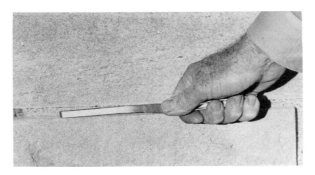

Use a flat end jointer as shown in the picture. Here the mortar is raked out to a given depth, generally about ½ inch.

If you face your fireplace with stone, you may want to use raked joints. A raked joint is not recommended for a chimney above the roof. Here raked joints tend to hold water, sometimes causing excessive moisture to be absorbed into the chimney, which then leaks out onto the room ceiling.

If you use faced stone for the chimney above the roof, it will be necessary to chip the exposed cut corners so as to resemble the face stone on the four sides of the chimney. The picture shows how this is done with a stone set and a hammer before the corner stones are mortared in place.

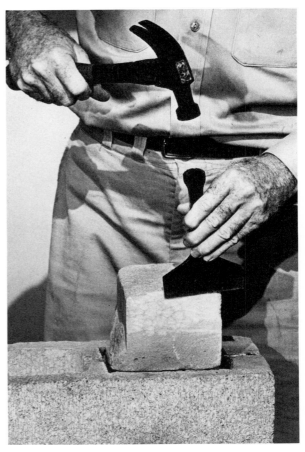

Mix the same kind of mortar for laying stone as for laying blocks described previously. Also the same rules for laying level and plumb apply to stone as to brick. CAUTION: Stains are harder to remove from stone than from brick. They can be avoided by not allowing the mortar to run on the face of the stone while in the process of laying. If some mortar does get on the stone, use a wire brush to clean as you lay. Under no circumstances clean stone with diluted muriatic acid. It may appear to remove some of the stains, but it actually burns the surface, eventually discoloring it.

F-5. A furnace flue is not required for electric heat. If your plans do not call for a furnace flue, skip the instructions for building one within the fireplace chimney.

F-6. Check your house plans before laying out the dimensions of the base. If a fireplace is not shown, figure out how many flues you require in the chimney. Because flues run up through the masonry making up the chimney, they help to determine the size of the base.

F-7. If you ever plan to attach a coal stove or coal furnace to this chimney, provide a soot clean-out door. Locate it so it will be in line with the bottom of the first section of clay flue liner. When the door is positioned properly, lay blocks around it on all sides, being sure the mortar makes a perfect seal between the blocks and the door frame. Next, put the first section of flue liner, with opening for furnace pipe, in place.

F-8. When you purchase flue tile, be sure to order a special section with the hole for the stovepipe or furnace pipe already cut. Otherwise, you will need to cut a section on the job. Since sizes of holes vary, you will need to know the flue-hole size required for the job.

F-9. For a flue to function correctly, the inside lining must be completely smooth all the way to the top of the chimney, free of projecting mortar at the joints as well as free of any other debris that might become caught within the flue liner.

Ensure a smooth inside flue by partially filling a gunny sack with sawdust so that when it is tied shut, with a heavy cord about 6 feet long, it fits snugly inside the initial flue liner. Then bring the cord up, through, and out of the top of second flue liner as it is being fitted onto the top mortar joint of the first flue liner. Be sure to tie a small weight to the free end of the cord to prevent it from falling back into the part of the flue already completed. Now as each section of lining is in place with blocks laid up around it, pull the sack up almost to the top of the joint. Continue this operation until the last section of flue liner and blocks are laid. Then pull the sack out of the

finished flue, which will have a smooth lining from bottom to top.

F-10. Know building-code requirements before establishing opening for furnace smokepipe into the flue. If code requirements do not exist in your locality, place opening no closer than 18 inches below the ceiling floor joists. Also be certain that woodwork of any kind is no closer than 6 inches.

F-11. Build the finished hearth so it will be flush with the finished floor.

F-12. Build the hearth approximately 4 inches thick, and construct it of reinforced concrete.

F-13. The hearth must be entirely supported by the fireplace itself. Do not under any circumstances allow any part of the hearth to be supported by the wood framework. Wood framing shrinks, and beams supporting a heavy load, such as a hearth, have a tendency to deflect. Sagging beams can damage walls and ceilings, and are likely to crack the fireplace, producing a fire hazard.

F-14. As concrete is being poured, locate reinforcement rods slightly above floor of form, so concrete completely covers the rods. Under no circumstances, however, should the rods be as high as the middle of the form.

F-15. Prepare a second sack for the fireplace flue liner as described in Key F-9 for the furnace flue liner.

F-16. Always doublecheck mortar joints, being sure that sections between flue tile are tight and that areas between blocks are completely bonded.

F-17. If your chimney does not come through the roof at the ridge, a metal cricket is required adjacent to the side of the roof facing the ridge so that rainwater and snow will not collect at this point.

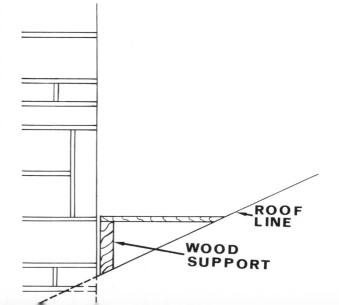

ROOF LINE

WOOD SUPPORT

First construct a wood base as shown in the left-hand picture. Then fashion cricket or saddle flashing as shown in the right-hand picture. Be sure to saw grooves along sides of chimney as well as bend, cut, solder, and caulk flashing.

F-18. You can make a slab for the top of your chimney if you prefer. First make a wood form 2¼ inches thick, with the inside dimensions the same as those outside the chimney. Next, place the form on an out-of-the-way flat surface. Using a piece of woven fence wire or concrete reinforcement wire, position it a fraction of an inch off the bottom. As you pour a concrete mixture of 1 part cement to 2 parts sand to 3 parts rock and clean water into the form, smooth the top with a trowel. After it has cured for about thirty days, install it on the top of the chimney in the same way as described for a stone slab.

F-19. Waterproof the brick or stone chimney area above the roof, or any other masonry area exposed to the weather. You can do an excellent job of waterproofing without marring or discoloring the finished product. When the mortar is thoroughly dry and the weather is dry, use a clean paintbrush to give the exposed area two coats of silicone sealer, obtained from a paint store. Be sure to follow the manufacturer's directions as listed on the can. Silicone sealer is a clear liquid, and it should not be confused with the black roof mastic that is frequently smeared over many well-constructed chimneys.

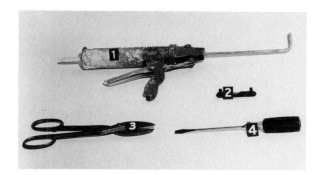

G

THE EXTERIOR FINISHING

G-1. In addition to some of the tools called for previously, you will need the following tools:

1. The caulking gun recommended consists of a metal frame in which tubes of caulking compound are placed. The size of the caulking bead is controlled by the amount of tip cut from the exposed end of the tube.
2. A line level is a small level approximately 3 inches in length with built-in hangers to fasten it over a tight-stretched line.
3. Metal snips are for cutting tin and light sheet metal.
4. The screwdriver is a common enough tool, though you may not have needed it up to this point.

G-2. The following list of materials is given to aid you in estimating material needs:

MATERIALS FOR EXTERIOR FINISHING

Name	*Description*
Finish facia	1 × 8s, finish-grade
Paint	Exterior paint for facia and soffit
Paint	Prime paint for facia and soffit
Metal starter strips	Either galvanized iron or aluminum
Ledger boards	1 × 4s, construction-grade
Lookouts	2 × 4s, construction-grade
Soffit material	¼-inch Masonite or weatherproof plywood
Ventilation screens	Screen wire or screens and frames designed for ventilating soffits
Roofing starter roll	Asphalt same color and weight as shingles
Roofing shingles	3-tab asphalt shingles
Metal valley (if required)	Aluminum or other nonrusting metal 10 inches wide
Roofing cement	A plastic cement that remains pliable
Ridge and hip shingles (if required)	Individual shingles same color and weight as regular roofing shingles

Name	Description
Nails	1-inch galvanized roofing nails
	8-penny box
	1-inch
	16-penny box
	6-penny box
Window units	Primed units ready for installation
Exterior door units	Primed units ready for installation
Exterior door locks	Outside door locks, keyed for single key
Exterior siding	Siding of your choice, including nails and other special materials recommended by the manufacturer
Guttering	White colored aluminum guttering. Figure number of pieces after comparing guttering areas of your house with gutters and fittings listed in Step 11-42

G-3. The picture in step 11-2 shows roof sheathing and felting above "rafter" and wall plates, studding, and outside Celotex wall sheathing as completed in Chapter 9.

G-4. The Masonite Corporation provides a pre-finished soffit called the Colorlok X-90 soffit system. Vent strips, providing 17 square inches of open area per lineal foot, are part of the system. It is compatible with all exterior siding materials. Soffits 2 feet or less in width require no lookouts for support. Wider soffits require lookouts as described in step 11-2. Wherever face nailing is required, use prefinished Colorlok nails or galvanized nails and touch-up paint.

G-5. Picture in step 11-5 shows cap plate and outside Celotex wall siding as completed in Chapter 9.

G-6. For clarity, top view of cornice framing is shown with roofing material and rafters removed.

G-7. For clarity, roof sheathing and felting are not shown in the picture with step 11-6.

G-8. Unlike metals have a tendency to corrode when they are in contact with each other.

G-9. Asphalt roll starter strip and shingles are manufactured by saturating heavy felt paper with hot asphalt. Then the top surface is covered with a fine layer of finely crushed slate. Because it is actually three shingles in one, the triple-tab shingle is recommended.

G-10. Be sure roll starter strip and shingles are of the same color and weight.

G-11. Use solid starter strip to give weather protection for the slots in the first course of asphalt shingles.

G-12. Nail only near the edge closest to the eaves, dropping back from the starter strip edge just far enough so as not to nail through the metal overhang.

G-13. Asphalt shingles are available in 3-in-1 thick-butt shingles and locking hexagonal tabs, varying in weights, and in colors to please the most discriminating eye. The writer does not recommend asphalt roll roofing (also available) for the kinds of houses described in this book.

The houses in the book were roofed with 3-in-1 thick butt shingles, weighing 235 pounds per 100 square feet, with each shingle coated by the manufacturer with a dab of roofing cement on the underneath side. The heat from the sun causes the shingles to remain flat and fast, preventing them from blowing off the house during a heavy wind.

G-14. If you have untreated asphalt 3-in-1 butt shingles, you can prevent them from blowing off the roof by raising a shingle at a time and applying a spot of roofing cement about the size of a quarter from a caulking gun just below the raised shingle. Then lower the shingle and stand on it for a moment to stick it in place. It is best to do this on a warm day after the roofing job is completed.

G-15. Do not lay asphalt shingles in either very hot weather or cold weather. In very hot weather, shingles can be damaged from pressure as you walk over the laid part of the roof. In cold weather, shingles have a tendency to become brittle and can crack when you walk on them.

G-16. To prevent walking excessively over the completed portion of the roof, bring up the required number of shingles to do the job. To keep handling at a minimum, place the bundles at various points over the roof.

G-17. Cutting every other starting strip shingle causes the joints to be staggered as additional layers of roofing are applied. Otherwise, joints would lay in an objectionable vertical line.

G-18. Read the packing slip found in each bundle of shingles regarding the amount of exposure for each shingle.

G-19. Be sure the nails are in a straight line and are covered by the following layer of shingles.

G-20. If a nailhead breaks off or you need to pull out a bent nail, correct the error. Either drive another nail, or place a small dab of roofing cement in the hole or over the nail without a head.

G-21. Before nailing, place a layer of roofing cement on the metal only where that part of the shingle will overlap. Also cover the last nailhead of the shingle (if exposed) with a dab of roofing cement. Then press the shingle firmly onto the metal valley.

G-22. As you lay shingles up the valley, use a rag and white gasoline to wipe away excess cement from the exposed metal.

G-23. Use enough roofing cement to make a watertight joint, being careful not to allow the cement to be squeezed out of the joint onto the roof proper.

G-24. Begin laying ridge shingles from the end of the ridge first struck by prevailing winds. This is a precautionary measure as winds blow rain away from where shingles lap.

G-25. Primed exterior door and window units were used for several reasons. From rough opening to completely hung door or window takes only a fraction of the time necessary to prepare and hang a door or window by other methods. All time-consuming work is done for you. There is no need for on-the-job notching, boring, or mortising. Components are cut, machined, and assembled accurately by the latest precision methods. By eliminating on-the-job labor, you save time to put to good use in other parts of the building operation.

G-26. Doors come in many different stock designs. Select a design of your choice if not specified on your house plans or specification sheets. Also, doors are either solid or veneered. Solid-core doors are made up of a system of softwood blocks in the core. Exterior doors are generally of the solid-core variety. Hollow-core doors are light in

weight and are generally cheaper than solid-core doors. Hollow-core doors make excellent interior doors.

G-27. Be sure the doorframe fits the rough opening for which it is intended. Before attempting the installation, check the various dimensions of the frame against corresponding dimensions of the rough opening.

G-28. Now is the time to doublecheck your floor plans with regard to door openings. Before proceeding, be certain that swinging doors will open in the correct direction.

G-29. The Masonite Corporation's Prefinished Colorlok X-90 siding is a prefinished hardboard siding made from a new fiber formula that provides superior stability and exceptional dent resistance. The surface of Colorlok siding is protected by a tough plastic film. It resists age, abrasion, fade, and stain, and its smooth outer surface washes clean with water. It is available in Frost, White, Desert Sand (Beige), Pearl Gray, and Willow Green. Its Lap Lok aligning strip gives it a clean no-nail appearance. To weatherseal the installation, lap siding also comes complete with joint moldings. It comes in 12-inch widths and 16-foot lengths with a nominal thickness of 7/16 inch.

G-30. Before applying paint be certain siding is perfectly dry. Otherwise, paint simply seals the moisture in the siding, causing it to peel.

G-31. While working with hardboard, follow these rules for sawing:

Cut with exposed surface up when using handsaw or power saw.

Use a 8-tooth-per-inch or finer crosscut handsaw.

Use a bandsaw, compass saw, or coping saw for irregular, curved, or inside cuts.

Use a crosscut or combination blade with circular power saws. Use a carbide-tipped blade for large jobs.

G-32. While building your house, why not build a little red barn for tools or play?

As a garden tool-storage shelter or a playhouse for the youngsters, a little red barn makes an attractive functional asset in a back yard. Although easy to build, it is sturdy and well designed, including a hinged roof for easy access to the loft, pegboard interior walls, and Masonite X-90 siding. For complete construction information, write

Courtesy Masonite Corp.

the Masonite Home Service Bureau, Box B, Chicago, Illinois 60690. Just ask for a free copy of Plan AE-109.

G-33. Masonite Corporation's Ruf-X-90 panels also may be secured with ½-inch square-cut grooves on 8-inch centers and shiplap edges.

G-34. You can easily make matching corner boards and batten strips by ripping strips approximately 2 inches wide from Ruf-X-90 panel boards.

G-35. White guttering is recommended. There are many good brands of quality guttering on the market for the homeowner who wishes to do his own work. For instance, Sears Roebuck supplies an excellent slip-joint galvanized guttering system with tough acrylic enamel baked on. The inside

is coated with acrylic lacquer. In any event do not buy steel guttering of less than 28 gauge, and 26 gauge is better. Aluminum guttering should be at least .027 inch thick, fittings .020.

G-36. Guttering comes in aluminum, steel, and copper. Do not combine unlike metals. To do so may result in corrosion.

G-37. Various brands of guttering may have fittings shaped slightly differently from those shown in the picture. This does not necessarily alter the quality of the product. For instance, gutters are generally fastened in one of three ways. I shows the spike and ferrule method, J shows the strap hanger method, and L shows the facia bracket hanger method.

G-38. Gutter styles are of two kinds, half-round and box-type or molded. The picture in step 11-42 shows the box-type, which is recommended because it adds a distinctive border around the cornice of a modern house. The half-round gutter is usually recommended for over-hanging roofs that do not have a finish facia board or where the roof extends 2 or more inches beyond the rafter edges.

G-39. Determine gutter and rainpipe sizes from the following table:

Gutter size (inches)	Rainpipe size (inches)	Square feet of roof surface on house
4	3	750 or less
5	4	750-1400
6	4	Over 1400

THE PLUMBING

facturers have fittings to meet every requirement. So the problem is to know which fitting to use for a specific situation and how to install it.

H-2. Copper pipe and fittings for the drainage and venting system come in 1½-inch and 3-inch sizes and in 10-foot lengths. Always use copper drain pipes above ground—never below. The parts are as follows:

1. Copper pipe, 1½-inch or 3-inch
2. Roof flashing
3. Vent increaser
4. Coupling
5. Tee
6. 90° bend
7. Slip-joint adapter
8. Tee with side opening (RH)
9. Tee with side opening (LH)
10. 45° bend
11. 45° street bend
12. Drum trap
13. 90° street bend
14. Threaded adapter
15. Toilet floor flange
16. C-I pipe adapter
17. Cleanout with plug
18. 45° Y

Courtesy Sears Roebuck and Co.

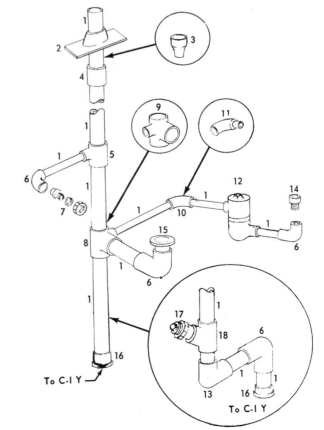

H-1. Check with the local building code to see what you may or may not do in the installation of residential plumbing. Also find out if there are requirements for specific kinds of water supply and sewage drainage parts.

Some codes require that plumbing installations be made only by a master plumber. If you live in a community with such a code, hire yourself in as a helper to a master plumber for your installation, for there is plenty of rough work that you can do in preparation for his work.

Other codes require only that the installation meet with the approval of a local health inspector.

Many rural communities have no code at all. If this is your case, it is still wise to talk over your installation plans with the county health officer. He can be most helpful in pointing out local situations and giving recommendations that will help protect your health and that of your family.

Actually, anyone who is handy with tools can do a good plumbing job himself. Plumbing manu-

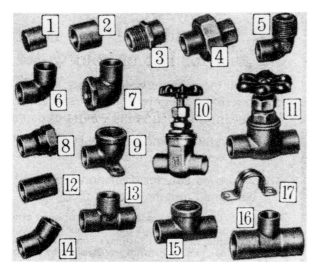

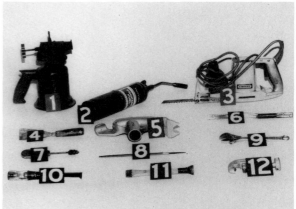

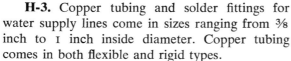

H-3. Copper tubing and solder fittings for water supply lines come in sizes ranging from ⅜ inch to 1 inch inside diameter. Copper tubing comes in both flexible and rigid types.

In flexible tubing, type L is used for indoor piping, while type K is used for outdoor and underground duty.

In rigid tubing, type L is used for indoor piping, while type M is designed for general-purpose use and for forced-hot-water systems. Only solder-type fittings are shown in the picture here. The parts are as follows:

1. Cap—copper
2. Reducing bushing—copper to copper (reduces fitting one size)
3. Adapter—copper to outside threads
4. Union—copper to copper
5. 90° Elbow—copper to outside threads
6. 90° copper to copper
7. 90° copper to outside threads
8. Adapter—copper to inside threads
9. 90° dropear elbow—copper to inside threads (½-inch copper to ⅜-inch inside threads)
10. Gate valve—copper to copper
11. Stop valve—copper to copper
    Stop and waste valve—copper to copper
12. Coupling—copper to copper
13. Tee—copper to copper to copper
14. 45° elbow—copper to copper
15. Tee—copper to copper to inside threads
16. Reducing tee—¾-inch copper to ¾-inch copper to ½-inch copper
17. Copper pipe strap

H-4. Some of the tools required for making plumbing installations have already been described. In addition, the tools shown here are required for installing copper water supply lines and an all-copper drainage system aboveground and a cast-iron drainage system belowground, including drain line leading from the house to community sewer. (If you plan to use plastic pipe and fittings instead of copper and cast-iron pipe and fittings, code permitting, refer to Key H-10.) The special tools for a copper system are as follows:

1. The blowtorch uses gasoline for fuel. This type of torch is used for heating copper fittings 2 inches or larger before soldering copper pipe into them.
2. The propane torch uses propane gas for fuel. This type of torch is popular among workmen for heating fittings under 2 inches in size before soldering small copper pipe into them.
3. The reciprocating saw is an all-purpose power saw. It is an ideal saw for making holes in floors and framing members where required for the passage of plumbing pipes.
4. The putty knife is ideal for packing commercial joint compound into hubs of cast-iron pipes.
5. Although the conduit bender is primarily used by electricians, it is an excellent tool for bending small copper tubing. Instructions for use are included with the tool.
6. A yarning iron is used to pack oakum into hubs of cast-iron drainpipes.
7. Wire brushes are used to clean the inside of

copper fitting hubs before soldering pipes into hubs.

8. A round tail file (8-inch) is used to remove burrs from inside of cut copper or plastic pipe.

9. An adjustable wrench or a set of wrenches comes in handy for tightening nuts when making plumbing installations.

10. Wood chisels come in different sizes. Select one to suit type of notching required for your particular jobs.

11. Cold chisels are used for cutting cast-iron drain pipes. Never use cold chisels and wood chisels interchangeably. Each is designed for a particular job.

12. A tubing cutter is especially designed for cutting soft tubing, such as copper tubing.

H-5. The following materials list is based on an all-copper plumbing system, with the exception of the drain leading from the bottom of the main vent stack to the sanitary sewer line.

PLUMBING MATERIALS

Name	*Parts and fittings*
DRAINAGE AND VENTING SYSTEM 3-inch copper drainage system for aboveground installation	3-inch and 1½-inch rigid pipe 3-inch tee with 1½-inch side opening or (for double bathroom) 3-inch double tee with two 1½-inch side openings Toilet floor flange Reducing tee—3-inch copper to 3-inch copper to 1½-inch copper Roof flashing Increaser (if required) made from 4-inch copper pipe 18 inches long soldered onto a 4-inch to 3-inch reducing coupling Pipe adapter for connecting main stack pipe to cast-iron drain system 1½-inch brass cleanout plugs if tees instead of elbows are to be installed along copper drain lines Drum trap Couplings, elbows, and tees to assemble your particular copper drain system
4-inch cast-iron drainage system for belowground installation	4-inch cast-iron pipes 45° Y-branch with cleanout, including cleanout ferrule with brass nut Floor drain with deep-seal trap for basement floor 45° and 90° elbows as required to assemble your particular cast-iron drain system
HOT AND COLD WATER SUPPLY SYSTEM	½-inch and ¾-inch type K flexible copper tubing for underground installation, type L for aboveground installation Pressure and temperature relief valve Outside water faucets Stop-and-waste valves, unions, tees, reducing tees, elbows, connectors, and adapters (copper to outside threads) to assemble your particular hot and cold water supply system

Name	*Parts and fittings*

**MATERIALS FOR INSTALLING DRAIN AND
SUPPLY LINES**

Copper pipe straps
¾-inch roofing nails
Strong rags
Fine steel wool
Solder, 50 percent tin and 50 percent lead
Flux designed for soldering copper
Small panel door to be located behind bathtub
Lumber used for some bathtub, lavatory, and toilet
　　installations
Wax or rubber ring and putty
Oakum for caulking cast-iron soil pipe joints
Joint compound or lead for sealing cast-iron soil
　　pipe joints
Type of insulation made for water supply lines

FIXTURES

Bathroom medicine cabinet
Toilet with flush tank and fittings
Bathtub with fittings (combined with shower if
　　desired)
Kitchen sink with fittings
Garbage disposal with fittings
Laundry tubs with fittings
Washing machine with fittings
Dishwasher with fittings
Ice-maker refrigerator with fittings
Hot water heater, with fittings, size to fit family
　　needs
Grab bars and holders for toilet paper, towels, wash
　　cloths, drinking glasses, electric shaver, and soap
　　dishes

H-6. To provide the best in the plumbing installation, copper tubing with sweat joints is recommended with the exception of the drain leading from the bottom of the main vent stack to the community sewer.

Copper is somewhat more expensive than galvanized iron or plastic pipes and fittings. However, copper is less affected by chemicals in water than other metals used for the same purposes. Still another advantage over galvanized iron is the sweat joint, which is easy to master and is used throughout the entire installation.

H-7. Install fixtures later, after the finished floors, walls, and ceilings are completed.

H-8. Certain general instructions are given in this chapter for fixture dimensions, such as minimum height from floor, distance from wall or other fixtures, and the location of holes in floor, wall, and ceiling for drain and vent pipes and water supply lines. However, for a proper job of installation, be sure to obtain specific measurements for each fixture from the plumbing supply house furnishing your fixtures.

H-9. Cast-iron soil pipes are 5 feet in length, and often must be cut for shorter lengths. Cut

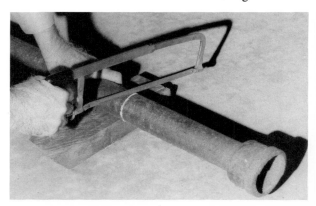

double-hub pipe when shorter pieces are required. This way each shortened piece has a hub. Accurately measure piece required, allowing additional length required to fit into adjoining hub. Using a piece of chalk, mark around, square with the pipe. For cutting service-weight pipe, make a 1/16-inch cut around pipe with a coarse-toothed hacksaw.

Complete cutting pipe by tapping pipe with a hammer until pipe breaks at cut.

For cutting extra-heavy pipe, mark pipe. Then lay it on a 2×4 on the floor. Using a cold chisel and a hammer, make a light cut all around the pipe. Then continue cutting around and around the pipe, striking chisel harder each time around, until pipe breaks.

Before connecting soil pipe, be sure it is clean

and dry. Soil pipes can be laid either in a vertical or horizontal position, but be certain that they are exactly in one of these two positions by checking with a level or a taut cord. The only exception is where pipe is laid purposely at an angle, usually a 45° angle. Place spigot (plain end) of next section into hub its full depth, securing pipe firmly in position.

Next pack joint partially with oakum. As you wrap the oakum around the pipe at the joint, drive it to the bottom of the hub space with a yarning iron, being sure you do not drive the

oakum out of the bottom of the hub into the pipe proper. A watertight seal forms when the oakum is packed tightly and evenly to within about 1 inch from top of hub.

Code permitting, use a putty knife to pack commercial joint compound inside remaining

space of hub. Smooth off the top and allow to set. I use Mitee Soil Pipe Cement, which is easy to handle and produces a tight waterproof joint.

If your code requires leaded joints, light a plumber's furnace and place the lead in the melting pot. Place ladle alongside melting pot. When the lead is molten, dip it out with the ladle, and pour it slowly into the hub for vertical joints only. Pour it evenly around the joint until the lead is about ⅛ inch above the top of the hub. Be sure

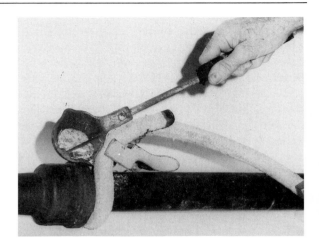

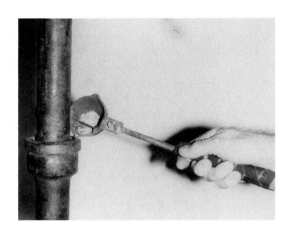

to dip enough lead to fill the joint in one pouring. CAUTION: Never dip a cold ladle into molten lead. To do so may cause an explosion. Now caulk the joint. Place the end of an outside caulking tool on the lead, striking it gently with a hammer as you tap around the leaded joint. CAUTION: Hard blows may jar the lead loose from the joint. Next use an inside-caulking tool, and strike heavy blows with a hammer. Complete caulking operation with a caulking tool that fits into space without binding.

For leading horizontal joints, use an asbestos joint runner to prevent lead from running out of hub. Begin by preparing joint with oakum as with vertical joint previously described. Next place asbestos joint runner around the pipe as tightly as possible, just above the hub. The clamp should be placed on top of pipe to form a funnel. Using a hammer, tap runner down against top of hub to prevent lead from running out. Pour a ladleful of molten lead in at top of joint to the point of overflowing. When the lead has cooled, remove the runner. Then cut off surplus lead with a hammer and cold chisel. (This lead can be reused in

another joint.) Complete joint by caulking lead into hub, using the same procedure as previously described for caulking lead into vertical joint.

H-10. Code permitting, you may want to install a plastic drainage and water supply system instead of a cast-iron and copper drainage system and a copper water supply system. If so, the only tools required are a saw, ruler, round file or pocket knife, and a small paintbrush. The following steps are the same whether you are working with large or small plastic pipe.

Using a hacksaw, carpenter's handsaw, or a power saw equipped with a fine-tooth blade (9 to 14 teeth per inch for a handsaw blade), cut pipe to exact length. See the first illustration in Key H-14 for suggestions on how to measure tubing exactly. Cuts must be square. You can make them like a professional by placing pipe in a jig and using jig cut as a guide for the blade. If you use a vise as a holding device, wrap held part of pipe with rags to prevent damage. Note: Use chrome-plated fixture pipes and connections where they will be exposed to view, such as kitchen sink and lavatory drain and water supply pipes and fittings.

Using a round file, pocket knife, or a standard reamer, remove burrs from all around inside edge of cut pipe.

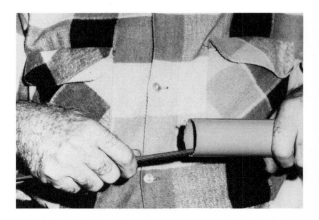

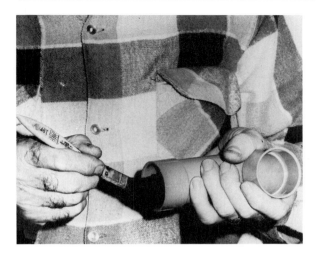

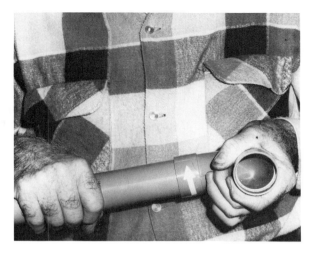

Be sure inside surface of fitting hub and surface part of pipe that is to fit into hub are clean. Then, using a small nonsynthetic bristle brush, apply a generous amount of solvent or cement (recommended for your particular type of pipe) to inside surface of fitting hub. Note: If you join plastic pipe or fittings to metal pipe use a metal adapter. Before joining spread a thread compound on thread side and plastic joining compound on smooth side of adapter.

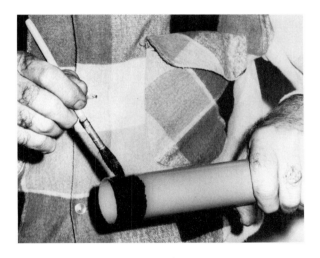

Brush solvent or cement on the outside surface of pipe to the depth of fitting hub.

Evenly distribute solvent by giving pipe a quarter-turn as you press it firmly into fitting hub. Hold pipe and fitting firmly until curing has begun, usually about 15 or 20 seconds, to prevent the pipe from pushing out from the fitting. Clean off any excess solvent. Generally, the joint sets permanently in five minutes.

If bolt-type fittings, such as flanges, are used, be sure to tighten all bolts evenly to prevent damage to plastic components.

H-11. If your house plans call for a concrete slab for the first floor, all supply and waste lines below floor level must be installed before the concrete is poured. In such installations encase water supply pipes and fittings in metal sleeves (cut from size larger pipes) so no concrete comes in direct contact with the pipes and fittings proper. Then position pipes securely in place so they do not move when the concrete is poured. Next temporarily pack top openings of pipes with rags to keep lines free of debris. Be sure to leave part of rag exposed at each opening so as not to overlook removing it when fitting is attached later.

H-12. If yours is to be a basementless house with crawl space, you do not need to install a floor drain. In this case support soil pipe between opening in floor with metal straps spaced 10 feet apart until ground level is reached. Be sure to drop pipe a minimum of ¼ inch per foot toward sanitary sewer.

H-13. At this point you may want to bring the water supply line into the basement. If so, skip to Key H-19. There may be two advantages in doing this: it gives a supply of water for drinking and building purposes, and if you need practice in soldering copper tubing to fittings, smaller jobs are a good place to start. The following steps make it possible for a novice to do a professional job.

H-14. Here are some guidelines for soldering (sometimes called sweating) copper tubing joints.

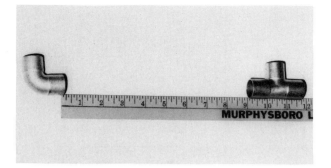

If this is your first job, practice on small tubing and fittings first, such as the ½-inch size.

Begin by measuring tubing required for connection. Mark tubing the distance between the location of the two fittings plus the depth of tubing that goes into each fitting. For example, the depth the tubing goes into the ¾-inch fitting in the picture is ¾ inch. (You will note the depth changes with different-size fittings.) The distance between fittings is 9 inches. Therefore, 10½ inches of tubing will be cut.

You can use a hacksaw with a blade with 24 to 32 teeth per inch for cutting small tubing, but a quicker and more efficient method is to use an inexpensive tubing cutter, which cuts tubing up to 1½ inches in diameter.

reamer. If cutter is without reamer, use a small round file or an old pocket knife.

For cutting 2-inch and larger pipe, use a jig for obtaining square cuts easily and quickly. This is simply a block of wood about 2-feet long with side boards nailed to it, each with a square cut in it. The cuts serve as a guide for the sawblade.

Place cutting blade on tubing where marked to be cut. Then slowly advance blade as you tighten screw and at the same time revolve instrument slowly around tubing. To make inside of cut ends smooth, ream out burr with built-in

Generally, elbows in the line are recommended to make right-angle turns and 45° fittings to make eighth turns. Whenever possible, the writer recommends bending copper tubing water supply lines instead. This is less time consuming,

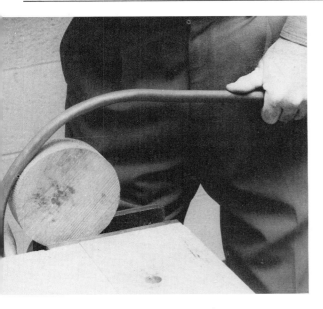

fine steel wool, but a quicker job is done with an inexpensive wire brush as shown. This kind of brush is specially designed for the purpose. Never use a file to clean end of tube or inside of fitting.

Read manufacturer's directions on can of flux designed for soldering copper. Then using a small paste brush or stick, apply a thin coat of flux to the cleaned end of tubing and to the inside hub of fitting to be soldered.

and the wide line bends reduce friction within the line. A conduit bender is ideal for making neat bends without flattening the tubing. If you do not have a conduit bender, you can make a substitute as shown in the picture.

Using a bandsaw or a keyhole saw, cut a 6-inch circular piece from a short piece of 2×6. Then to make a 45° or 90° turn, gently bend tubing around the curved end of the 2×6 until the desired angle is reached. Bend tubing slowly so as not to flatten tubing.

Even though tubing is new and bright, clean ends going into fitting hub with fine steel wool. Also inside hub of fitting can be cleaned with

Put tubing into fitting, being certain end fits against stop inside fitting hub and remains there during soldering operation. Note: The end of a long length of horizontal tubing being soldered into a fitting has a tendency to creep away from the stop, even though tubing may remain inside fitting.

Using a propane gas torch (a blowtorch may be used for heating fittings 2 inches or larger in diameter) apply even heat all around hub of fitting only. Never apply heat to the pipe itself.

Next apply wire solder to joint. (Use 50-50 solder, half tin and half lead.) At correct amount of heat, end of wire solder melts on contact, flowing into joint. For best soldered joint, do not feed solder continuously all the way around. Rather,

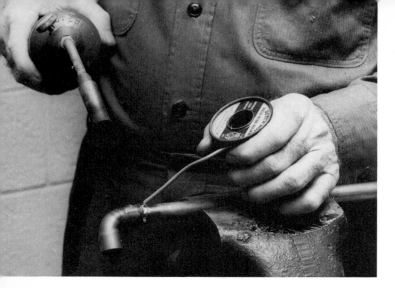

apply it at no more than two points, opposite each other. The trick is to have the fitting hot enough to cause solder to flow by capillary action between end of tubing and hub of fitting. Therefore, remove flame from fitting while applying solder. Return flame only if liquid solder is solidifying without filling joint. Overheating may destroy action of flux as well as cause the liquid solder to flow on through joint into pipe. This is what happens when a blowtorch is used for soldering small tubing to fittings, unless the flame can be made fine enough to avoid overheating the fitting hub.

Because heating the fitting only causes liquid solder to flow into the joint by capillary action, melted solder is drawn into the space between tubing and hub of fitting even if solder must flow uphill, as in a vertical installation.

To obtain a well-soldered joint on tubing larger than 1 inch, it may become necessary to tap or move the tube slightly during the soldering operation.

Feed solder until a line forms completely around joint. Then immediately use a rag or brush

to wipe away surplus solder. A bright ring of clear solder without pitholes indicates an acceptable joint.

If you find that solder melts in a completed joint while you are making a soldered joint to a different hub on the same fitting (such as a tee), wrap damp rags around completed joint(s). CAUTION: Do not allow any part of damp rag to come into contact with hub being soldered.

By giving a little thought to planning and by taking of accurate measurements, you can make up several fittings and pipes at one time on the workbench. Then you can fasten each end of the unit to the proper connections. This is especially helpful when several fittings and pipes are required in a location that is hard to work in.

Allow each soldered joint time to cool before soldering the following joint. However, it is necessary only for the liquid solder to solidify before proceeding to the next joint. When this occurs, proceed even though the previous one may be quite warm.

H-15. If you did not plan ahead for the plumbing installation when the joists and studs were framed, it may be necessary to cut some of these members now, especially if you plan to conceal pipes inside walls and under floors. Of course, it is obvious that if you can run pipes between joists and studs instead of across them that weakening of the framing is reduced to a minimum.

Often, though, you cannot avoid cutting or partially cutting joists and studs to get the type of plumbing installation desired. Here, then, are a few rules-of-thumb to consider in maintaining acceptable strength within the house framework.

If you must bore a hole in a joist, be sure it is centered between top and bottom and that its diameter is not more than ¼ the width of the joist at the point of bearing. The picture shows an 8-inch joist with a hole slightly less than 2 inches in diameter (maximum allowed in this case)

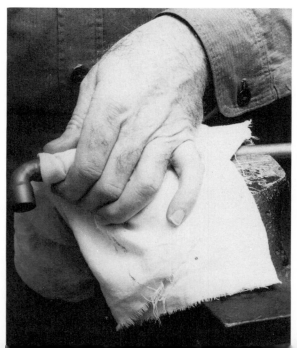

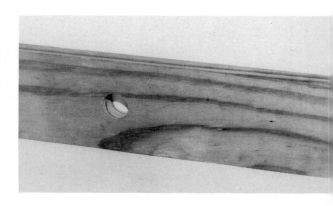

drilled exactly in the center of the face of the joist. Make such a hole no larger than adequate for a 1½-inch copper vent or drain pipe.

Although some plumbers exceed this recommendation, for guaranteed flooring strength do not notch a joist more than ¼ its width at its point of bearing. And then keep the notch within the width of the joist from the face of support. Note: As you move away from the point of support, cut notches progressively shallower if they must be cut at all. For example, if a large notch, such as the one in the picture here, was located near the center of the joist, the floor would definitely be weakened, unless the joist was given additional support.

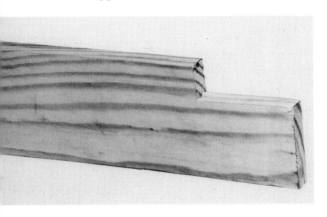

If you must cut away a large notch in a supporting joist, the floor will not be weakened if it is braced well. In one of the houses in this book, here is the way a 3-inch copper pipe runs through a large notch in the middle of a floor joist. First a knot-free 2×4 4 feet long was spiked with 16-penny nails to bottom of joist, centrally located below the proposed notch. Then the joist was notched to receive the pipe.

Sometimes it is necessary to cut out an entire section of a floor joist, such as in installing a toilet elbow drain where the opening in the floor is located directly over a floor joist. In such a case, brace the joist structure by building a well, similar to the well described in step 7-12 when framing sills and floors. The well need only be large enough to accommodate the elbow and to provide room to work around it.

Generally speaking, do not notch studs of supporting walls more than ¼ their depth or drill a hole larger than 1¼ inches in diameter in a 2×4 stud. If larger notches are required, reinforce the stud.

H-16. Locate sanitary tee on stack pipe A so that when 90° elbow B and toilet drainpipe C are connected to it, top of elbow will set level with bottom of floor.

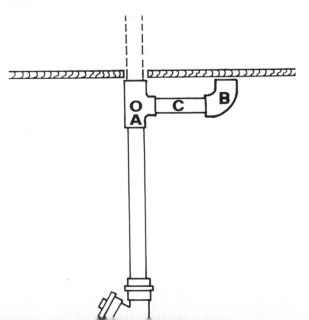

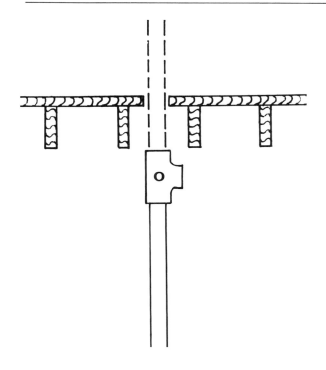

H-17. Sometimes, because of floor joist direction, it is not possible to install top of sanitary tee to bottom of floor without running toilet drain pipe through the joists. If you encounter this problem, do not cut holes in floor joists. Simply proceed as previously instructed with the exception of sanitary tee location onto soil stack. Solder it onto vertical soil stack so that top of tee sets level with bottom of floor joists as shown in drawing above.

H-18. The hole should be only large enough so the lower part of flange can slip through while the wider upper part will sit on top of the floor.

H-19. If there is no code objection, and you installed a plastic drainage system, you will want to use flexible plastic pipe for branch drain pipes and vent pipes. The mirrorlike surface cannot lime up or corrode, and very little friction is created inside the pipe. No additional tools are required than those recommended previously for the installation of the plastic drainage system.

H-20. If you encounter long runs between right-angle turns in drain lines, install a tee instead of an ell. Next solder a short nipple into one hub of the tee, and onto this solder an adapter, copper to inside threads. Then screw a brass pipe plug into adapter. Right-angle turns so designed provide easy access for cleaning rods all along the drain system, if they should ever get stopped up.

H-21. All venting can take place through the main vent stack. However, in most cases it is less time-consuming and less expensive to install a separate 1½-inch vent pipe through the roof for venting the kitchen sink.

H-22. Drum trap may be installed either right side up or upside down as pictured in step 12-16. Upside-down installation makes future cleaning from basement a simple task. In either type installation, a pocket of water must always remain in trap, unless line is being cleaned.

H-23. If your house plans call for additional bathroom fixtures, drain and vent them as described thus far.

H-24. Install drain and vent pipes for kitchen sink in the same way as previously described for the bathroom lavatory.

H-25. The route the water service line takes to the house as well as the planning of all other water lines should be made with the location of the hot water heater in mind. Minimize long inside runs by having the water heater as close to the bathroom and kitchen as possible. Sometimes this presents a bit of a problem, especially if the heater requires a chimney, such as is required of a gas-fired hot-water heater.

H-26. To prevent damage later if trucks drive over the service water line or in planting shrubs or trees over the line later, dig ditch a minimum of 3 feet deep.

H-27. The connection to the water main is made by the local water company. It may or may not install a meter. Also it may install the meter near the tap, or it may make the installation inside the basement. The company also installs a shut-off valve near the meter.

H-28. Use a ¾-inch copper service line if you plan 10 or fewer fixtures. A 1-inch line is required to supply an adequate supply of water if you plan to have between 11 and 20 fixtures.

H-29. Generally copper pipe can be secured in sufficient length so that no joints are required

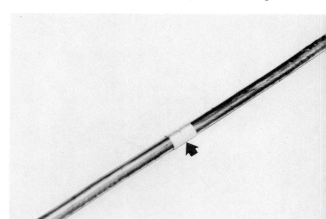

between water tap on city main and entrance to basement. If this is not possible and connections are required, join pieces of tubing together by soldering ends inside hubs of copper couplings, shown by arrow.

H-30. Water supplied at 40 pounds per square inch (psi) is a convenient pressure. If pressure is considerably higher, such as 80 pounds per square inch, or if pressure fluctuates greatly, install a pressure-reducing valve at this point. Then adjust it to the pressure most suitable for your installation.

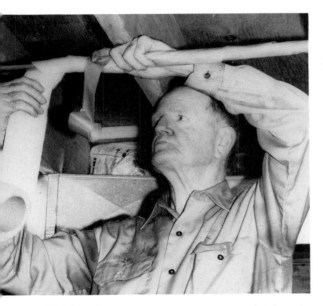

H-31. Here are some common mistakes to avoid when installing service hot and cold water lines.

Never run uninsulated hot and cold water lines closer than 6 inches apart. To do so causes the cold line to sweat while absorbing heat from the hot line.

Even though electric cables are insulated, plan water pipe installation so that when installing the wiring it will not come directly in contact with the water pipes.

If your area experiences humid weather during the summer months, always insulate cold water lines. This prevents sweating.

If your area is subject to freezing temperatures during winter months, avoid installing uninsulated water pipes within exterior walls, unless the pipes are installed between wall insulation and finish walls.

H-32. For copper supply lines, use ¾-inch copper tubing for main hot and cold water supply lines. Branch off with ⅜-inch tubing only for toilets and lavatories. Make all other branch lines to fixtures with ½-inch tubing.

H-33. Run lines between joists and studs whenever possible. It is not advisable to notch joists for running pipes across them. Rather, use furring strips to bring ceiling below bottom of pipes. (Chapter 14 explains how to install furring strips.) On the other hand, if drop ceilings are to be installed, you have no problem.

H-34. Plan water lines to run as directly to fixtures as possible with the least number of joints, fittings, and sharp turns. Such planning results in a cheaper operation, less work, and less reduction in water flow due to friction.

H-35. If horizontal or vertical lines are to be exposed within the living quarters, use rigid copper tubing. It is neat in appearance and will not sag, causing water pockets when line is drained.

H-36. Using copper pipe straps and ¾-inch roofing nails, fasten tubing approximately every 10 feet along runs, including those underneath joists.

H-37. Unions make it easy to disconnect water heater and other appliances for service when required.

H-38. Plan to connect hot water lines to left faucet when facing fixture, cold water lines to right faucet. Crossing of pipes may be necessary when fixtures are back to back.

H-39. A rule of thumb is to use copper tubing about 12 inches long, capped on top, and one size larger than the line the antihammer serves. Then solder this unit into a reducing tee

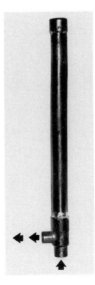

located in the line near the fixture connection. (Black arrows show where to connect water supply line leading to fixture.) If you wish, copper antihammers can be purchased from plumbing supply houses all complete for soldering directly into copper tees.

H-40. CAUTION: Code or no code, install temperature and relief valve to prevent the heater from exploding if the pressure inside becomes too great. The purpose of the tubing leading away from the valve is to prevent someone from getting scalded if too much pressure builds up.

H-41. No hot water line is required for toilet fixtures. In fact, doublecheck to be sure the single line will carry cold water.

H-42. Care of fixtures begins with unpacking. Open crates by applying pressure of hammer claw or wrecking bar to wood crating only. Never put pressure of unpacking instruments on fixtures proper.

H-43. If built-in holders are desired for toilet paper, towels, washcloths, drinking glasses, toothbrush holders, and soap dishes, mark locations and do roughing-in if required.

H-44. Before permanently fastening fixtures in place, be sure to remove rag or tape from waste-pipe openings and water supply pipe openings placed earlier to keep debris from entering open pipes.

H-45. Even though you do your own plumbing, keep fixtures covered until bathroom is complete. Old blankets or several thicknesses of newspaper glued or taped together make good protective coverings.

H-46. When setting bathroom fixtures upside down, protect them by placing a heavy pad, such as an old blanket, between them and the floor.

H-47. If finished floor is yet to be installed, place wood blocks of correct thickness under flange so face will be flush with finished floor.

H-48. Generally, two bolts are recommended by the manufacturer to come up through the floor flange for fastening stool in place. Where four bolts are recommended, two special bolts are placed through two holes in front of bowl. These bolts have wood threads at one end and machine threads at the other. The wood threads are screwed into floor.

H-49. If your house has a concrete floor, place machine bolts, head down, in prepared holes. Next set in place with mortar. Then install bowl.

H-50. Heights of lavatory installations are a matter of personal choice. Generally, they vary from 29 inches for small children to 36 inches for some adults.

H-51. Install grab bars for safety's sake in shower stalls and on walls adjoining bathtub.

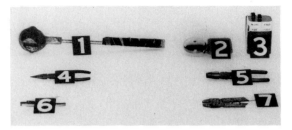

WIRING
AND
FIXTURE
INSTALLATION

I-1. Many of the tools required for general wiring have been shown in previous chapters and their usage explained. The picture here shows the additional tools required.

1. A plumber's ladle was shown in the previous chapter as an alternate tool. In this chapter the ladle can be used in conjunction with a plumber's furnace or a blowtorch to solder connections of electrical wires twisted together.
2 and 3. A doorbell and a 6-volt lantern battery wired together are used to do low-voltage testing of electrical circuits.
4. Long-nosed lineman's pliers are used for gripping locknuts and twisting wires.
5. Regular pliers are used for general purposes, such as gripping wire, cutting wire, etc.
6. A pocket knife can be used for cutting insulation.
7. A multi-purpose wiring tool is used for cutting and skinning wires, attaching terminals, etc.

I-2. The following list is given as a guide in figuring materials needed for electric installations:

ELECTRIC INSTALLATION MATERIALS

Name	Description
115 230-VOLT SERVICE INSTALLATION	
Service wire	To run from meter box to service panel, size as approved by local utility company
Service wire conduit and fittings	To run from meter box to service panel, size as approved by local utility company
Ground wire	To run from meter box to ground rod, size as approved by local utility company
Ground wire conduit and fittings	To run from meter box to ground rod, size as approved by local utility company
Service panel	200 amperes, unless smaller size is approved by local utility company
Ground rod	Located in ground directly under meter box

Name	*Description*
115-VOLT INSTALLATION	
Metal boxes	Switch, service outlet, junction, and lighting metal boxes designed for nonmetallic sheathed cable; outlet and switch cover plates. If either conduit or armored cable is used, secure boxes designed for it. Purchase number required in your house plans
Metal hangers	Designed to fasten between studs and joists for the purpose of supporting metal boxes
Nails	2-inch nails used for fastening box hangers in place
Weatherproof receptacles	Specially designed for mounting outdoors (optional)
Wire	Three-wire (two wires plus ground wire) nonmetallic sheathed cable, unless armored cable or conduit is used. If your plans call for a two-wire 115-volt system, purchase this type of wire
Conduit or armored cable and fittings	Use only if nonmetallic cable is not approved by local code
Large staples	Specially designed for holding nonmetallic cable in place on wood framing members
Armored cable straps	Use only if armored cable is used
Conduit pipe straps	Use only if conduit is used
Switches	Single-pole, three-way, or four-way as called for in your house plans (mercury switches if you desire noiseless operation)
Switch plates	Color and number as required
Service outlets	Number as called for in your house plans
Service outlet plates	Color and number as required
Electrician's plastic tape	As many rolls as required
Plastic cable (code permitting)	Covered wire designed to run underground (optional)
Chimes or bell-buzzer	Single-tone for back door; multi-tone for front door (optional)
Push buttons	Accessories for chimes or bell-buzzers
Bell wire	Insulated wire designed to connect chimes or doorbells to transformer
Bell-wire staples	Designed for surface mounting of bell wire along runs
Transformer	115-voltage A.C. and D.C. voltage as called for in your plans
230-VOLT INSTALLATION	
Service outlets and outlet boxes	For 230-volt nonmetallic sheathed cable unless conduit is required
Three-wire cable	Nonmetallic sheathed cable (unless code requires conduit), sizes as called for in your plans for various heavy-duty accessories
Pigtails	Three-wire cable designed for connecting major appliances to service outlets
OPTIONAL LARGE INSTALLATIONS	
Electric heating	Kind and number of materials required are generally found on the individual instruction sheets or in installation booklet accompanying a particular unit
Electric air conditioning	
Central vacuum system	
Home security system	

I-3. Seldom does one find a community that has no code requirements for the installation of electric wiring. Even if no code exists where you live, for safety's sake, check with the local electric utility company to find out if there are any conditions required before it will bring the electric lines to your house if you do the wiring. Also it is a good idea to check with your fire-insurance company to see if it has any requirements that must be met before it will give you a fire-insurance policy.

Some codes will permit anyone to do the wiring as long as it passes inspection by a building or housing inspector. Other codes require all wiring to be done by a licensed electrician. If your community has such a code, you can save money if you can hire yourself out as a helper to a licensed electrician for the length of the wiring job.

I-4. Rather than having overhead wires coming from power source down through roof into meter box fastened onto side of wall, request an underground service cable to meter box. Generally, this type of installation is no more expensive to the customer than the old-fashioned overhead job, and, of course, the lack of overhead wires is more pleasing to the eye. Also, underground wiring reduces danger from lightning.

I-5. Be careful with electricity! It can be worked with in perfect safety, or it can become a killer. Do not touch any electric wire until you are absolutely sure it is not a hot wire, connected to a power source. Both 115-volt and 230-volt lines are dangerous if you are not cautious.

I-6. Plan to begin the wiring operation at the service entrance after you have checked with the local power company for their recommended location. Usually the meter mounting device is located on the side of the house about 5 feet above finished grade.

I-7. Local power company installs service wires from power source to meter.

I-8. Standard electrical wiring symbols are shown here. If they are unfamiliar to you, learn them so you can understand your house wiring plans. Write proper symbols on framing or floor to designate location of lights, service outlets, and switches. Also, indicate locations of electrical appliances, power equipment, heating and air conditioning units, etc.

I-9. Saving by installing a minimum number of circuits is one of the best examples of false economy that you can demonstrate in building a new house.

I-10. If you design your own 115-volt circuits, remember that #14 wire is rated for 15 amperes, 1600 watts; #12 wire is rated for 20 amperes, 2400 watts. Otherwise, be sure wire sizes correspond to sizes recommended on wiring diagram of house plans.

I-11. Generally, place dining room, laundry, and kitchen on separate circuits. Also, it is good practice to place service outlets and ceiling lights of the same room on different circuits.

I-12. If code in your area does not permit nonmetallic cable, you have two other choices. Either armored cable, commonly called by its trade name BX, or thin-wall conduit is generally accepted.

FIRST CHOICE. Armored cable is made up of type T wires, each wrapped in a spiral layer of water-repellent paper. A flexible galvanized steel armor serves as a protective covering for the wires, which come in different number and different sizes to suit different electrical installations. A bare copper grounding strip is located between the paper and the armor. Use armored cable only for indoor wiring and only in dry locations. Also, use only steel outlet and switch boxes fitted with a cable connector specially designed for armored cable. If you already have steel boxes without built-in clamps, you can use connectors for making the connections. Make all splices inside steel junction boxes.

Generally, the principles of wiring and the testing of circuits are the same as for nonmetallic cable, but there are some important differences to consider.

While installing armored cable, make necessary bends such that if completed would form a complete circle at least 10 times the diameter of the cable. CAUTION: Never make sharp bends.

Using a fine-tooth hacksaw, remove about 8 inches of the spiral wound steel armor. Hold the saw at right angles to the strip of armor, not the cable itself. Carefully cut through one section of armor, making sure blade does not penetrate either the grounding strip or the insulation of the

Symbol	Name	Symbol	Name	Symbol	Name
◯	CEILING OUTLET	F	CEILING FAN	▪	PUSH BUTTON
⊣◯	WALL OUTLET	F	WALL FAN	▯◯	DOORBELL
◯	CEILING LIGHTING OUTLET	J	CEILING JUNCTION BOX	▯	DOOR BUZZER
⊖	DUPLEX CONVENIENCE OUTLET	J	WALL JUNCTION BOX	R	RADIO OUTLET
⊖s	SWITCH – CONVENIENCE OUTLET	S	CEILING PULL SWITCH	TV	TELEVISION
⊖wp	WEATHERPROOF OUTLET	C	CLOCK OUTLET	S	SINGLE POLE-SWITCH
⊖R	ELECTRIC RANGE	T	THERMOSTAT	S₂	DOUBLE-POLE SWITCH
⊖D	ELECTRIC DRYER	G	GENERATOR	S₃	THREE-WAY SWITCH
◯	230-VOLT POLARIZED OUTLET	M	ELECTRIC MOTOR	S₄	FOUR-WAY SWITCH
▲	SPECIAL PURPOSE OUTLET	◫	NIGHT LIGHT	Swp	WEATHERPROOF SWITCH

wires. Then give it a twist to break the short end away, exposing the insulated wire for making connections. CAUTION: Be sure not to cut off grounding strip under armor. Allow an inch or more to project beyond armor. Then fold this grounding strip back over the outside of cable.

With the removal of the armor, the water-repellent paper is exposed around the wires. To prevent the raw edge from breaking the insulation, insert a protective fiber bushing at the cut end of the cable between paper and wires. First, unwrap paper from around wires up to a couple of turns under the armor. Next, tear wrapping off inside armor. Then insert bushing between the paper and the wires. CAUTION: Do not overlook bushing installation, as no electrical inspector will pass on armored cable installations if bushings are not used.

Fasten armored cable by tightening the clamp screw located inside metal box, being sure that grounding strap is folded back over the cable. If steel boxes that you want to use do not have built-in clamps, use cable connectors. Slip the connector over end of cable with the bushing installed (threaded end out). Next, tighten holding screw. Remove the knockout slug from the box and insert connector firmly inside box to assure a good ground.

Hold cables in place with straps or staples at 4½-foot intervals and within 6 to 12 inches of every steel box.

SECOND CHOICE. Thin-wall conduit comes in different diameters for different wire sizes and in unthreaded 10-foot lengths. It can be used indoors, or in masonry (except where cinders are one of the ingredients) in damp or dry locations.

Generally, the principles of wiring and testing the circuits are the same for conduit wiring as for nonmetallic cable, but there are some important differences to consider.

First connect conduit to metal boxes (never use porcelain or bakelite) by fitting threaded end of connector over conduit. Then insert connector through box knockout, tightening lock nut securely. Join sections together with conduit couplers.

Use a fine-tooth hacksaw to cut conduit where required, reaming cut ends inside and tapering with a round file. Be sure to make necessary bends with a conduit bender especially designed for the purpose. A conduit bender is also a useful tool for bending copper tubing.

Use pipe strap, held in place with 1-inch roofing nails, spaced 4 feet apart on exposed runs and 6 feet apart on unexposed runs.

When the conduit is installed, pull wires through it into proper metal boxes. Then continue the wiring operation as described for non-metallic cable. Note: For long runs of wires through conduit, use a fish-tape tool for an easy pull-through operation. To pass through bends, work the tape back and forth. If there is a lot of resistance, use a lubricant such as soapstone or talcum powder. Fish tape is available from electrical supply houses in 50 and 100 foot lengths.

I-13. Be sure all boxes are designed for the kind of wiring called for in the house plans—nonmetallic cable, conduit, or flexible armored cable. Two-wire nonmetallic cable was used in the houses in this book.

Another kind of box that in appearance is similar to metal boxes pictured in Chapter 13 is made of bakelite or porcelain. They are used by some builders instead of metal boxes. Porcelain boxes do not require a grounding wire, and the cable is not anchored to the box as when using metal boxes. However, it is necessary to anchor cable to a surface within one foot of each box. CAUTION: If you use armored cable or conduit, do not use this type of box. Use metal boxes.

I-14. Sometimes there is an advantage in having more than one device mounted side by side, such as a service outlet and a switch, three switches, four switches, etc. If you plan to mount two devices side by side, form a "two-gang" box by unscrewing one side each of two boxes. Then screw remainder of the two boxes together. The picture shows a three-gang box being assembled. Here one side was removed from each of two

boxes and two sides from a third box. With the four superfluous sides discarded, shown at bottom of picture, the remainder of the three boxes are fastened together to form a three-gang box.

I-15. Install switch and outlet boxes at a height convenient for all members of the family. In the houses in this book, switch boxes were installed 4 feet from finished floor line to top of box. In kitchen, outlet boxes were installed 38 inches from finished floor to top of box. All other outlet boxes were installed 16 inches from finished floor to top of box.

I-16. Permanent fastening of switch and outlet boxes is made at time of finished wall installation. At this time, box is centered between panel joints (if paneling is used) and made flush with the finished wall. The added foot of loose cable located at each box recommended during the installation makes this adjustment possible.

I-17. A rule-of-thumb recommendation is to place a service outlet in the middle of every 12 feet of running wall space, except over kitchen counter space, where an outlet should be placed every 4 feet. Also install a minimum of one weatherproof outdoor receptacle, as shown in picture, for each side of the house. Such outlets are most convenient for appliances and holiday lighting.

I-18. You may wish to use "grip-tight" boxes, which require no hangers, to be mounted between wall studs. These boxes are installed after finished walls are completed. For now only the wiring is completed.

When finished walls are completed, connect cable to box through opening in wall. Then push box with connected cable into opening. Next tighten side screws to bring side brackets up tightly against wall.

I-19. Make a final comparison check between boxes installed and those called for in the wiring diagram. For instance, are all boxes for switches, outlets, and lighting in place where required, including those outside the house?

I-20. The extra cable allows for moving the box sideways for centering between vertical lines of panel boards when they are installed later.

I-21. With staples recommended for fastening nonmetallic cable, use one every 3 feet on supporting surfaces, such as joist, stud, wall, or ceiling. CAUTION: Never use fence staples. When line crosses joist, pull cable through predrilled holes, similar to those described for pulling cable through studs. For fastening armored cable or conduit see I-12.

I-22. When outlet boxes are some distance apart, you can save time in connecting them by running connecting cables up, then across ceiling joists and down the studs. In this type of installation, you drill holes through top and cap plates rather than through each stud between boxes.

I-23. Protect nonmetallic cable at all times. Make bends carefully so as not to damage covering. Run cable through a piece of conduit, extending 6 inches above surface, when passing through floor or ceiling. Be sure to use a bushing at each end of the piece of conduit.

I-24. Here are some helpful hints for making nonmetallic wire splices and taps. CAUTION: Do not use on unexposed runs or if junction violates local code.

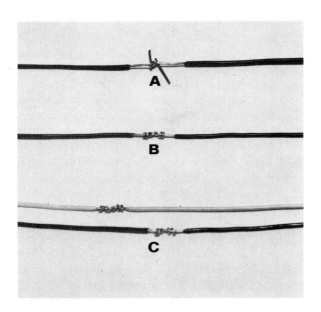

To splice, remove about 2½ inches of insulation from wires to be spliced. If exposed wires are dirty, clean with fine emery paper. Now cross wires at about midpoint A. Then turn them tightly in opposite directions with fingers and pliers B. Now make six to eight turns, using fingers and pliers C.

Use a tap if there is no strain on tapped wire. Remove about 1 inch of insulation from continuous wire. Now remove insulation from end of second wire as if preparing a splice. Then wrap tightly around bare area of continuous wire. CAUTION: When using armored cable or con-

duit, make splices and taps only inside a junction box.

Coat joint area of wires with soldering paste, especially made for soldering copper. CAUTION: Never use an acid flux for soldering copper. Then

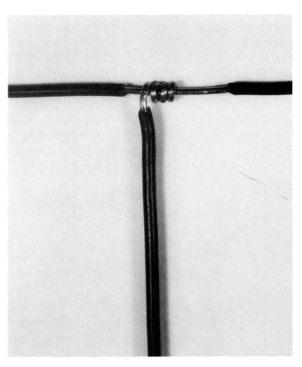

heat with an electric torch, applying solder until joint is completely tinned. Note: Do not allow solder to "pile up" on joint.

Complete joint by wrapping with electrician's plastic tape, which does the same job as both rubber and friction tape when used together.

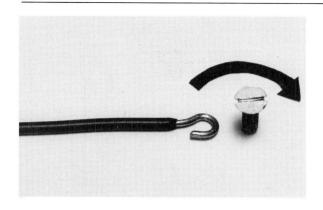

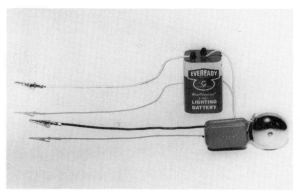

I-25. For making connections at screw terminal, cut ½ inch of insulation away from end of wire as if sharpening a pencil. Be sure not to remove tin coating from wire. Then, using a pair of pliers, bend end of wire clockwise into a loop to fit around screw. Note: Never fasten bend of wire counterclockwise around screw.

I-26. Here are some guidelines pertaining to switch wiring—single-pole, three-way, four-way, and other residential type switches:

1. Always run neutral wires to current-consuming devices without interruption by a switch or fuse.
2. Always attach hot wires to switches.
3. Always join black wires to black wires, never to white, except at switch loops where end of white wire should always be colored black.
4. Connect hot wires to dark (brass-colored) terminals and white wires to light (silver-colored) terminals.

I-27. Use two three-way switches to control one or more lights from two different points, such as from either end of a corridor, either of two room entrances, or either top or bottom of a stairway.

I-28. Use two three-way switches and one four-way switch to control one or more lights from three different locations. To control one or more lights from more than three points, use an additional four-way switch for each point, connected.

I-29. You can make a simple testing device to test the circuits with low-voltage electricity. All you need are a door bell, a 6-volt lantern battery, some wire, and a pair of alligator clips.

A short circuit can be caused in various ways. A black and white wire could be making contact somewhere in the circuit. If metal conduit is used,

a black wire could be in contact with it or the metal box. If a two-wire nonmetallic cable with a ground wire is used, a black wire could be in contact with the neutral wire or metal box.

I-30. If bell fails to ring, it could indicate that switch wires in boxes were either incorrectly fastened together or were not twisted tightly enough to make good contact.

I-31. The transformer reduces the 115-volt alternating current (AC) line voltage to low-voltage direct current (DC) of 6, 12, or 16 volts, depending upon the purpose it is to serve. Generally, two-chime installations require a line reduction to 16 volts DC.

I-32. Lightly insulated bell wire is satisfactory for connecting transformer to push buttons and chimes or bell buzzer.

I-33. Do not fail to add wattage for chimes when you figured the capacity of circuits. For example, list 16-volt transformer serving two chimes at 15 watts.

I-34. Later when power is on, do not become alarmed if transformer case feels warm while someone presses push button. This is normal.

I-35. Solderless connectors make wiring connections easier and quicker. Also, later if fixtures require replacement, the job can be done quickly if solderless connections have been made.

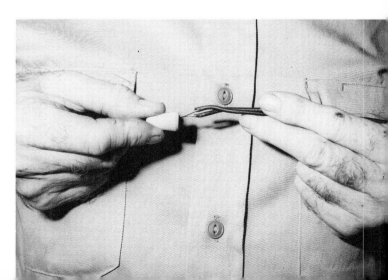

I-36. Each major appliance, such as electric range and clothes dryer, operate on a separate 115/230-volt three-wire circuit. Hot water heater operates on a 230-volt circuit only.

I-37. Use type of wire similar to that used in previous wiring, such as nonmetallic sheathed cable.

I-38. An electric range operates on 115/230 volts. It operates on 115 volts at low heat and 230 volts at high heat.

I-39. Before installing major appliances, check local code with regard to the wiring and grounding diagram you plan to use.

I-40. Because of the way individual burners and ovens are connected, the neutral wire to the range does not carry as many amperes as the two hot wires. You may use a neutral wire one size smaller than the hot wires. If yours is a small range you may use two #8 wires with a #10 neutral. However, if at a later date you decide to install a larger range, it will be necessary to install two #6 wires with a #8 neutral.

I-41. Electric ranges, clothes dryers, and hot water heaters are considered heavy appliances. If the heavy appliance in question is connected to a circuit also serving other electrical needs and if the circuit is protected by fuses (not plug fuses) mounted on a pullout block or by a circuit breaker similar to the ones shown in the early part of this chapter, no additional installations are necessary. On the other hand, if the circuit is protected by plug fuses, a separate fused switch is required for *each* appliance. The ampere rating must not be greater than that which protects the branch circuits. It is well to note that any amperage device protecting a circuit must not have a greater capacity than one and a half times the ampere rating of the appliance. A 15-ampere overcurrent protection is a minimum recommendation even though the appliance is rated less than 10 amperes.

I-42. A double-element electric water heater is recommended because it permits a constant supply of hot water.

I-43. When the utility company completes installation of service cable to meter, turn disconnect switch in service panel to on position. Then turn each circuit, one at a time, to on position. As you turn circuits on, have a helper turn on at least one light or appliance connected to that circuit. If a circuit fails to function properly, make some tests as follows.

If your service panel is the fused type, do these five steps to change a fuse:

Disconnect all items, such as small appliances and lights on a circuit.

Then be sure main housepower switch is turned to off position.

Unscrew blown fuse, replacing it with a new one of correct number of amperes. Never substitute a metal object, such as a penny, for a fuse unless you first put in a call to the fire department and cancel your fire insurance policy.

Now return main house power switch to on position.

Test the circuit by connecting appliances or lamps, one at a time. If the fuse blows again with any one item, you have located the trouble. Make proper repairs before proceeding. If each item operates as an individual unit, this points to an overloaded circuit. In this case remove enough items from the circuit to keep it within the rated wattage.

If your service panel is the circuit-breaker type, do these things to reset a circuit breaker:

Disconnect all items such as small appliances and lights on a circuit.

Push circuit-breaker handle or switch from its center position to the off position. Notice words "on" and "off" stamped on the surface on either side of handle.

Then return handle or switch to on position.

Test the circuit by connecting each appliance or lamp one at a time, just as when testing a fuse-protected circuit.

I-44. Markell manufactures other types of electrical heating equipment. The picture here shows the installation of one of their recessed fan-forced residential and light-commercial heaters.

Courtesy Markell Electric Products, Inc.

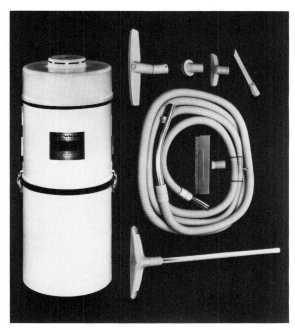

Courtesy Whirlpool Corp.

I-45. Ease of installation and quiet, efficient operation are only a few features of the Whirlpool Central Vacuum System. Called the Jack-Vac, Whirlpool's central vacuum systems are now available as packaged kits containing everything required for complete home installation. Individual kits are available for each of the two dry pick-up systems and the wet-and-dry system. Complete set of cleaning tools provided with each of the three units includes crevice tool, dusting tool, rug nozzle, upholstery tool, hard floor tool, two 20-inch interlocking stainless-steel wands, 25-foot hose with fingertip suction adjustment in the handle, and handy case for storing or carrying.

I-46. The installation fittings shown in the picture are part of the items furnished by Whirlpool Corporation. The number of items depends upon the unit purchased.

1. Flexible tubing
2. Rigid tubing
3. 45° Y
4. Wall valve bushing
5. 90° street ell
6. 90° ell
7. Slip coupling
8. 45° street ell
9. Wall valve assembly
    A. Wall valve
    B. Exterior mounting bracket
    C. Wall section opening
    D. Interior mounting bracket
    E. "O" ring
    F. 90° adapter elbow

I-47. If you previously did not provide an opening in foundation wall to accommodate main line, use a star drill and hammer to make opening.

I-48. Be sure to check for interference from other utilities, and tube extension below floor to facilitate hookup to horizontal runs.

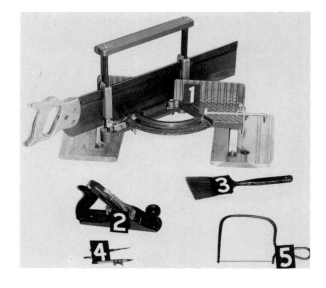

J

INSULATION AND INTERIOR FINISHING

J-1. Most of the tools used in insulating and finishing the interior have been shown and their usage explained in previous chapters. The picture here shows additional tools required.

1. A miter box is a machine used to saw miter joints. The all-metal miter box shown is more accurate than a homemade wood miter box and can be used to cut wood to any angle from 45° to 90°. Legs screwed to short pieces of boards make for easy temporary fastening to the saw horse with tray as shown in Fig. C-4.
2. The smooth plane, 9 inches long, is the most generally used plane. However, a jack plane, 14 inches long, produces better results when planing large areas, such as edges of interior and exterior doors.
3. A varnish brush of good quality is recommended, width to suit the job. For general work, a 2½-inch or 3-inch brush is satisfactory. If your color scheme requires painting or enameling, also use a second good-quality brush, width to suit the job.
4. A compass or dividers have several uses. In interior finishing, either one can be used to scribe the face of one trim board against the face of a second trim board in preparation for making a coped joint.
5. A coping saw is used for cutting irregular shapes or patterns, such as cutting a coped joint on the end of a piece of molding.

J-2. Use the following table as a guide to figure the materials required for insulation and interior finishing:

MATERIALS FOR INSULATION AND INTERIOR FINISHING

Name	Description
Ceiling tiles	
	Polyethylene, 4 mil.
	½-inch staples for fastening polyethylene to bottom of ceiling joists
	9/16-inch staples for fastening ceiling tile to furring strips
	1 × 4-inch furring strips
	8-penny box nails for fastening furring strips to bottom of ceiling joists
	Ceiling tiles, size and color of your choice
Insulation	
	Type and amount as required to insulate walls, above ceiling in attic, and below floor joists

Name	Description
Hardboard panels	
	Hardboard panels, size and color to suit
	4-penny finishing nails or 1-inch colored nails to fasten panels in place
	Hardboard panel adhesive, also used to fasten hardboard panels in place
	Inside and outside corners, colors to match walls
	Colored putty sticks
Plank walls	
	Knotty-pine, oak, or cedar planks
	2×4s to provide cross members between wall studs
	16-penny common nails for fastening cross members to wall studs
	Finishing nails, size to suit, for fastening planks to cross members
Hardwood floors	
	15-pound asphalt-saturated felt paper
	Oak flooring
	10-penny casing or finishing nails
Bathroom	
	Hardboard panels, ceiling tiles, and accessories as described in Chapter 14
	Comb spreader, if Marlite adhesive is used for fastening wall panels
Darkroom, sewing room, recreation room, etc.	
	Hardboard panels, ceiling tiles, and accessories as described in Chapter 14
Door jambs and swinging doors	
	Door jambs
	8-penny finishing nails for fastening door jambs to wall studs
	Interior doors
	Thresholds, if desired
	Door hinges
	Door locksets and/or latch sets
Sliding doors	
	Sliding-door units, including hardware as specified in instructions with unit
	Interior doors
Casings and other trim	
	Door and window casings
	Door stop
	Baseboards
	Base shoe or carpet strip
	Molding for application between walls and ceiling
	4-penny finishing nails for fastening trim, with exception of outside edge of casings
	6-penny finishing nails for fastening outside edge of casings
Finishing the woodwork	
	Colored sealing stain
	Clear spar varnish
	Latex interior paint or enamel, if desired
	Sandpaper, grade 6-0, or steel wool, grade 00
	Steel wool, grade 0000
	Stain sealer and varnish brush
	Paint or enamel brush if paint or enamel is part of the color scheme

J-3. Polyethylene can be purchased in varying widths from 8 feet to 20 feet. Laps are permissible, so use a width most convenient to your handling. If you have a helper, polyethylene as wide as the ceiling can be conveniently installed.

J-4. Because fiber tiles are quite soft and are easily soiled, they should be installed after interior walls are completed.

J-5. Generally, ceiling tiles come in full 12-inch or 16-inch widths. This, however, is not always true. Weldtex wood ceiling tiles, for example, are only 11⅞ inches square.

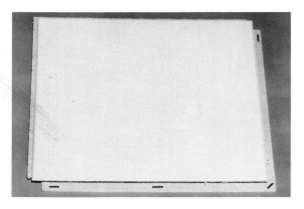

J-6. Some carpenters prefer to insulate the walls after applying polyethylene and furring strips to the bottom of the ceiling joists. Following insulation of the walls and completion of the finish walls, they fasten ceiling tile to the furring strips with four staples to the 12-inch tile as shown in the picture here.

J-7. First snap a chalk line down the center of the second furring strip, forming a guideline for one set of border tiles. Then snap a chalk line at

right angle to the first chalk line (parallel to the ceiling joists), forming a guideline for the second set of border tiles. Before proceeding be sure the two border lines form a perfect square.

Begin tile installation in the corner of the ceiling. Measure and cut each border tile individually. Then begin installation in the A, B, C order shown in the picture. When beginning, remove only tongue edges from tiles, leaving flanges intact for stapling. Place cut side of border tiles against wall with edges aligned with chalk lines. CAUTION: Cut tiles with finish side up, using a sharp knife or a crosscut saw. Using a table saw really makes cutting border tiles a breeze.

Pay particular attention to the installation of tile A. This is the only one aligned with both chalk lines, and it must be perfectly aligned before proceeding. When the border is reached opposite from where you began, remove stapling flange (the one nearest wall) from each tile. Such tiles can be face-nailed close to the wall with 1-inch nails. Be sure nails are close enough to the wall so as to be hidden when moldings are applied between the ceilings and walls.

J-8. ALFOL comes in several different types, each designed to provide maximum insulation for the purpose intended.

Check with your building-materials supplier for the correct types of ALFOL to be used for the insulation jobs you have in mind.

J-9. If your plans call for plank wall installation, see step 14-33 for proper application of wall insulation.

J-10. ALFOL is quite flexible. Little insulation effect is lost because ALFOL will open to its full depth within 3 inches of passing over any obstruction that tends to close it up. Merely open the insulation to its full width and apply it as if the obstructions were not present.

J-11. For attics, 8 inches of insulation is a minimum recommendation for homes heated with electricity.

J-12. Although careful cutting of corners can provide a neat joint without using inside metal corners, a more professional job can be done by using them. And it can be done in less time.

J-13. Masonite inside and outside corner moldings come in either vinyl-clad wood or metal. Edging and division moldings come only in metal. All moldings are color-keyed to all Masonite hardboards.

J-14. Although a handsaw can be used to cut hardboard, a power saw is recommended if more than one room is to be paneled.

J-15. Knotty-pine panels are tongue-and-groove boards of several widths. They can be fastened either vertically or horizontally. Paneling of random widths makes for an attractive room.

J-16. If some boards are difficult to join together, position the groove edge of a scrap piece of plank over the bead edge and drive home with a mallet or hammer.

J-17. When walls are completely installed, fasten molding of your choice between top of wall and ceiling edge. Then install door and window casings. Also install baseboard and shoe around bottom of walls. These installations are made in the same way as shown in steps 14-59 to 14-69.

J-18. Finish with a color of your choice. If you like a clear natural finish, first apply one coat of good-quality lacquer sealer. (This type of sealer does not darken the wood.) Then apply one or two coats of clear satin varnish. Satin varnish gives a beautiful finish without the high gloss usually associated with varnishes. For more on varnishing see step 14-70.

J-19. Hardwood flooring is milled in various widths and thicknesses with tongue-and-groove edges and ends. Widths vary between 1½ to 3¼ inches, increasing by intervals of ¼ of an inch. Thicknesses vary between ⅜ (11/32), ½ (15/32), ¾ (25/32), and 1 (33/32). It is bundled in lengths ranging from 2 feet to 16 feet. The 13/16-inch plain-sawn 2¼-inch face of a clear grade red oak is generally used for residential flooring laid over a subfloor.

J-20. As the floor is being laid, arrange the pieces on the subfloor so that there is a variation of end joints and that both grain and color blend well.

J-21. Unless you have had experience using a floor sander, it is best to employ a qualified floor finisher for sanding and finishing the floor. Oil, shellac, floor varnish, and gym finish are common finishes applied to hardwood floors. I recommend two coats of a good-grade gym finish. Whenever worn spots appear later, all that is required is a washing of grease and dirt from the worn spots. Then simply apply gym finish with a clean paintbrush. The old and new finishes blend together. If you wish a more glossy floor finish, use any good grade of floor wax according to directions on the container.

J-22. Marlite comes in 4-foot sheets or in Random Plank. Your lumber dealer can recommend Marlite especially made for shower and moisture areas as well as Marlite for areas not affected by moisture. There are even Marlite murals that give any room a custom decorator look.

J-23. Never use butt joints or leave unfinished edges. There is a molding designed for every joint. Moldings are essential, since they allow panels to expand or contract. For this reason never use nails for fastening panels.

J-24. With bathrooms 8 feet or less in length and width, standard 8-foot panels can run the full length of walls, providing only one joint running the length and width of the room at the 4-foot level. Also, with this type of layout you can arrange the 4-foot levels in a pattern of different colors, as shown in the picture with step 14-39.

J-25. The Marlite decorator panels were installed over a ½-inch backing of interior plywood nailed to the wall studs. Also, the sheets may be installed onto 1×4-inch furring strips, which have previously been nailed onto the wall studs.

J-26. Soon after installation, remove excess adhesive and smudges with a soft cloth and white (unleaded) gasoline. Also, this is a good procedure for keeping hands free of adhesive.

J-27. The ceiling may be covered with acoustical tile as previously described in Chapter 14 for ceiling installation, or you can use Marlite 16-inch square blocks. These are a durable, low-upkeep, prefinished covering that blends well with the wall panels. The blocks are cemented in place and small metal clips (provided with blocks) are nailed to a rabbeted lip of each block. In addition, these blocks are tongue-and-groove and interlock with each other.

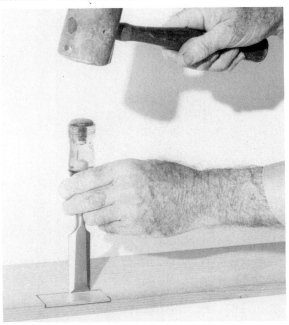

J-28. Lay out gain outline with a knife or a sharp lead pencil. Then, using a 1-inch wood chisel struck with a wooden mallet, cut around gain to its depth. Be sure to keep beveled side of chisel out.

J-29. Holding chisel at angle as pictured and striking hard blows with mallet, chip wood from end to end of gain.

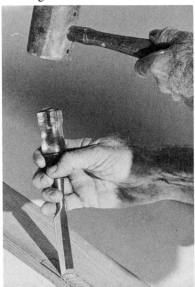

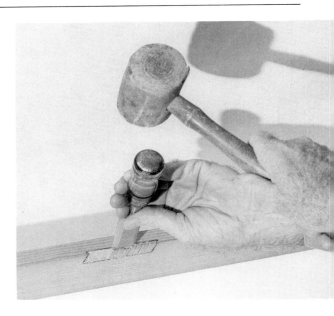

J-30. Holding chisel horizontally and striking lightly with mallet, cut out chipped material. Be sure depth of finished gain is such that top surface of hinge (when mounted in place) will be approximately 1/32 inch below adjoining surface.

J-31. You can finish your window and door casings, baseboards, base shoe, and cove molding or you can purchase them prefinished to match the color of your walls. The added cost of purchasing them prefinished over purchasing them unfinished is well worth the difference if one considers the time saved plus the expense of purchasing sealing stain and varnish or enamel.

If you do decide to finish your trim, do it before fastening it in place. Refer to steps 14-70 and 14-71 for finishing trim to match or harmonize with the walls. In any event, you will need to finish the interior areas of the windows and window frames and doorjambs. Do this before nailing the door and window trim in place.

J-32. If your walls are finished hardboard, stain and varnish or paint casings and door stops to match before fastening them in place.

J-33. For a quick way to scribe a true margin along the edge of the jamb, set the combination square so that the blade projects 3/16 inch beyond face of the square's head. Then use the square as a gauge to mark margin.

J-34. By nailing only part of a casing at a time, you can move it slightly for making a perfect joint, if the joint doesn't quite close. Even though such movements may cause casings to vary slightly from the gage lines, the job still looks as if it were done by a pro.

J-35. Also, casings may be fastened in place with contact cement or color-matched nails.

J-36. Coping means to shape the end of a piece of molding or board so that it will fit with a butt joint against an adjacent member.

J-37. Never nail base shoe to baseboard. To do so will cause a crack (dirt collector) if either baseboard or flooring shrink.

J-38. How you finish interior trim depends upon the quality of the wood and the decorative scheme of each room. You have a choice of using wood stain, natural finish, or paint or semi-gloss enamel.

J-39. Consider the following painter's dozen when using either sealer stain or varnish.

1. Be sure the wood is clean, dry, and free of grease or oil.
2. Since sealing stain requires no wiping with a rag, it is much easier for the beginner to use.
3. To match walls and trim perfectly, take a sample of your hardboard along with a sample of the kind of wood you plan to color to your paint dealer. He will continue to add the right colors to a stock sealer stain until your hardboard color is matched perfectly on your sample board.
4. Edge grain of wood absorbs more sealer stain than other areas. To keep this from happening, brush a mixture of half-and-half linseed oil and turpentine or paint thinner to the edge grain before applying the sealer stain.
5. If sealer stain requires thinning, mix a small amount of turpentine or paint thinner with it.
6. Temperature at around 70° with average humidity is ideal for varnishing. Cold weather makes for a poor flow of varnish, while hot weather causes varnish to dry too quickly.
7. If the varnish does not dry as quickly as the label on the container claims it will, have your paint dealer add a small amount of dryer to it.
8. If the temperature and humidity are ideal and the varnish flows too stiff, mix a small amount of paint thinner or turpentine to it.
9. Work varnish over a small area at a time. You may get a better spread by brushing across the grain as well as with the grain. However, always finish by lightly stroking the varnish with the grain.
10. Constantly watch for runs. Stroke them out before they have an opportunity to set.
11. To turn out a professional job may require two or even three coats of varnish. Always rub surface lightly between coats with grade 6-0 sandpaper or grade 00 steel wool. Rub final coat lightly with grade 0000 steel wool. Always be sure surface is perfectly dry before doing any rubbing.
12. At the end of each sealing stain or varnishing session thoroughly clean brush in paint thinner or turpentine.

J-40. Select a clean brush large enough to do the job, but not too large. Also, do not use a single brush for varnishing and painting. Rather, keep one brush for varnishing, another for painting.

J-41. Latex paint or enamel is much easier to work with than oil-base paint or enamel. Also, the clean-up job is much easier. Removing latex paint splashes and drips as well as cleaning the brush is a simple matter of using ordinary tap water. Oil-base paints and enamels require paint thinner or turpentine during the clean-up process.

J-42. There are a number of excellent caulking materials for bathtubs, sinks, lavatories, and shower stalls carried in stock by lumber yards and hardware stores. Be sure to follow the manufacturer's directions on the container.

GLOSSARY
OF
HOUSEBUILDING
TERMS

ACROSS THE GRAIN   At right angle to the direction of the grain.

ANCHOR BOLTS   Bolts imbedded in fresh concrete to which framing material is fastened when the concrete is cured.

ANTIHAMMER   A section of water pipe installed in the line, about 1 foot long and one size larger than the line and capped at one end, used to prevent hammering noises.

APRON   A piece of finish or molded board located under a window sill to cover the joint between the wall and the bottom of the sill.

ASBESTOS JOINT RUNNER   A jig made of asbestos and a metal clamp, used to prevent melted lead from running out of the joint while caulking soil pipe in a horizontal position.

ASBESTOS MASTIC   A material used to waterproof surfaces, such as outside basement walls.

ASHLAR STONE   A building stone cut true on all faces facing other stones.

ASH-PIT CLEANOUT DOOR   A metal door installed near the base of a chimney and used for removing ashes.

ASH-PIT DUMP   A metal trap located in the fireplace floor, used to release ashes to the basement or to a tunnel leading to the outside of the house.

ASPHALT ROOFING PAPER   Heavy paper used in construction for insulating and waterproofing purposes.

BACKER BOARDS   Boards with partial overhang nailed to the plate parallel with the ceiling joists. These boards serve as nailers for ceiling boards at opposite ends of a room.

BACKFILLING   The operation of filling the space between the foundation and the sides of the excavation with dirt.

BACKING ANGLE   A double slope cut on the top edge of a hip rafter so as to provide two surfaces to receive the ends of roof sheathing from two adjacent sets of roof rafters.

BARGEBOARD   Finish board located on face side of gable framing.

BASEBOARD   A molding used to cover the joint between the floor and wall.

BASE SHOE   A molding located at the bottom of the baseboard, used to cover the gap between the carpet and baseboard. Sometimes called carpet strip.

BATTEN STRIPS   The narrow finish boards or hardboards fastened over panel joints on exterior walls to give a finished effect.

BATTER BOARDS   Horizontal boards nailed to upright stakes and set in pairs at right angles to each other a short distance back from each corner of a proposed building. The boards are used to show the first-floor level and as a support for various guidelines before framing the house.

BEARING POSTS Posts that partially support the girder(s) of a house.

BEARING SEATS Rectangular recesses formed in foundation walls, giving partial support to the girder(s) of a house.

BEARING WALL A wall that supports other objects, such as floors, ceiling joists, or roof.

BELL TILE Sectional tile, bell-shaped at one end, used to lay in ditches to carry waste water to a lower level or to a community drain system.

BELL WIRE Small copper wire used in the wiring of doorbells and door chimes.

BENCHMARK A known point of elevation, generally a known height above sea level.

BEVEL-CUT To cut or shape a board to a desired angle.

BEVELED SIDING A type of exterior wall siding made by sawing boards diagonally, producing two wedge-shaped pieces or boards.

BIRD'S-MOUTH A name used by carpenters to denote the notch sawn into a rafter where it is located on the plate.

BLOWER COIL A device in the air-conditioning system that brings in warm air and discharges it as cool air.

BLUEPRINT A copy of a drawing, usually a tracing, showing the working plans as they were drawn in ink or pencil. The terms "blueprints," "plans," and "working drawings" are used synonymously. See *working drawings*.

BOOT A sheet-metal receptacle making the connection between ductwork and a register, such as the connecting receptacle between the air-supply duct and the floor register as part of an air-conditioning system.

BOXED CORNICE A cornice made up of finish material.

BOX GUTTER A gutter shaped like a box.

BOX NAIL A nail like a common nail but thinner; used where common nails might split the wood.

BOX SILL A built-up sill located on the foundation with the sole plate resting on the floor joists rather than on the sill proper.

BRAD A small slender nail with a deep head, generally used in wood when either a finishing or a casing nail would be too large.

BRANCH CIRCUIT One of the electric circuits connected to the service panel.

BRANCH DRAIN A section of pipe that serves as a drain line for one fixture only.

BRANCH WATER LINE A water line serving one fixture only.

BRIDGING A method of stiffening floor joists, ceiling joists, and partitions. Sometimes small wooden braces are placed diagonally between the larger timbers. At other times timbers of the same size are placed at right angles, fitting snugly between the joists or partitions.

BUILDING CODE A collection of rules and regulations covering various phases of building construction.

BUILDING DRAIN A drain line from the foot of the stack to the sanitary sewer.

BUILDING LINES In this book the building lines refer to the outside and inside edges of the foundation. Such lines are generally shown solid on building plans.

BUILDING PAPER Heavy asphalt-saturated paper used over sheathing or subfloors.

BUSHING A device screwed tight against the end of a piece of conduit to protect insulated wires from abrasion.

BUTT To join boards together so that all points of the joint, such as the ends or edges, touch.

BUTT HINGE A hinge, usually used for doors, consisting of a loose pin holding two metal leaves together. One leaf is mortised into the jamb, while the other one is mortised into the edge of the door.

CANTILEVER Any rigid structure, such as a beam, floor, or roof, extending beyond its vertical support.

CAPILLARY ATTRACTION The attraction of a solid surface to a liquid. The inside of a copper fitting attracts the melted solder, making for a sealed joint between pipe and fitting.

CAP PLATE The horizontal timber of a house frame located on top of top plate of outside walls and partition framing. This is a means of locking top adjoining sections of outside wall framing and partition framing together into one solid unit of framing.

CARPET STRIP See *base shoe*.

CASING A molding to cover the joint between the jamb of a door or window and the wall.

CASING NAIL A nail like a finishing nail, but slightly smaller in gauge and with a slightly tapered head.

CAULKING COMPOUND Material used to make a seam or joint watertight.

CAULKING GUN A metal frame in which tubes of caulking compound are placed.

CEILING JOISTS Timbers fastened to cap plates and running across the narrow dimensions of the house. These are the main ceiling joists. Short ceiling joists running at right angles from the last main ceiling joist to a cap plate are called stub ceiling joists.

CEILING NAILER Generally 2-inch planks nailed to cap plate so they extend as an overhang to which ceiling material is nailed later.

CEILING TILE   Square or rectangular blocks especially designed to make a finished ceiling.

CENTRAL VACUUM SYSTEM   A vacuum-cleaning device with the electric power unit and tank located in the basement, garage, or utility room.

CHALK LINE   Chalk impregnated into a cord so that when it is snapped over building material a chalk line is formed.

CHEEK CUT   Side cut at end on both sides of certain rafters, such as hip rafters.

CIRCUIT BREAKER   An electric device that trips and opens the circuit when an overload occurs.

CLEANOUT   A removable drain fitting permitting cleaning out of obstructed soil pipe.

CLEAT   A wedge-shaped piece of wood nailed to a surface to serve as a check or support.

CLOSURE BLOCK   A concrete block, cut to size if necessary, to fill a course of concrete blocks.

COLD CHISEL   A wedgelike tool made of steel with a cutting edge on one end used for cutting or shaping metal.

COLLAR BEAM   A board to help keep the rafters from spreading apart. It also helps to prevent the roof from sagging under extra weight, such as snow.

COMBINATION SQUARE   A steel blade (marked off in fractions of inches) set at right angles to the inside face of a wood or metal stock.

COMMON NAIL   The standard nail for general use.

COMMON RAFTER   A rafter that runs at a right angle from the ridge to the plate.

COMPASS OR DIVIDERS   Instruments with many uses. In interior house finishing, either one is acceptable to scribe the face of one trim board against the face of a second trim board in preparation for making a coped joint.

CONCRETE   A mixture of Portland cement, rock, sand, and water.

CONCRETE BLOCKS   Blocks made of concrete, used for walls in some basements and foundations.

CONCRETE NAIL   A nail especially made to fasten wood to concrete or concrete blocks.

CONDENSER   A device in the air-conditioning system that reduces the gases to a liquid form.

CONDUIT   Thin metal pipe through which electric wires or cables run.

CONDUIT BENDER   A tool designed to bend soft pipe such as conduit or copper tubing.

COPED JOINT   A joint in which the end of one member is cut to fit the surface of another, such as a piece of molding cut to fit against the face of a second piece of similar molding.

COPING SAW   A saw used for cutting irregular shapes, such as in making a coped joint at the juncture of two pieces of molding meeting at an internal corner.

COPPER PIPE STRAPS   Copper straps used to fasten copper water and drain lines in place.

CORNER POST   Framing elements located at corners of wall and partition frames, made up of three full-length studs and three spacer blocks 12 to 16 inches long.

CORNICE   Top part of a wall located directly underneath the eaves.

COUPLING   A plumbing fitting used to join two pipes together.

COURSE OF MASONRY   A layer of concrete blocks, bricks, stone, or a combination of masonry.

COVE MOLDING   A molding with a concave surface, such as is commonly used between the walls and ceiling of a room.

CRAWL SPACE   The area between the floor joists and the ground in a house with no basement.

CRICKET   A small gable roof located where it can divert drainage. Sometimes called a saddle.

CRIMPED PIPE END   Small, regular folds pressed into one end of a pipe, such as a round air-supply pipe for an air-conditioning system.

CRIPPLE JACK RAFTER   A rafter that extends from a hip to a valley, never reaching the cap plate or the ridge.

CRIPPLE STUDS   Shortened studs located above or below an opening. Those located above the header are called upper cripple studs; those below the rough sill, lower cripple studs.

CROSS MEMBERS   Framing material fastened at right angles to other framing material, such as 2×4s nailed between wall studs on which plank wall covering is fastened.

CROWN   The highest point of any construction, such as the high point of a warped board.

CROWN OF RAFTER   The top edge of a rafter.

CRUSHED STONE   Particles of stone that will not pass through a ¼-inch screen.

CURING CONCRETE   Treating freshly poured concrete by sprinkling water at favorable temperatures on it periodically for one month.

D   Abbreviation of the word "penny" in the classification of nails. For example, 16d means 16-penny.

DARBY   A flat tool 48 inches long by 3½ inches wide with a handle located on the blade at midpoint. It is used after the striking-off process to further press down rocks and to bring to the surface fine material, including mortar.

DEEP-SEAL TRAP   A device located in the main soil-pipe drain line to prevent sewage from backing up and flooding the basement.

DIAGONAL THICKNESS   Thickness of a board or timber diagonally rather than vertically or horizontally.

DIFFUSER   A cover, such as a cover for an air-conditioner register, made up of narrow, slanted slats that are usually controllable from a closed to a wide-open position.

DISCONNECT SWITCH   A switch wired in a circuit to disconnect an electrical appliance when desired.

DOOR JACK   A homemade device used to hold a door while the edge is being planed to fit a door opening.

DOOR UNIT   Door jambs, outside casings, door, and hinges fastened into a unit, ready for immediate installation into rough door opening.

DORMER   A window whose framework is a gable-type intersecting roof.

DOUBLE FRAMING   The nailing of two framing members together to furnish added strength, such as the joist framing around a stairway.

DOUBLE-HUNG WINDOW   Two window sash, each capable of sliding up and down the window frame.

DOUBLE JOIST   Two joists fastened together to give added strength.

DRIP CAP   A thin board or piece of metal located over the top of a window to keep water running down the wall from entering the house.

DROP OUTLET   A metal outlet fastened through a hole in the gutter to which a piece of rainpipe is fastened.

DUCT   A sheet-metal pipe by which air is conveyed, such as the ducts of an air-conditioning system.

EASEMENT   A right held by a person, company, or corporation to make use of the land of another for a specific purpose, such as a right of a telephone company to set poles on land owned by another person, company, or corporation.

EAVE   That part of the roof extending beyond the wall, sometimes called the overhang.

EDGE PULL   A door pull mounted flush on the edge of a sliding door.

EIGHTH-BEND (⅛-bend)   A short piece of soil pipe in the form of a 45° angle.

ELBOW   In rainpipe, an elbow with a 60° angle. In plumbing, a water pipe or a drain fitting with a 90° angle.

ELECTRIC CONDUIT   A special pipe used for the protection of electric wires.

ELEVATION   A geometrical drawing or design that represents an object as being projected on a vertical plane parallel to one of its sides. Essentially, a straight-on view of an object.

EMERY PAPER   A stiff paper coated with powdered emery.

END CAP   A metal cap fastened to the end of a piece of gutter.

END GRAIN   Grain on ends of boards.

ESCUTCHEON   A decorative metal plate around faucets and pipes, on both sides of a door lock set or latch, etc. set.

EXCAVATION LINES   Lines used on working drawings to show the outside and inside edges of footings. Such lines are generally shown dotted on building plans.

FACE OF RAFTER   The bevel cut located at the end of a rafter.

FACE SHELLS   The outer sections of a concrete block.

FACIA   The face side of a board nailed over the lower ends of rafter tails.

FACIA BOARD   The board nailed across the rough facia at right angles to the rafter tails.

FACIA BRACKET HANGER   A hanger fastened to the facia to hold some types of box gutters in place.

FALL   To move from a high point to a lower point, as in the case of seep water moving from a high point on a basement floor toward the drain.

FERRULE   A metal sleeve placed around the wood handle of a tool to prevent splitting.

FIELD TILE   Short lengths of drain tile, usually laid with a ¼-inch gap between each length.

FILLER BOX   Boxlike forms of wood constructed to the size of required openings, such as windows and doors, in the finished concrete foundation wall.

FINISH FLOOR   The final floor surface.

FINISHING NAIL   A nail with a much smaller head than a common nail, used in lumber where head is to be countersunk.

FIRE BRICK   A brick made of fireclay, used for lining fireplaces.

FIRECLAY   A refractory clay used for making fire bricks and as a mortar for laying them.

FIREPLACE UNIT   A prefabricated metal structure lining the three sides of a fireplace.

FISH TAPE   A flexible steel tape about ⅛-inch wide and 1/16-inch thick. It is springy enough so that it will not buckle when it is pushed through a conduit. It is used for pulling wires through an installed conduit.

FIXTURE DRAIN   A section of branch drain with a built-in trap adapted to the special requirements of a particular fixture.

FIXTURE SUPPLY LINE   A section of pipe from a branch water line.

FLASHING   Strips of nonrusting metal that are let into both sides of a joint to prevent water from entering.

FLEXIBLE COPPER TUBING   A pliable copper pipe put up in rolls, used as water supply lines.

FLOAT   A small flat tool used by concrete finishers to press down rock and to bring fine material to the surface of freshly poured concrete. Sometimes a float is used for giving the concrete its final finish. This is the case when a rough finish is desired, as for a concrete driveway.

FLOATING   Smoothing the surface of poured concrete to a rough finish.

FLOOR DRAIN   A fitting located in the basement floor and connected to a drain system to discharge waste water to a sanitary sewer.

FLOOR FLANGE   A metal plumbing fitting fastened to the drain line and resting on top of the floor to which the toilet bowl is fastened.

FLUE LINER   A clay liner on the inside of a flue.

FLUSH   Even with a surface to form a single plane.

FLUSH ELL   A fitting used to fasten the toilet bowl to the water bowl.

FLUSH JOINT   A joint level with the masonry surface.

FLUSH PULL   A door pull mounted flush on the side of a sliding door.

FLUX   A preparation used to remove oxides from metal as well as to prevent further oxidation during the soldering operation.

FOOTING   The base of a foundation that rests on the ground. Generally, footings are twice the width of the thickness of the foundation wall.

FOOTING PADS   Independent footings that provide a base for bearing posts.

FORMS   Wood or steel structures wide enough and heavy enough to hold concrete in place during the pouring and setting-up process.

FOUNDATION   A prepared base on which the house is built.

FOUR-WAY SWITCHES   An electric device used in conjunction with two three-way switches so that an electric device, such as a light, can be controlled from three different locations.

FRAMING SQUARE   A square with a 24-inch part called the body and a 16-inch part called the blade, both divided into fractions of inches.

FRAMING SQUARE BODY   The widest part of a framing square. This is the part of the square used to measure the run of a roof.

FRAMING SQUARE TONGUE   The narrowest part of a framing square, sometimes referred to as the blade. This is the part of the square used to measure the rise of a roof.

FREEZELESS WATER FAUCET   An outside faucet that when shut off automatically drains the last 12 inches of the water line.

FRIEZE BOARD   A finish board sometimes located near the top of the wall directly beneath the eaves.

FULL-LENGTH STUD   The tallest of timbers used in wall framing and partition framing.

FURRING STRIPS   Wood or metal strips fastened to a ceiling, wall, or other surface to serve as nailers for ceiling tile, laths, or hardboard, to form an air space, or to make it thicker.

FUSE   An electric protective device containing a piece of metal that melts under a specified amount of heat, breaking the circuit.

GABLE   The triangular portion of the wall directly under a gable roof.

GABLE RAFTERS   The two end rafters of a gable roof.

GABLE ROOF   Two roof surfaces coming together, forming a ridge with gables at each end.

GABLE STUD   A stud that extends from top of wall cap plate to gable rafters.

GAIN   A shallow rabbet for receiving the leaf of a butt hinge or half-surface butt hinge.

GALVANIZED IRON   Iron coated with zinc to help prevent rusting.

GANG BOX   Two or more electric outlet boxes mounted side by side.

GASKET   A firm material such as cork or rubber placed around a joint to make it watertight.

GIRDER   A large timber, either single or built up, or an iron I beam used to support heavy loads, such as joists or walls over a house opening.

GRAB BAR   A metal bar located in shower stalls and near bath tubs to help prevent accidents.

GRIP-TIGHT BOX   An electric outlet box held to the wall by two clamps.

GROUND ROD   A metal rod buried deeply into the earth to furnish a conducting connection between an electric circuit and the earth.

GROUND ROD CLAMP   A clamp designed to make a tight connection between the ground wire and the ground rod.

GROUND WIRE   An electric wire intended to make connection with the ground.

GUTTER   Concave material for carrying away rainwater as it comes off the roof.

GUTTER GUARD   A wire screen or perforated metal strip fastened underneath the roof shingles and to the outside edge of the gutter to prevent leaves and other debris from clogging up the guttering system.

GYPSUM BOARD SHEATHING   Panels used as sheathing with a core of gypsum located between two faces of water-repellent paper.

HACKSAW   A saw with a blade especially designed for cutting metal.

HALF-ROUND GUTTER   A gutter shaped like a pipe split down the center.

HARDBOARD   A panel made from wood fibers compressed into sheets.

HEADER   A short joist that supports one or more cut-off joists (tail beams) where they terminate at a well hole, such as a chimney well or stairwell. Also, two pieces of timber fastened together with small strips of wood between them so as to make the assembly the same thickness as the rest of the wall framing as it is located horizontally over a rough door or window opening.

HEARTH   The floor of a fireplace that extends into the room.

HIP JACK RAFTER   A rafter that extends from a cap plate to a hip rafter.

HIP RAFTER   A rafter that connects two intersecting planes of a roof at the hip.

HIP ROOF   A roof with the same slope or pitch on four sides.

HOLLOW-CORE DOOR   A door with an air space between its two faces, suitable for indoor use.

HOT WIRE   An electric wire or cable with current passing through it.

HUB   The end of a soil pipe having a flare.

HYDRATED LIME   Also called slaked lime, used as an ingredient in mortar.

I.D.   Abbreviation for "inside diameter."

INSULATING BOARD   Panels made of insulating material fastened on roof rafters and wall studs, serving a dual purpose of sheathing and providing a certain amount of insulation.

INTERSECTING ROOF   Where one roof passes through another roof, as a gable roof intersecting a hip roof.

JACK PLANE   A plane 14 inches long, used to plane large areas, such as edges of interior and exterior doors.

JAMB   Either of the sides or the top of an opening.

JIG   A tool designed especially for a particular job.

JOINT GAUGE   A board with uniform markings, used to assure uniform joints while laying bricks or concrete blocks.

JOIST   One of several parallel beams, supported in turn by larger beams, such as girders or bearing walls.

K COPPER PIPE   A copper pipe suitable for carrying water underground.

KEYWAY   A V groove in the center of the basement wall footing. This provides a way of bonding the foundation wall to the footing.

KNOCKOUT   A round piece of metal partially stamped out of a metal electric box so that it can be knocked out.

LAP JOINT   A joint in which two pieces of wood overlap, forming a single surface on both faces.

LATCH SET   A knob and latch assembly for doors that do not need to be locked.

LATH STRIPPING   Thin, narrow strips of wood, used temporarily to hold edges of building paper in place on roof decking.

LAYOUT   An arrangement or plan of a house or part of a house.

L COPPER PIPE   A copper pipe designed to carry water above ground.

LEDGER BOARD   A board located on the wall to receive one end of the lookouts.

LEVEL   A rectangular body of wood or metal in which glass tubes, partially filled with a nonfreezing liquid, are recessed in its side and near its end.

LINE LENGTH   The distance between the center of the ridge and the rafter tail cut.

LINE LEVEL   A small, light level with small hangers to be attached onto a cord for establishing a horizontal position between two distant points.

LINEMAN'S PLIERS   A long, narrow pair of pliers used for gripping locknuts and twisting wires in electrical work.

LINE VOLTAGE   Number of volts supplied by the service wires coming from the utility company's power supply, such as 115 volts to supply current for the house lighting system.

LINOLEUM KNIFE   A knife with a curved blade and a wood handle, designed for cutting linoleum.

LINTEL   A piece of metal angular in form, used to support the masonry above a fireplace.

LOCKNUT   A nut designed not to come loose after being tightened.

LOCK SET   A knob and latch assembly with a lock.

LOOKOUTS   Short pieces of 2×4s fastened horizontally between the lower end of the rafters and the ledger board located on the side of the wall.

LOUVER   A series of slanting overlapping slats fitted into a framework.

MAIN RIDGE BRACE   A brace located between cap plate of a partition wall and ridge board to furnish a support for the common rafters.

MAIN WATER LINE   A water line serving two or more fixtures.

MAJOR RIDGE   The ridge of the main roof.

MALLET   A hammerlike tool with a wood, leather, or plastic head, used to drive tools with wood handles such as a wood chisel.

MANTEL   A shelf above the top of a fireplace.

MASONRY BIT   A bit designed to drill holes in concrete or masonry.

MEASURING LINE OF RAFTER   A line parallel to the top edge of a rafter, running through a point indicating the depth of the bird's-mouth cut.

METAL HANGERS Metal pieces designed to fasten outlet boxes or junction boxes to the house framework.

METER BOX A metal box, usually mounted on the outside of the house, to contain the electric meter.

MINOR RIDGE Ridge of the intersecting ridge.

MITER An angle cut on a piece of wood to butt against an angular cut on a second piece of wood.

MITER BOX A machine used to saw miter joints.

MIXING BOX A box specially built for use in mixing concrete.

MIXING VALVE A valve used to mix hot and cold water to the desired temperature.

MODULAR CONCRETE BLOCKS Concrete blocks of standard measurement.

MOLDINGS Long, narrow boards with ornamental surfaces, such as door and window casings.

MORTAR A mixture of Portland cement, hydrated lime, sand, and water, used for bonding masonry.

MORTARBOARD A board used by a mason at the job site for holding mortar.

MORTISE A hole or slot cut into a piece of wood to receive another piece, formed exactly to fit.

MULTI-PURPOSE TOOL An electrician's tool designed for cutting and skinning wires, attaching wires to terminals, etc.

MURIATIC ACID A corrosive liquid used in diluted form as a soldering flux for soldering sheet metal. Also, used in a diluted form to clean mortar from laid brick.

NAIL SET A tool designed for driving heads of finishing nails, casing nails, or brads below the surface of wood.

NEUTRAL STRIP An electric ground-wire connector, generally designed for several connections.

NONMETALLIC SHEATHED CABLE Electric wires covered by a nonconducting material, available in various sizes for circuits of different capacities.

NYLON BUSHING A nylon lining for a hole in an electric device through which electric wires pass.

OAKUM A loose fiber used in caulking cast-iron soil pipes before sealing them with melted lead.

O.C. Abbreviation for "on center." For example, wall studs are generally positioned 16 inches O.C.

O.D. Abbreviation for "outside diameter."

O-RING A round rubber ring, such as is used as a seal in a central vacuum system.

ORTHOGRAPHIC VIEW A single-plane view of an object as it really is, such as a top view or side view of a house.

OUTLET BOX A box constructed of metal, porcelain, or bakelite used to mount an electric outlet.

PARALLEL WIRING A method of wiring that provides that if one device breaks down it will not affect the quantity of electricity received by other electric devices on the same circuit.

PARTITION An inner wall that subdivides space within a house.

PARTITION JUNCTION STUD Three full-length studs nailed together so as to form an inside corner on each side of a partition frame.

PEGBOARD Hardboard having holes into which hooks can be placed.

PERSPECTIVE VIEW A view of an object as it appears to the eye, sometimes called a pictorial view.

PILASTER An upright column, rectangular in shape, combined with a wall.

PIPE STRAP A strap of metal used for holding rainpipe in place.

PITCH The angle or slope of the roof from the ridge to the cap plate.

PLANCIER MATERIAL Material, such as plywood, that fits frame on both sides of ventilating screen located on the underside of the eaves.

PLENUM A main duct made of sheet metal, box-formed, used either to carry cool air from the blower coil in an air-conditioning unit to the branch cold-air ducts or to carry warm air from the branch warm-air ducts to the blower coil.

PLIOBOND One of several adhesives used to fasten plastic tubing together.

PLUMB A perfectly upright position. For instance, the wall of a house should be at right angles to the plane of the horizon. If so, the wall is said to be plumb.

PLUMB BOB A small mass of metal tied to a line, used to ascertain a vertical line.

POLYETHYLENE Clear or black sheeting that remains pliable at extremes of heat and cold. It is used in the building trade as a vapor barrier and to protect building materials from the weather during the building program.

PREFABRICATED FORMS Forms, generally made of steel, manufactured to take the place of wood forms, made on the job, for holding poured concrete in place.

PRIMING COAT The first coat of paint.

PUNCH LIST A list made by the home builder at a late stage of construction, detailing exactly what is required before the house can be called completely finished.

PUTTY RING A ring of beeswax or putty placed around the discharge opening located on the bottom of a toilet bowl.

PUTTYSTICK A manufactured colored stick used to fill countersunk nail holes.

QUARTER-BEND (¼-bend)   A short piece of soil pipe in the form of a 90° angle.

QUARTER-ROUND   A three-sided molding with a curved face and a 90° angle formed by the remaining two sides; in cross section it is a quarter circle.

RABBET   A groove cut in one piece of wood to receive a second piece of wood.

RAFTERS   Sloping timbers of the roof.

RAFTER TAIL   The section of a rafter between cap plate location and the lower end of the rafter.

RAINPIPE   Round metal tubing used to lead rainwater from gutter to the ground.

RAKE   The sloped edges of a gable roof.

RAKED JOINT   Mortar raked out of a masonry joint to a specified depth before it sets.

READY-MIX CONCRETE   Concrete properly mixed in special trucks between source of supply and the job.

REAMING   The operation of widening or opening holes, as in beveling the openings in conduit pipes.

RECIPROCATING POWER SAW   A power saw with a narrow blade moving to and fro as cuts are made. Suitable for wood, plastic, or metal, depending on type of blade in use.

REDUCING COUPLING   A fitting designed to receive a pipe of a certain diameter at one end and to receive a smaller pipe at the opposite end.

REINFORCEMENT ROD   A steel rod with a ridged surface, put in fresh concrete to provide added strength.

REINFORCEMENT WIRE   A heavy woven wire designed for placing in fresh concrete to give added strength.

RESIN NAIL   A coated nail with greater holding power than an uncoated nail.

RE-VENT PIPE   A bypass for air and gases between a branch drain and the vent portion of a stack.

RIDGE BOARD   A board located between the uppermost ends of common rafters, which are then spiked together from opposite sides of this board.

RIGID COPPER TUBING   Stiff copper pipe, generally used as water lines where they are exposed to view.

RISE OF THE BUILDING   The number of inches that the roof rises for every foot of run. Rise is figured by multiplying the pitch by the unit of span.

RISER   The vertical height of the face of a step.

ROOF DECKING   Boards or sheets of plywood used to cover the rafters before applying shingles or other finish roof cover.

ROOF FELTING   An asphalt paper fastened to roof sheathing before applying shingles.

ROOFING PLASTIC CEMENT   A waterproof cement used between overlapped asphalt shingles or roll roofing.

ROUGH FACIA   A timber nailed to the bottom ends of rafters.

ROUGH-IN MEASUREMENTS   Measurements showing locations of plumbing fixtures and other building accessories.

ROUGH OPENING   An opening in the framework of a house, such as the opening between the studs of a window or doorway.

ROUGH SILL   A timber located on top of lower cripple studs of a window rough opening.

RUBBING BRICK   A brick manufactured for rubbing to give concrete surfaces a finished appearance.

RUN   The horizontal dimension of a step.

RUN OF THE BUILDING   The shortest horizontal distance that a common rafter is permitted to cover.

SAFETY VALVE   A combination pressure and temperature relief valve installed in the hot water tank.

SANITARY CROSS   A soil-pipe fitting containing two tapped drain openings located opposite each other.

SANITARY SEWER   A sewer especially designed only for sewage disposal.

SANITARY Y BRANCH   A drain fitting in the shape of a Y installed between base of stack and soil-pipe drain line leading to the sanitary sewer.

SASH   The framework that holds a pane of glass in a window frame.

SAWHORSE   Also called a sawbuck. A movable frame made with two pairs of legs fastened to a single piece of wood used to support boards being sawed or planed.

SCAFFOLD   An elevated platform erected temporarily for holding workmen and materials during the building operation.

SCALE DRAWING   A drawing of an object in precisely reduced proportion, so that, for example, ¼ inch on the drawing equals 1 foot of the object.

SCORING   Cutting a notch on both sides of a concrete block with a stone set and hammer.

SCREED   A guide made by supporting an iron pipe on top of wood stakes driven into the ground to a specified position, used in smoothing a freshly poured concrete surface.

SCRIBE   To mark with a pointed instrument, such as a set of scribers or compass, as a guide in cutting a piece of wood to a pattern.

SEALING STAIN   A combination of sealer and stain, making the job of sealing and staining a single operation.

SERVICE CABLE   The electric cable running from the electric utility pole to the meter and thence to the service panel.

SERVICE PANEL   A box with a series of circuit breakers or fuse blocks from which emanate the electric circuits for the house.

SEWER PIPES The pipes used for conveying sewage from the house to the community sanitary sewer line.

SHEATHING Panels or boards nailed over studding or rafters to serve as a base for siding or roofing.

SHED ROOF A flat roof with a single slope.

SHEET METAL Galvanized iron sheets, available in a variety of thicknesses.

SHIM A strip of material or a wedge used to fill a small space.

SHINGLES Roof covering made of pieces of tapered wood, slate, metal, or asbestos.

SHORTENING The distance between the line length and the true length of a rafter.

SHORT VALLEY RAFTER A rafter that extends from a cap plate to the supporting valley rafter.

SHUT-OFF VALVE A hand-operated valve installed in a water line whenever a cut-off is required.

SILICONE SEALER A liquid used to waterproof masonry above ground level.

SILL The bottom of a door or window frame.

SILL PLATE The part of the side wall of a house that rests horizontally, directly upon the foundation.

SINGLE-POLE SWITCH An electric switch breaking one of the wires to an electric device such as a light.

SLAB A large concrete section such as a basement floor or driveway.

SLIDING DOOR A door attached to a set of rollers located on a track fastened to the top doorjamb.

SLIP COUPLING A short plastic tube, slightly larger than the plastic tubing in general use. Used with adhesive to fasten two pieces of tubing together.

SLIP JOINT A gutter joint made by holding two pieces of guttering together with a grooved piece of metal.

SLIP NUT A nut used in plumbing, designed to fit over a drain pipe flared at the end and to make a watertight connection by being screwed tight against a joining drain pipe fitted with male threads.

SMOKEPIPE THIMBLE A metal or other noncombustible material mortared into a chimney flue to receive a furnace or stove smokepipe.

SMOOTH PLANE The most generally used plane, about 9 inches long.

SOFFIT The horizontal surface between the end of the rafters and the outside wall of the house.

SOIL PIPE A pipe that carries discharged materials from the house to the sanitary sewer.

SOIL PIPE ADAPTER A short connector designed to receive a 3-inch stack pipe in one end and a 4-inch soil pipe in the other end.

SOIL STACK Called "stack" for short. A vertical pipe in the plumbing system extending up through the roof as a vent, through which sewer gases escape to the outside.

SOIL TESTS The sampling of soil at various depths to determine the type of footings necessary for certain kinds of buildings.

SOLDER An alloy of lead and tin used in fusing two pieces of metal together.

SOLDERLESS CONNECTOR A hollow plastic device designed to fasten two or more electric wires together without the use of solder. Also called a wire nut.

SOLE PLATE The horizontal timber of a house frame on which the outside wall studs and partition studs rest.

SOLID-CORE DOOR A door that has softwood blocks filling up the space between the two door faces.

SPAN The distance between the supports of a beam, arch, or truss.

SPECIFICATIONS A document prepared by an architect to explain many of the details about a house not possible to include on a set of working drawings.

SPIGOT The plain end of a cast-iron soil pipe.

SPIKE AND FERRULE SET A device consisting of a spike and a small metal tube used to fasten some types of box gutters to the facia.

SPIKE NAIL A nail thicker than a common nail. Spikes range from 3 inches to 12 inches in length.

SPINDLE The part of a latch set or lock set that extends through the door.

SPLASH GUARD A piece of concrete, board, or composition material located below a downspout to prevent water from washing away the topsoil.

SPLICE The twisting together of two electric wires.

STACK See soil stack.

STAPLER A heavy-duty stapler designed to shoot staples to fasten certain building materials together, such as building paper to roof sheathing, ceiling tile to furring strips, etc.

STAR DRILL A steel shank with one end flared in the shape of a star, used with a hammer to make holes in concrete or masonry.

STARTER STRIP A metal strip especially designed for fastening to the bottom edge of roof sheathing. Also, a narrow strip of roll roofing applied to the lower end of the roof sheathing before laying roof shingles.

STONE SAW A power-driven saw fitted with a blade designed to cut masonry.

STOOL The ledge forming the finished bottom of a window frame.

STOP A molding located on the jamb of each side of a window sash, each side of a sliding door, and each side and top of a swinging door.

STOP AND WASTE VALVE A hand-operated valve located on the water supply line where it enters the house.

STORM SEWER   A sewer especially designed for rainfall disposal.

STRAIGHTEDGE   A board with a truly straight edge used for measuring and drawing straight lines.

STRAINER   An assembly of several wires to be placed in the top of a drop outlet to prevent leaves and debris from clogging the rainpipe. A strainer is not necessary if gutter guard is installed.

STRAP HANGER   A piece of metal strap used to hang half-round gutters in place.

STREET ELBOW   A 90° elbow with male threads on one end and female threads on the other end.

STRIKE PLATE   A plate mounted on the jamb to receive the latch from a lock set or latch set.

STRIKING OFF   The operation of leveling concrete to the top of forms or bringing it to a desired contour. Generally, the striking-off operation is performed by sawing a straight 2×4 or 2×6 back and forth over the tops of the forms in which concrete has been poured.

STRINGERS   The framework of a flight of stairs.

STUDDING   Upright framing material used in partitions and outside walls.

STUDS   The small, upright timbers used in partitions and outside walls. Usually, 2×4s are used to frame sides and partitions of houses. Also, projecting metal pins or lugs.

SUBFLOOR   Rough floor consisting of boards or panels under the finish floor.

SUPPORTING VALLEY RAFTER   Extends from a cap plate to hip rafter at right angles.

SWINGING DOOR   A door fastened to a doorjamb with hinges.

SWITCH BOX   A box of metal, porcelain, or bakelite used to mount an electrical switch.

TABS   Metal prongs inside the electric service panel onto which circuit breakers are fastened.

TAIL BEAM   A short joist supported in a wall on one end and by a header on the other. Generally found in fireplace framework.

TAIL PLUMB CUT   The cut on the lower end of a rafter.

TAMP   To position freshly poured concrete firmly in all parts of the form.

TAP   The twisting of one electric wire tightly around another wire.

TAPERING   The operation of making something smaller at one end, such as in cutting a board narrower at one end than at the other.

T-BAR HANGER   A metal hanger fastened to outside wall to hold rainpipe in place.

T FITTING   A water pipe or drain fitting in the shape of a T, used to start a branch line from the main line.

TEMPLATE   A pattern, usually made of paper or a thin piece of wood or metal, used as a guide by the home builder.

TERMINAL   A mechanical device used for making a connection in a piece of electric equipment.

TERMITE SHIELDS   Metal shields formed over foundation walls to prevent termites from entering the house from the ground.

TESTING DEVICE   A doorbell and a 6-volt lantern battery wired together, used to test electrical circuits.

THERMOSTAT   An electric device that is designed to establish and maintain a desired temperature automatically.

THREE-WAY SWITCHES   Two switches used to control an electric device, such as a light, from two different locations.

THRESHOLD   The bottom part or sill of a doorway.

TIE RODS   Special steel rods used to hold inside and outside of forms together while concrete pouring and setting up are in progress.

TOENAIL   To nail at an angle through one member into a second member.

TONGUE-AND-GROOVE   A joint between two boards in which a tongue on one fits into a groove on the other.

TOP PLATE   The horizontal timber of a house frame located on top of the outside wall studs and partition studs.

TRANSFORMER   An electric device used to reduce voltage.

TRAP   A plumbing fitting constructed so as to allow waste material to pass through a pipe on the way to the sewer and at the same time retain enough water to prevent sewer gas from entering the house.

TRIMMER JOIST   A carrying joist that supports an end of a header.

TRIMMER STUDS   Two shortened studs each nailed to a full-length stud and located on each side of a rough opening prepared for a window or door.

TROWEL   A hand tool consisting of a metal blade and handle used for smoothing the surface of poured concrete or mortar. The blade of a bricklayer's trowel is triangular, while a concrete finisher's trowel is rectangular.

TROWELING   Smoothing the surface of poured concrete or mortar to a slick finish.

TROWELING MACHINE   A machine powered by a gasoline motor for the purpose of smoothing the surface of poured concrete.

TRUE LENGTH   The actual length of a rafter; the line length minus one half the ridge thickness.

TUBING CUTTER   A piece of apparatus designed for cutting soft tubing, such as copper tubing.

UNDERGROUND CABLE   Electric cable with an insulating covering designed to be laid underground.

UNION   A plumbing fitting used to join two pieces of pipe together with a slip nut.

UNIT RISE   The rise in inches that the common rafter extends in a vertical direction for every foot of unit run.

VALLEY   The angle formed by the joining of two inclined roof edges.

VALLEY GUARD   A piece of metal bent at a right angle and fastened to the gutter corner beneath the valley.

VALLEY JACK RAFTER   A rafter that extends from the ridge to a valley rafter.

VALLEY RAFTER   A rafter that connects two intersecting planes of a roof at the valley.

VAPOR BARRIER   Material such as polyethylene used to prevent the passage of moisture.

VENT PIPE   A pipe used in plumbing to release sewer gas to the outside at a level above the roof line as well as to prevent back pressure and siphonage.

VIBRATOR   A tool used to make walls smooth during the pouring of concrete.

WALERS   Timbers placed along the studs of long sections of concrete forms. Walers help to prevent the forms from bulging, align and strengthen the forms, and provide bearing points for the top of the side braces.

WALL PLATE   A covering of an electric switch or outlet located in a box.

WASHERS   A flat metal ring placed over a bolt to give tightness when the nut is drawn tight.

WEATHERSTRIP   A narrow strip of wood, plastic, rubber, or fiber placed between a door or window sash and its frame to keep air and rain from passing.

WEDGE   A piece of wood or metal thick on one end and thin on the other, such as a wood shingle.

WELLS   Openings, such as stairwells and chimney wells.

WINDOW UNIT   Window jambs, outside casings, other trim (excluding inside casings), and window mounted into sash making up a unit ready for immediate installation into a rough window opening.

WIRE CABLE   A series of wires woven together.

WIRE NUT   A solderless connector; a plastic device used to fasten two or more electric wires together.

WIRING DIAGRAM   A drawing showing the nature of a particular wiring system, such as the wiring used in an air-conditioner unit.

WOOD CHISEL   A wedgelike tool made of steel with a cutting edge on one end and a wood handle on the other end, used for cutting or shaping wood.

WORKING DRAWINGS   Drawings made by an architect for showing exactly how a building should be put together.

WRECKING BAR   A tool used for pulling spike nails and prying nailed boards apart.

YARNING IRON   A plumbing tool used to pack oakum into hubs of cast-iron soil pipe.

Y JOINT   A joint having the shape of the letter Y, used for connecting two diverging drain branches to a principal drain line.

INDEX